DYNAMITE AND SIX-SHOOTER

DYNAMITE AND SIX-SHOOTER

The Story of Thomas E. "Black Jack" Ketchum

Facsimile of 1970 Edition

by
Jeff Burton

New Foreword
by
Marc Simmons

SOUTHWEST HERITAGE SERIES

SUNSTONE PRESS

SANTA FE

New Material © 2007 by Sunstone Press. All Rights Reserved.

No part of this book may be reproduced in any form or by any electronic or mechanical means including information storage and retrieval systems without permission in writing from the publisher, except by a reviewer who may quote brief passages in a review.

Sunstone books may be purchased for educational, business, or sales promotional use. For information please write: Special Markets Department, Sunstone Press, P.O. Box 2321, Santa Fe, New Mexico 87504-2321.

Library of Congress Cataloging-in-Publication Data

Burton, Jeff.
   Dynamite and six-shooter : the story of Thomas E. "Black Jack" Ketchum : facsimile of 1970 edition / by Jeff Burton.
     p.cm. -- (Southwest heritage series)
   Originally published: Santa Fe, N.M. : Palomino Press, 1970.
   ISBN: 978-0-86534-576-8 (softcover : alk. paper)
   1. Ketchum, Black Jack, 1863-1901. 2. Outlaws--West (U.S.)--Biography.
3. Criminals--West (U.S.)--Biography. 4. Frontier and pioneer life--West (U.S.)
5. West (U.S.)--History--1860-1890. 6. West (U.S.)--History--1890-1945. I. Title.

F595.K4B8 1970
354.15'0929aB--dc22
                              2007061710

WWW.SUNSTONEPRESS.COM
SUNSTONE PRESS / POST OFFICE BOX 2321 / SANTA FE, NM 87504-2321 /USA
(505) 988-4418 / ORDERS ONLY (800) 243-5644 / FAX (505) 988-1025

The Southwest Heritage Series is dedicated to Jody Ellis and Marcia Muth Miller, the founders of Sunstone Press, whose original purpose and vision continues to inspire and motivate our publications.

CONTENTS

THE SOUTHWEST HERITAGE SERIES / I

FOREWORD TO THIS EDITION / II

FACSIMILE OF 1970 EDITION / III

I

THE SOUTHWEST HERITAGE SERIES

The history of the United States is written in hundreds of regional histories and literary works. Those letters, essays, memoirs, biographies and even collections of fiction are often first-hand accounts by people who wanted to memorialize an event, a person or simply record for posterity the concerns and issues of the times. Many of these accounts have been lost, destroyed or overlooked. Some are in private or public collections but deemed to be in too fragile condition to permit handling by contemporary readers and researchers.

However, now with the application of twenty-first century technology, nineteenth and twentieth century material can be reprinted and made accessible to the general public. These early writings are the DNA of our history and culture and are essential to understanding the present in terms of the past.

The Southwest Heritage Series is a form of literary preservation. Heritage by definition implies legacy and these early works are our legacy from those who have gone before us. To properly present and preserve that legacy, no changes in style or contents have been made. The material reprinted stands on its own as it first appeared. The point of view is that of the author and the era in which he or she lived. We would not expect photographs of people from the past to be re-imaged with modern clothes, hair styles and backgrounds. We should not, therefore, expect their ideas and personal philosophies to reflect our modern concepts.

Remember, reading their words and sharing their thoughts is a passport back into understanding how the past was shaped and how it influenced today's world.

Our hope is that new access to these older books will provide readers with a challenging and exciting experience.

II

FOREWORD TO THIS EDITION
by
Marc Simmons

I first visited the old mining town of Cerrillos in 1958. A resident pointed out to me the historic Palace Hotel. "Up on the second floor," he said, "Dr. Palmer once had his office. When Black Jack Ketchum held up a train east of town and got shot for his trouble, he was brought in so that Palmer could patch him up. Black Jack bled all over the doctor's floor, and you can still see the stain."

Regrettably, I never got to view it. The hotel burned in 1968, and this bloody memento of New Mexico's outlaw days was lost. I've been unable to find proof that Tom "Black Jack" Ketchum ever tried to hold up a train in the vicinity of Cerrillos. However, he did stage other robberies across the Southwest, and railroad companies posted a reward for his capture.

Tom and his brother, Sam, had been raised near San Saba, Texas, and became working cowboys. But Tom had a mean streak. He killed a rancher in 1895 and fled west. Sam followed him a short time later. They seem to have landed in southeastern Arizona. At that time, a notorious outlaw named William "Black Jack" Christian led a gang operating in the area. The gang was caught in a gun battle with a posse in April 1897, and Christian was killed. As it happened, with his dark and sinister look, Christian bore a strong resemblance to Tom Ketchum from Texas. As Tom gained fame for banditry, people began to refer to him as Black Jack.

With lawmen breathing down their necks, Tom, Sam and an accomplice named Spindel slipped into New Mexico. Near Socorro, Spindel rode into town for supplies. Sheriff Holm O. Bursum recognized him, they shot it out, and the county paid for Spindel's burial expenses.

Black Jack and his brother continued on to northeastern New Mexico. On September 3, 1897, the pair held up the Colorado & Southern train west of Raton, between Folsom and Des Moines. The location was at a place called Twin Mountain Curve, where the engineer had to slow to a crawl. Afterward, they conducted other robberies in West Texas and New Mexico.

Sam was back in the Des Moines country in 1899 with a gang to stick up the same train again at the Twin Mountain Curve. This time a posse caught up with the thieves, and Sam Ketchum was wounded in a blazing fight. Taken to the penitentiary in Santa Fe, the desperado refused treatment. To the doctor, he said grimly, "I'm not going to let you cure me and then break my neck." He knew that the New Mexico legislature had recently passed a law making train robbery a capital offense.

Shortly after, Sam Ketchum died from infection and was buried in Santa Fe's Odd Fellows Cemetery. Knowing nothing of the fate of his brother, Black Jack returned to northeastern New Mexico, and attempted another heist on the Colorado & Southern at Twin Mountain Curve. This time, he was alone. A plucky conductor, however, winged him with a sawed-off shotgun. Black Jack escaped into the brush but was easily captured the next day.

The outlaw was transported to Trinidad, Colorado, where his arm was amputated. Then he was moved to Santa Fe for safe keeping.

On September 6, 1900, Black Jack the train robber got a one-way ticket to Clayton, where he stood trial for "felonious assault upon a railroad." The jury found him guilty and sentenced him to hang. After appeals were exhausted, the condemned man was escorted to a Clayton gallows surrounded by a stockade fence. Spectators were admitted by ticket. The date was April 26, 1901.

As he climbed the wooden steps, Black Jack said to his captors: "Better hurry up boys, because I'm due in Hell for dinner."

While he was languishing in jail, Mr. Ketchum had eaten well and put on extra weight. Thus, when the trap was sprung and he hit the end of the rope, his head popped off. A mortician sewed it back on the body before burial.

A photographer took a series of grisly pictures of the execution, before and after. They have been published repeatedly, and the last time I looked, copies were on public display in Clayton.

Black Jack Ketchum was the only person ever hanged under the territorial law that imposed the death penalty on train robbers. His grave can be visited in the cemetery on the east side of Clayton. It is marked with a tombstone placed by the Union County Historical Society.

III

FACSIMILE OF 1970 EDITION

DYNAMITE AND SIX-SHOOTER

Jeff Burton

My advice to the boys of the country is not to steal horses or sheep, but either rob a train or bank when you have got to be an outlaw, and every man who comes in your way, kill him; spare him no mercy, for he will show you none. This is the way I feel about it, and I think I feel right about it.

TOM KETCHUM

26 April 1901

palomino press
AN IMPRINT OF
THE PRESS OF THE TERRITORIAN

First published 1970 by
PALOMINO PRESS
an Imprint of
THE PRESS OF THE TERRITORIAN
Box 1847, Santa Fe, New Mexico.

Contents

	ACKNOWLEDGMENTS	
	THE BOLDEST OUTLAWS	1
1.	"I COULD KILL A BUZZARD A-FLYING"	9
2.	VAGRANT YEARS	16
3.	THREE MURDERS AND A DEAD RINGER	23
4.	EASY MONEY AND HARD RIDING	31
5.	CROSSED TRAILS	39
6.	THE STEIN'S PASS IMBROGLIO	48
7.	FRAMED	53
8.	DYNAMITE AND SIX-SHOOTER	61
9.	SEPARATE WAYS	67
10.	ANOTHER INCIDENT AT TWIN MOUNTAINS	73
11.	BULLETS IN TURKEY CREEK CANYON	79
12.	THE SIXTEENTH OF AUGUST	91
13.	DEAD TO RIGHTS	104
14.	POINTS OF LAW	110
15.	AN AMBUSH FOR GEORGE SCARBOROUGH	132
16.	"WILL YOU DIE GAME, BOYS?"	138
17.	OFF WITH HIS HEAD	145
18.	EMPTY SADDLES AND LONELY GRAVES	158
	TALES THAT WERE TOLD	171
	NOTES	188
	BIBLIOGRAPHY	215

Frontispiece: Tom Ketchum before he became an outlaw. Other illustrations between pages 90 and 91.

TOM KETCHUM
It is not known when or where this picture was taken, but Ketchum's appearance, and the style of the clothing, would place it within the period 1887-1890.

ACKNOWLEDGMENTS

This book could not have been written without the generous assistance of many people who made available to the author much of the raw material from which this study of Tom Ketchum and his times has been fashioned. Writing is hard work that has to be borne alone; research, more often than not, is the sum of an author's indebtedness to others. This author can but hope that he has made good and conscientious use of all the help given to him.

A special word of thanks, first, to Phil Cooke, of Santa Fe, New Mexico. Over a period of several years he interviewed, read, transcribed —well, what I should say is that without his efforts and exhortations the book might not even have been started; more latterly, he and Mrs Cooke, Nena, even bestirred into useful activity a guest who, left to his own inclinations, might cheerfully have whiled away sun-laden hours with the dreams no stuff was ever made on.

Mrs Joyce Hines, of East Ham, London, deserves a particular word of praise for turning a manuscript that was written almost entirely in longhand into a neat final typescript.

I was fortunate enough to encounter, either in person or through correspondence, many other helpful and thoughtful people. Through them I obtained a great deal of information from both primary and secondary sources.

Rose Marie Alderete, Clerk of the Court, and Glenna Lawrence, Assistant, Supreme Court of New Mexico, Santa Fe; Mary Arnett, Librarian, *The Light*, San Antonio, Texas; Joseph "Mack" Axford, Tombstone, Arizona; J.E. Baker, Warden, and Tom J. Trujillo, Records Supervisor, State Penitentiary of New Mexico, Santa Fe; Larry Ball, of Boulder, Colorado; Xanthus "Kit" Carson, of Albuquerque, New Mexico; Mary G. Eckhoff, Assistant Director, Diplomatic, Legal, and Fiscal Records Division, National Archives, Washington, D.C.; S.C. Kay Evatz, University of Colorado Libraries, Western Historical Collection, Boulder,

Colorado; Frank A. Eyman, Superintendent, Arizona State Prison, Florence, Arizona; Bill Farringdon, of Santa Fe, New Mexico; George Fitzpatrick, of Albuquerque; Jeanette Harris, Public Library, San Antonio, Texas; Susie Henderson, Museum Library, Santa Fe; Virginia P. Hoke, Southwest Reference, Public Library, El Paso, Texas; Myra Ellen Jenkins, Archivist, State Archives of New Mexico, Santa Fe; the staff — I don't know any of their names—of the Photoduplication Service of the Library of Congress, Washington, D.C.; Lady Luck, of no fixed abode, who smiled from time to time, and not always to deceive; Louis E. Montgomery, Brady, Texas; Kathleen Pierson, State Historical Society of Colorado, Colorado State Museum, Denver; Colin Rickards, now usually in Toronto, Ontario, with whom I discussed the shape of the projected book on a number of occasions, and who offered much good advice; G. Martin Ruoss, Special Collections Librarian, Coronado Room, Zimmerman Library, Albuquerque; and Margaret Sparks, Research Librarian, Arizona Pioneers' Historical Society, Tucson, Arizona.

My grateful thanks to them all.

J. B.
10 May 1970

THE BOLDEST OUTLAWS

The oral tradition of fable and ballad, out of which the patterns of legend were woven through the countless centuries of the past, was fading in Tom Ketchum's own lifetime. He will never become one of those folklore villains whose violent and lawless ways have been burnished with an illusive romance. If he is remembered at all, it is mostly for the peculiar circumstances which attended the curtailment of his earthly career. Yet, as a man who was noted in his own day, and who stood out above most others in his profession, he is worthy of more than passing mention. He and his companions were the boldest outlaws ever to ride the Southwest, and almost the last of their line.

Tom Ketchum and his older brother Sam were on the dodge in Texas, New Mexico, and Arizona for less than four years; their career of banditry lasted for little more than two years. But at least five men—perhaps as many as seven or eight—were killed by the various members of the gang; and seven trains were held up—four in New Mexico, and three in Texas. The death of Sam and the capture of Tom did not end the story, for their associates continued to ride and rob for several years more, usually in the company of some of the principal outlaws from the Northern Plains.

During most of the period between the spring of 1897 and the summer of 1899, there were only four in the gang: Tom and Sam Ketchum, Will Carver, and Dave Atkins. As long as this combination held together, Tom was leader, although, as he once stated, "everybody was consulted in most things". His was always the dominant personality until the others found at last that they could stand no more of him and told him so.

Dark skinned and black haired, he was six foot two inches tall and weighed about one hundred and eighty pounds. "At close range", wrote Jack Culley, recalling his journey in the train which carried the convicted bandit to the penitentiary, "Tom Ketchum struck me as being one of the most powerful men I've ever seen, with corresponding activity. I had a feeling he could have taken the two sheriffs and everyone else on the coach and thrown us out onto the track... Every inch... seemed to me brawn and muscle". Leonard Alverson, who was wrongfully convicted of taking part in one of the gang's hold-ups, also spoke of Tom's "wonderful physique".

He was devious and cunning, and his instinct for concealment when in flight was a sharp as that of the wolverine. Though he was not much given to laughter, he sometimes showed a dry, sardonic twist of humor; while the childishness in him was as apt to manifest itself in a practical joke as in a swirl of rage. Opinions differed as to whether his features connoted the intelligence he undoubtedly possessed. "Tom Ketchum's face", commented Culley, "did not impress me as being that of a particularly intelligent man; it was the face essentially of a man of action. The small black eyes were the most notable feature of it, shining and piercing, and possessed of an extraordinary alertness, like that you see in the eyes of some wild animals. This feature it was doubtless that accounted for his ability to detect, and draw a bead on, an object simultaneously". According to one newspaperman, they were "marvellous eyes . . . small, brown or greenish gray as his mood changed and indefinably swift and menacing". Another reporter noted that Ketchum had "an intelligent face and a pair of bright, piercing eyes".

Behind those eyes lay a nimble mind, an uncertain temper, and a sullen and malevolent disposition. Most of the Western outlaws, like most of the criminals of any time or place, were quickly caught or killed because they liked or trusted too many people. Tom Ketchum was taken because he liked or trusted practically no one. Both his unbounded nerve and his bouts of wanton cruelty may be set down to his lack of regard for anything that breathed, not excluding himself.

Sam Ketchum, nine years his elder, was different in nearly every respect. He was a big man, more than six feet tall but an inch or so shorter than his brother. He was fair skinned, with reddish-blond hair, blue eyes, and heavily freckled face and arms. "I picture him vividly", wrote Culley, "as the finest figure of a man in my recollection". Bob Lewis, who knew both of them, said this: "Sam Ketchum was a brave and courageous man and if his brother hadn't been such a bad influence he would have been all right". He was always popular and his later career mystified many people who had known him on the range. But his decision to take the left-hand trail cannot be attributed wholly to Tom's "bad influence". After Tom and several companions had murdered a rancher in Texas, Sam followed them west, presumably in order to avoid having to answer questions. To this extent, Tom Ketchum was the cause of his brother's outlawry. What was more significant, however, was that Sam was forty-one years old at this time, and he had nothing to show for a life which had been chiefly devoted to honest toil. This may go far towards explaining why, in the spring of 1896, he threw in with Tom. Thereafter, one thing followed another until soon there could be no turning back. Eventually he assumed leadership of the gang, only to demonstrate that there was little point in pulling a successful outlaw coup unless the getaway was to be handled as skilfully as the robbery itself.

The third member of the gang, and the only one of the original four to venture into the far more dangerous field of bank robbery, was Will Carver. Lighthaired and fair-complexioned, but deeply sun-tanned, he was of medium height and wiry build, weighing about one hundred and forty pounds. Leonard Alverson, an Arizona cowpuncher who was well acquainted with the outlaws and their ways, characterized Carver as "a nice fellow but very melancholy over the death of his wife." Albert Thompson, who never met Carver but who came to learn a good deal about the gang, depicted him in terms much harsher than those of Alverson and others: "cold, fiendish, calculating and a dead shot". There is plenty of corroboration for Thompson's last assertion, but otherwise the assessment is a poor one. Whatever else he may have been, William Carver was not "fiendish". Although cool-tempered and usually level-headed, he seems not to have possessed the shrewdness of the "calculating" man. Amiable on the surface, with a quick turn of wit, he was inwardly reticent—apparently unable or unwilling to enter into close friendships—rather than "cold". There was nothing of the firebrand in him; he avoided gunplay whenever he could. But when he was forced into a position where he really had to fight, he was as game and deadly a gunman as ever looked down the sights of a Winchester. An article in the *San Angelo Standard* sums him up best.

> Will Carver... was a plain, unassuming, quiet sort of desperado, of a very retiring disposition, and rather shunned than courted notoriety. He was adverse to society, and preferred to dwell in the solitudes of the great southwestern plains, with a few choice spirits...

That newspaper story was, in effect, Carver's obituary notice, and it was written because, a few months earlier, the bandit, throwing aside his customary reserve, had taken to deserting the "solitudes of the plains" for the hurly-burly of the red light districts, consequently to become either contemptuous of danger or merely careless in his movements. Survival, for an outlaw, depended upon constant watchfulness. Will Carver grew casual and walked into trouble, with the usual result.

Dave Atkins is the least known of the band, but he took part in five hold-ups before he broke with Tom Ketchum. He was five feet eleven inches in height, slimly-built, and weighed about one hundred and fifty pounds. His complexion was "very dark"—the inheritance no doubt, of an Indian strain which Joseph Axford, who met him in Arizona, believed to be Comanche. His hair was brown and he sometimes wore a thin mustache. The description compiled by the Pinkerton National Detective Agency observed that he "drops his head when talking," and called attention to his "peculiar slouchy walk." Rather quaintly, the gang dubbed him "Tommy Atkins". He tried to go straight, and Axford believed that "he had the quality to make it that way"; but the law does not lightly forgive, and he was swiftly located in Montana and taken to Texas to stand trial for the murder, committed by him in conjunction with Tom Ketchum and others, which had set him upon the outlaw path.

Three other men rode with the gang, though only briefly. They were William E. Lay, Bruce "Red" Weaver, and Ed Cullen, whose correct family name may have been Bullion.

"Elza" Lay, already wanted for armed robbery in Idaho and Utah, was with the gang for some three or four months. Many people, including a Territorial Governor, were genuinely impressed by his fortitude and gallantry. If others took a more critical view of his ability to charm authority, they have left no testimony to that effect. Almost alone of the truly notorious outlaws of the West, he was accorded sympathetic treatment. To his credit, he never reneged upon the trust placed in him.

Although, in the opinion of "Butch Cassidy", Weaver lacked sand and was fit only to act as messenger, he probably took part in one hold-up, at least. Loud mouthed and aggressive, he was also much wilier than he appeared to be. He was arrested on three or four occasions, but never convicted; and at one stage he played a double game without being detected. There was a retributive irony about the manner of his death.

All that needs to be said about Ed Cullen at this point is that his active career as a road-agent lasted for less than three hours.

Such were the men who were responsible for the most lucrative series of train robberies ever accomplished in the Southwest. Among their few trusted allies were four who themselves took up outlawry after the fall of the original gang. Three of them—Ben, Ed, and George Kilpatrick—were raised near the Ketchum place, in southwest Texas. They knew Tom,

Sam, Carver, and Atkins long before any of the four ventured into serious crime. At least two of the Kilpatricks rode into New Mexico to make contact with the gang. Thomas S. Capehart was a cowboy whose origins are unknown. The name appears to have been his real one and the claim that it was merely an alias for Harvey Logan is entirely without foundation. Unlike most, Tom Capehart was, to some extent, pushed into crime.

Tom Ketchum was not "Black Jack" and his gang was not the "Black Jack gang". But an unwitting fusion of identities, springing from a complexity of coincidence and controversy, established him in the popular mind as the celebrated Black Jack. Doubtless he will be Black Jack in scores of magazine articles as yet undreamed of.

Because of the fallacious belief that he was Black Jack, Ketchum has been connected with many crimes in New Mexico and Arizona, such as the robbery or attempted robbery of the bank at Nogales, which were the work of others. In contrast, his operations in Texas, where he was most successful, have been given scant attention or none.

It is broadly true that the representatives of law and order were not outstanding for their integrity, their courage, or their sense of duty. The question of integrity was hardly paramount. People who have been robbed do not really care very much whether a thief-catcher is a drunkard, a whoremaster, and perhaps even a bit of a thief himself, just so long as he gets his man. Many of the officers who ought to have been keeping close tabs on the outlaw gangs of the Southwest simply did not even try very hard. Their failings placed a heavy burden upon the relatively few lawmen who sought to do all that was required of them and sometimes more. There were other handicaps, moreover. Successive United States Marshals of New Mexico and Arizona, Democratic and Republican, were not making empty excuses when, every so often, they wrote to Washington to outline the difficulties of getting close to such outlaws as the Ketchums. The following, from William Griffith, Marshal of Arizona, is typical of their letters:

> . . . The country in which these parties operate is of great extent, parts of it very rough and mountainous and all of it very sparsely settled. The posse in search of them must be in condition to travel fast and far at a moment's notice. This necessitates their being unincumbered with a pack train. They must, therefore, depend upon the country for food. The only places where this food can be obtained are at cattle ranches scattered throughout the country from 30 to 50 miles apart. Some of the owners are in sympathy with the outlaws and the news of a visit of a posse to their ranches could be scattered far and wide as fast as horseflesh could carry it. Even were the pro-

prietors of all these ranches favorably disposed, they dare not sell or give aid to the posse. Did they do so their lives and property could pay the penalty as has happened in the past. . .
I would respectfully request. . . that the posse be allowed to purchase supplies in the field without being required to furnish receipts therefor. I am liable to be called upon any moment to put a man in the field and am unwilling to do so unless allowed to exercise my discretion as to the method of supplying such men when on duty. I do not wish to uselessly jeopardize the lives of my men or the residents of the country in which they must operate, nor do I intend to put a force in the field unless there is a fair prospect of ridding the country of these outlaws. . .

Tom and Sam sometimes hid out on the ranch of their elder brother, Berry, near San Angelo, Texas, and the gang were well known at numerous ranch houses and horse camps in southwest Texas, New Mexico, and southeast Arizona. Bill Lutley, who ran a few cattle under the Bar Boot brand and who lived near Wildcat Canyon, the band's favorite retreat in Arizona, saw a great deal of the outlaws and kept his mouth shut. There were many like him. Always, though, there was the danger that someone might betray them, either deliberately or inadvertently. The capture of Elza Lay was the eventual outcome of the gang's long-standing acquaintance with V.H. Lusk.

In all probability, the Ketchums first met Virgil Hogue Lusk when they were working as cowboys in the Pecos Valley. He ranched at Chimney Wells, some twenty-five miles east of the town of Eddy (later Carlsbad), New Mexico. It became their habit, in later years, to stop by at Lusk's place for a meal and a change of horses. They might trade horses with Lusk; or they might leave their worn-out mounts (usually stolen from one or other of the large cattle companies) somewhere in the vicinity of Lusk's range, intending to recover them the next time they passed through, perhaps several months later. This went on for two or three years until, in the end, Old Man Lusk decided that he had seen enough of it.

The cowboys, even more than the ranchers, took sides with the outlaws. Some, certainly, were fugitives themselves; but they were in the minority. The general attitude was governed mainly by a deep prejudice against all lawmen and by the fact that almost all of the bandits of the Great Plains had punched cows at one time or another.

It should not be overlooked, either, that the ranch women were more kindly disposed toward the outlaw than to the lawman. The outlaw, we are told, would usually offer to help with the dishes and would eschew rough language, whereas quite often the officer was a graceless, coarsely-spoken fellow.

As a group, the Ketchum gang were anything but extrovert. "They are known to the officers as bushmen", said one report, "as they rarely go into a town, and spend all their time in the bush on ranches, where they are not likely to be found". They were fond of gambling but, for a while at least, they kept away from liquor. Their abstinence, although amounting to no more than common sense, is testimony to the authority or persuasiveness of Tom Ketchum, who rarely drank anything stronger than coffee: after the others had got rid of Tom, they began to hit the bottle hard and to behave ineptly in other ways, inevitably hastening their own downfall.

In two years and three months the gang stole more than $100,000—probably as much as $180,000. In one robbery only were there as many as five men to take a share of the loot. In most instances the booty was to be split four ways, although on one occasion circumstances intervened to arrange matters in such a way that nearly all of the loot fell to one man.

The comments of Jack Potter, comming from a man who knew the outlaws, are oddly wayward. "I figure", he wrote, "that every member of the Black Jack [Ketchum] gang was a cowboy and [they] blundered by not having a yegg or dynamite man".

In the first place, dynamite was a readily obtainable commodity and quite often a cowboy might become familiar with its use in the course of his duties on the range. It required no extraordinary skill to blow up an iron safe.

Apart from this, whenever the gang forced their way into an express car, the safe was cracked without undue difficulty. There is no doubt at all that they were a capable bunch.

Almost the one question that defies an answer concerns their personal expenditure. It is known only that they paid for their clothing, supplies, guns, ammunition, and the like. The acquisition of one or two items of jewelry seems to have marked the limit of their extravagance. During his time with the Ketchums, Will Carver, the only man to take part in all five of the successful hold-ups, "earned" something between $30,000 and $50,000. Tom Ketchum's share, from four robberies, could not have been less than $15,000 and may have been double that amount. These were vast sums for men who pursued "a solitary outdoor life". Some of the money may have been impounded by people who had undertaken to hold it in safekeeping for the gang. While the outlaws were habitual gamblers, it would be unrealistic to suppose that they were consistent and heavy losers; in any case, very often their opponents were each other. Most of the money stolen by these outlaws simply cannot be accounted for.

Their story is one of violence and ultimate futility, with few softening lines of sentiment or humor. But it is a story which sheds light upon a facet of their times. These men were desperadoes, the most daring of their kind; the individual must judge how much of what they did was worse than what could be done against them in the name of the people.

Chapter One

"I COULD KILL A BUZZARD A-FLYING"

If the early direction of a man's life is resolved by the coalescent forces of ancestry, environment, and upbringing which help to determine the pattern of his character, his ultimate course must still depend upon choice, subject only to the random interference of mere chance. The actions of maturity are not ruled by the lottery of hereditary and childhood. Somewhere a choice has to be made and, like everyone who reaches his middle years, Sam and Tom Ketchum made theirs. A study of what is known of their formative influences furnishes some insight into the character of these men without explaining what it was that led them, in their prime years, to stake their lives on their six-shooters.

They came of old Anglo-American stock. By the middle of the last century the Ketchum/Ketcham family tree had sprouted branches in New England, Virginia, Illinois and Tennessee. Their story is essentially a reflection in miniature of the great theme of settlement and migration.

The first of the clan to penetrate the frontier country of Texas arrived there in 1846 from Illinois. They were James Ketchum, twenty years old, a native of Illinois; his wife Mary, nineteen and originally from Kentucky; and their baby daughter Elizabeth, born in Illinois. Within months of their arrival Mary E. Ketchum gave birth to a son, George W.

Some two years passed before they were joined by an elder brother of James, Green Berry Ketchum; his wife Temperance; and their one child, a one year old girl, also christened Elizabeth.

Green B. Ketchum was born in Alabama, circa 1822. A year or two later his parents moved to Illinois, where they settled. Evidently they must have had neighbors from Kentucky, for Green, like Jim, married a girl from that Commonwealth, leaving Illinois very shortly after the arrival of the first-born.

It is not known where the Ketchums lived during their first few years in Texas. By the time they cast their eyes on the fine grazing lands near the historic but long deserted Spanish mission of San Saba, Green and Temperance Ketchum had added two sons to the household. They were

— 9 —

Green Berry, junior, born in 1851 or 1852, and Samuel W., whose advent occurred in 1854, probably in the month of August.

Richland Creek rises in western San Saba County, almost the geographical center of Texas. For six months of the year it is dry. When there is a flow, it runs nearly due east for thirty miles to empty into the San Saba River, a western tributary of the Colorado, at a point five miles west of San Saba town. There were almost no settlers along the creek when Green and James Ketchum built their cabins a few miles above the mouth of the creek and began to establish themselves as cattlemen. Until the appearance of several white families at old San Saba during the first years of Texas statehood, the country had long known no human imprint save the marks of nomad Indians in passage. These Indians naturally viewed the intruders with resentment and tried to encourage them to leave but the newcomers fought, stayed, prospered, and multiplied.

In July 1860 the census taker for San Saba County, Assistant Marshal W.B. Coffee, noted that Green B. Ketchum, a stock raiser, owned personal estate to the value of $4534. There were four offspring, the youngest a girl six months old, Nancy B. Ketchum. The next house visited was that of John L. Harkey, a farmer, who had the same number of children as Green Ketchum but very little money. James Ketchum, another stockraiser, now had six children and was worth $3734. John Harkey's place was located directly between the ranches of the two Ketchums. Their other near neighbor, James C. Rogan, was a physician.

On or about October 31st, 1863, a fifth child was born to Green and Temperance Ketchum. He was given the names Thomas Edward.

Almost directly thereafter misfortunes started to gather at the doors of the Ketchums. Tom had barely progressed beyond the crawling stage when his father died. He was four when the next blow fell.

James Ketchum and his bachelor brother John, who had joined them a few years earlier, were returning from a cattle drive to New Mexico, their saddlebags loaded with money received from the sale of the herd. Two cowboys were with them. Near the stage stand on the Concho River they were ambushed and killed by a band of Kickapoo Indians. The widow, the grown daughter, Elizabeth, and the oldest of the boys, George, were left to cope with the ranch and the other seven children.

By 1870 there were still only about ten families living along the creek. The census returns for that year give a fair indication of the difficulties experienced by the two Ketchum households: the personal estate of each was worth less than half of what it had been ten years before. Even so they were very much better off than most of their neighbors. Green B. Ketchum, Junior, always known as "Berry", was now nineteen years old, Sam was about sixteen, and Thomas E., six. Sheriff J. Frazer Brown, the enumerator, if he was not in a great hurry, must have been endowed with astonishingly weak powers of observation, for he classified young Tom Ketchum as "female".

Two years later Temperance Ketchum died and Berry assumed sole charge and the bulk of the responsibility.

For Tom Ketchum there were several years of schooling. The nature and scope of his formal education is a subject worthy of more than idle interest, since in later years stories of his being a college graduate were unblinkingly filed by correspondents to the city newspapers, inspiring one imaginative gentleman of the press to designate Harvard as Ketchum's alma mater.

Now, there was hardly anything in San Saba County which owned to the name of "school". But there were any number of "academies", "colleges", and "seminaries". The local pedagogues wrote out high-sounding credentials for themselves, and offered most impressive curricula for the young gentlemen and young ladies of San Saba and environs. They knew very well that no one in the locality would apply for his offspring to be guided joyously through the classics or edified by instruction in the social refinements; but they knew, too, that the more imposing the pretensions, the readier the parents would be to believe in the professor as a fellow who could be trusted to impart a working knowledge of the three R's, or of one or two of them, anyway. So it was at just such an establishment that Tom Ketchum received his college education and, like Berry and Sam before him, learned to read and write.

Although religion was not a softening influence in San Saba County, the people were fervent churchgoers. Perhaps they needed to be; but there were the social aspects to be considered, too. Baptists, Methodists, and members of the Church of Christ sect were the most plentiful groups. The Ketchums were of the Baptist faith. Tom Ketchum, in his later life, had no use for any form of religion, yet his almost total abstinence from strong drink and his reflections on the nature of Hell might have owed something to those Sundays in the pew.

There may have been only a handful of families living by Richland Creek in 1870, but they were large ones. Mose numerous were the Harkeys, among whom was a four year old boy, Daniel Riley "Dee" Harkey, who in time would become a controversial figure in Carlsbad, New

Mexico, first as a peace officer and then, much later, as an author. Then there were the Halls, the Weavers, and the Browns. Finally there were the Duncans.

Tom Ketchum's sister Elizabeth had married Abijah S. "Bige" Duncan a year or two prior to 1870. In his book Dee Harkey states that the Duncan boys, Bige and Dick, were first cousins of Berry, Sam, and Tom Ketchum, that the Duncans were thieves, and that they "got to be vicious criminals". The first assertion is almost certainly a mistaken one. If the second is true, it is demonstrably true also of most of their neighbors. The third is half true: Richard Duncan was perpetrator of one of the foulest crimes on record in Texas, but Bige eventually became an honest and respected cattleman.

As the threat of Indian trouble receded, the settlers of San Saba County concentrated increasingly upon harassing each other. Horse-theft was commonplace; cattle rustling a habit. Many a rancher registered several different brands and owned one which bore a distinct similarity to that of some neighbor. There was ill-feeling between the big cattlemen and the small ranchers. All of them stood arrayed in angry opposition to the grangers who began to move into the rich valley lands during the late seventies. To the thieving was added, occasionally, violence. Successive editor-owners of the little local weekly, *The San Saba News*, usually refrained from covering the incidents in depth or detail. Sometimes the paper spoke for the cowmen, sometimes for the grangers. Bald summaries of District Court proceedings, together with accounts of such episodes as the editor deemed deserving of more than a brief word or two in passing, afford no more than a glimpse into the extent of the thievery. One week, a man would be flatteringly portrayed as a fine citizen; the next week, his arrest in an adjoining county while in charge of a band of stolen horses would be reported without comment.

Tom Ketchum first crossed the law, for all the law could tell, at the age of sixteen. Then record discloses bleakly that his case was called on March 17th, 1880, as number 29 on the docket. There is no note as to charge or disposition. Many years afterwards it was said that, in his youth, he failed to attend court when summoned as a witness. If this be so, the charge would have been one of contempt.

In the Fall elections that year 104 votes were cast in the Richland Springs precinct. The Richland Springs community, sixteen miles northwest of San Saba, now comprised "a post office, three stores, a school house, blacksmith shop and several residences". Though not much of a town yet, remarked the *News*, it has "fine possibilitys". One unnamed ranchman had owned only eleven cows and calves ten years before; now his herd numbered four or five hundred.

In this period several other Ketchums moved into the county. A Dr. N. Ketchum set up store in San Saba town to sell cantaloupes and five-cent cigars, twenty-five dollar sewing machines and "Champion Lamps, giving the light of sixty candles, and warranted not explosive". Dr. Ketchum, the "practical druggist", was also one of the stoutest pillars of the Baptist church. Henry Ketchum arrived at about the same time, lent his support to the Methodist church, joined a Prohibition Convention, and taught school "for the good people of Wallace Creek", fifteen miles from San Saba. The doctor, who had at least two grown sons, and the school teacher may have been uncles of Berry, Sam, and Tom.

Berry and Sam Ketchum, in the early eighties, were a pair of stalwart young bachelor ranchmen; first-rate cowmen with a flourishing herd and excellent range, more honest than most of their neighbors. Both, seemingly, were headed for success, but Sam was becoming restive.

Pitiably little is known or can be inferred of the relationship between the brothers at this time. Berry was to say that both Sam and Tom were "wild". But Berry was master and Sam might naturally have felt unsettled and perhaps slightly jealous. Tom, very much the junior, would have been allowed little or no voice in the running of the place. It is a fair surmise that Sam, himself discontented, began more and more to side with his younger brother.

As Tom grew to young manhood, he steadily won notice for his skill as a marksman. Nearly twenty years later, when his notoriety had struck its peak, a correspondent in Austin wrote that Tom was "widely known in this section as a dead shot with rifle and pistol." Tom himself did not gainsay this assessment.

"I was counted as fine a shot as ever fired a gun", he once recalled. "I could take a rifle and kill a buzzard or anything that was a-flying; take a tomato can and shoot it up into the air and then hit it again before it came down."

Besides devoting a lot of his time to the expenditure of powder and lead, he got through a good deal of hard work and became a good cowhand.

There is nothing to show that any of the Ketchums engaged in larceny during the early 1880s, but someone in the vicinity of Richland Springs was a persistent horse thief. Israel Harkey and Sam Ketchum were innocent but perhaps reticent witnesses to an affair reported by the *News* on Saturday, January 28th, 1882:

> A suspicious looking man was seen by Mr I. M. Harkey on last Tuesday crossing the river about four miles above town [San Saba]. He was riding a large sorrel horse branded LHF, connected, and leading a roan horse. He asked Mr Harkey for directions to some place on the Colorado. Mr Harkey came on to town and notified the authorities. Messrs. Alex Doran and M. J. Murray went in pursuit, and soon lost his trail, but went to the place he said he was going to, and there learned that no such man had been seen. In about an hour after he was seen by Mr Harkey, Mr Sam Ketchum saw a man riding a horse and leading one, that suited the description given by Mr Harkey, going into the Longley pasture. It is thought he is the same man who stole Messrs. Murray and Bagley's horses last week. Horse stealing is getting to be quite common in those parts, and it is thought one man is doing it. It is strange that he can't be caught.

No doubt the neighbors did not have to read too closely between the lines to understand exactly what had happened.

Such stories, with variations, were coming in from all over the county. Early in the spring of 1882 some of the cattlemen got together and formed the San Saba County Stock Association. Cattle rustling and horse-stealing continued apace. On December 15th, 1883, the editor went as far as he dared toward naming some of the culprits:

> We are sorry to say there are one or two parties in the county who think their brands are "too well known" and that it is not good policy, more especially for small owners, to make their brands and range locations known through the papers. . . .

From there he argued at length that the reverse was true, and practically accused the smaller ranchers of rustling. In the same issue he commented approvingly on an Article recently passed by the Legislature "for the benefit of the wild and woolly and hard to curry" who could not restrain themselves from "wilfully disturbing a congregation of worshippers". The benefits came in the form of a $25 fine and, at the discretion of the jury, up to thirty days in the county jail. Every now and then the editorial displeasure would be directed at the young fellows, mostly "from the western portion of the county", who came into town week-ends and signalled their departure with a crackle of revolver fire, but nothing seems to have been done about them.

As nearly as can be determined, it was in 1884 or the early part of 1885 that Sam and Tom Ketchum became known as rustlers. They were indicted and fled the county. Joseph M. Harkey, the sheriff, sent his brother Dee and Jim Hall to bring them back. The brothers were traced to Cow Valley, in McCulloch County, some twenty miles west of Richland Springs. Dee Harkey relates in his book that the Ketchums saw them coming and escaped on race horses.

It is improbable that Berry Ketchum's decision to leave San Saba County was brought about by the dereliction of Sam and Tom. The county was becoming thickly settled, allowing no elbow-room for a well-to-do rancher eager to expand his interests. Some of the Halls, the richest cattlemen in western San Saba County, had already left for New Mexico and California. Berry moved his headquarters no more than a hundred miles west of Richland Springs. His new ranch was located in Tom Green County, several miles south and slightly west of the hamlet of Knickerbocker and near the eastern line of Irion County. This was the place Sam and Tom called home for the next two or three years and continued to visit at intervals for almost as long as they remained free men.

Their brother-in-law, Abijah Duncan, followed them to Tom Green County a year or so afterward. In December 1885 Bige stood trial for "theft of cattle", was found guilty of "illegal driving", and fined $100. He and Elizabeth did not stay in San Saba County for very long after that. George Ketchum, eldest son of their uncle James, was actually the first of the family to arrive in Tom Green County, having taken his Mexican bride to live there in the late seventies.

Too much weight should not be attached to the early errors and misdemeanors of Sam and Tom Ketchum. Aside from the argument that many small men become big by successful pilfering of one kind or another, there is abundant evidence that most of the San Saba ranchers were thieves one day and victims the next. Sheriff Joe Harkey, too, was in trouble soon enough. Shortly after he was beaten for re-election in 1886 it was noticed that his accounts were defective. In December 1887 a grand jury found that Harkey had embezzled several hundred dollars, in which endeavors he was aided by the County Commissioners. Even this was only a minor impropriety compared with the murderous activities of the San Saba Mob, successor of one or other of the local Associations, which dealt in assassination and intimidation for some twelve or fifteen years from its inception in the early eighties.

Whatever might be charged against Tom Ketchum, it cannot be said that he made San Saba County a better place simply by betaking himself elsewhere.

Chapter Two

VAGRANT YEARS

Among the pertinacious but unsubstantiated stories about Tom Ketchum is the one in which he is said to have gone to Arizona and gambled away an inheritance of $1500. In its original form this yarn would have it that Ketchum hailed from New Jersey and came into the money upon the death of a relative there. Since this is palpably absurd the rest of the tale scarcely commands heed. What may have happened is that Sam and Tom arrived at some sort of a settlement with Berry.

During the two or three years which followed their departure from Richland Springs, they had worked with Berry on and off, hired out to various cattle outfits near San Angelo and in the Devil's River country to the south, and taken part in round-ups in the vicinity of Eldorado and Ozona. Probably, too, they had trailed cattle along the Yellow Houses route to New Mexico. By 1886 or 1887, when they decided to cut adrift from Berry, they were familiar with the cow country of much of Texas to the south and west of Abilene. At this juncture they did leave the State, and they may well have passed through Arizona on their way north. Their destination was Snake Valley, a tract of desert forty miles west of Milford, in south-eastern Utah.

In this remote and inhospitable locale, singularly unfitted for the raising of cattle and commending itself only to outlaws in dire need of a bolt hole, Sam and Tom Ketchum started a "ranch". Most of the time they were away from the valley, trading in livestock stolen from others. When they were at home they were host to such hard characters as Tom McCarty and Willard Christiansen, alias Matt Warner, a pair of horse thieves who later carried out a number of audacious bank robberies in Colorado, Oregon, and Washington.

After a year or so the climate, or the paucity of the profits, or perhaps even the inquisitiveness of the law, persuaded the brothers to withdraw from Snake Valley. By the close of 1888 they were back in Tom Green County.

Early in the following year Tom Ketchum was arrested by Sheriff

VAGRANT YEARS

Gerome W. Shields for disturbing the peace of the Sabbath in the manner so heavily frowned upon by the San Saba editor and expressly prohibited by statute. More explicitly, he pursued a dog with such tenacity of purpose that the distracted hound was driven to seek sanctuary. The dog tore down the aisle, and Tom charged after it, turning the service into utter disorder. Undeniably the peace had been breached; and wilfully so.

Nearly seven years were to pass before the authorities heard of any further transgression by Tom Ketchum and his crime, then, would be that of murder.

Soon after the dog-chasing episode Sam and Tom lit out for eastern New Mexico. Both brothers were hired as cowhands by the LFD, whose ranch headquarters were near Tascosa, in the Texas Panhandle.

Unlike many of those who wound up as outlaws, the Ketchums had not moved swiftly through the different gradations of crime. For the next six years they worked steadily as cowpunchers and trail hands. If they had felt themselves drawn toward outlawry, or committed to it, they would surely have turned bandit during the late eighties. In this period the Burrow gang, the Cornett-Whitley outlaws, and sundry others were responsible for a dozen hold-ups in Texas. There were numerous robberies in Arizona and the Indian Territory. Further north, so called "cowboy bandits" robbed the bank at Grover, Wyoming; a Northern Pacific train at Big Horn, Montana; the bank at Telluride, Colorado; a Denver and Rio Grande Western train near Thompson Springs, Utah; and, in 1890, another Northern Pacific train just outside New Salem, North Dakota. A train was robbed near Tascosa at about the time the Ketchums were working for the LFD. Nearly a year later one was stopped three miles south of Trinidad, Colorado, and the fireman was shot through the head— "for being sassy", as the conductor once put it. That New Mexico, almost alone among the western States and Territories, experienced no serious activity from outlaws during the late eighties and early nineties may be attributed, in part, to a law enacted a few years previously, under which the death sentence was mandatory for anyone convicted of holding up a train. This law was retained by successive Territorial Legislatures. It was still in force in 1899, when Tom Ketchum protested that he had never heard of it. But, in 1889 and 1890, neither Tom nor Sam had any cause to step wary of this law or any other. During these years, and the next four or five, they worked hard and saved little.

With the construction of the Fort Worth and Denver railroad during the late eighties, Amarillo became the shipping center for ranchers in the

DYNAMITE AND SIX-SHOOTER

Panhandle of Texas while Clayton, founded in March of 1888, similarly served the interests of the cattle and wool industries in eastern New Mexico. In the autumn of 1889 when Tom Ketchum first came up to Clayton with the trail herds, the town could offer three stores, two respectable hotels, one church, and a fair number of brothels, saloons, and gambling houses.

Tom and Sam, both of them votaries of Faro and Poker, made Charlie Meredith's saloon their favorite haunt. One of the resident gamblers, Frank Martinez, was "agreeable to play with", in Tom's view, "though Sam could beat him anytime dealing Monte". Whereas Sam, in common with most trail hands, had a liking for hard drink, Tom practically never touched the bottle. He had, at one time or another, sampled most forms of liquor, finding none of them to his taste.

There was no serious misbehavior from the brothers either in town or out on the range, but an incident described by James F. Hinkle, who met them on several occasions when he was wagon boss for the CA Bar outfit, provides another instance of Tom's boisterous and somewhat roguish sense of fun:

> Tom Ketchum got behind a pile of ties near the depot and with a beanshooter took it out on an engineer who was oiling his engine. He hit the engineer with buckshot while the trainman was stooping over and kept it up for a time. Finally the engineer located the trouble, got out his gun, and Tom hit it for the back end of a saloon.

As nearly as can be stated with chronological exactitude, Tom trailed cattle to Clayton with the S Cross in 1890 and the Carrizozo Cattle Company in 1891. The year after that he drove through Clayton and on to Cold Springs, in what is now the Oklahoma Panhandle, with the G-G herd, owned by Frank Garst, one of a number of ranchers who leased pasture in the Cherokee Outlet. There is no memorabilia of his personal life in these years other than a story in the "persistent rumor" category which casts him in the role of household predator. Although the girl's husband soon heard about the liaison he stood quietly aside until she became pregnant. Then, since it was obvious to all that the credit for her condition belonged to Thomas Ketchum, the cuckold reacted sharply by persuading the courts to undo the parson's work. There are no further details, except that the girl lived "somewhere above Amarillo".

In 1893 Tom went up to Clayton with a herd owned by W. G. Urton, who had extensive holdings north of Roswell. The following year found him in the employ of the VV ranch, a Lincoln County outfit. He was now nearly thirty-one years old and no better off than he had been five years earlier. This, he promised himself, would be his last season on the trail. An account of how Tom held himself to his vow comes from the pen of Jack Potter, another of the VV hands on that drive.

One of Ketchum's peculiarities, according to Potter, was his habit of administering self-punishment as a corrective to his mistakes. Awaking one morning to find that his horse had strayed during the night because the stake rope had not been secured, Tom made amends by directing a stream of abuse at himself as he walked down to the round-up camp, a mile away, occasionally reinforcing the catechism by beating himself about the head with his six-shooter. Only a few weeks after this he had far stronger cause for self chastisement.

For three seasons Tom had been lying adroitly and convincingly to a girl in Lincoln County. Each time he swore that he would save up his wages and marry her upon his return. At the outset of this particular drive, when "ranch folk for miles around" congregated at Fort Stanton to see off the outfit, Tom's girl "wept a little on his shoulder and told him that she would wait for him and that she could never love another". Tom rode away, assuring the other boys that this time he meant what he had told her.

Some days later the herd reached Fort Summer and Potter went for the mail which was awaiting collection from the Post Office. Ketchum was expecting a letter from the girl, and was mortified to learn there was none. He sat down gloomily and wrote her a long letter of reproach. When they got the cattle moving again Potter noticed that Ketchum was missing and turned back to look for him.

> I found him pulling his hair and cursing like a sailor. He began by swearing at the ugly weather and scarcity of water and then started out about his sweetheart, saying that if she "throwed him" he would go to the Hole in the Wall country and hide from women and hate them the rest of his life.

But less than a week later, when they camped on Perico creek, within sight of Clayton, Tom was in his best humor as he waited for the messenger boy to return with the mail. He grabbed the letters and feverishly sorted them through until he found the one addressed to him. He read it in silence, then took down his rope and strode away. Soon the sounds of "the most terrible cursing" arose from below the bank of the creek.

"There was old Ketchum", recalled Potter, "holding the letter in one hand and the doubled rope in the other. While beating himself over the head he was cursing himself for having confidence in women".

Someone tugged the rope away and asked him what the trouble was.

"Plenty", he replied, and give the letter to Potter, who read it out to the men:

> Tom Ketchum
> Trail Driver
> With John G. Bose.
>
> Sir:
>
> Yours from Fort Sumner received. Had I not received this I would never have written you You will remember the day that I bid you farewell and wept a little and told you that I could never love another.
>
> That was a little bait fixed up especially for your benefit. C. G. Slim was standing nearby looking on and you had no more than got out of sight when we went down to [Fort] Stanton and got married.
>
> He is a fine man and how I admire him! I hope that you will realize that you taught me how to lie and you will feel that you are now getting the results.
>
> Mrs. Cora Slim.

Tom immediately settled up with Bose and cut his two horses from the remuda. As he was packing his possessions onto one of the horses he was threatening some unseen or imaginary foe: "I dare you to make a move. You are liable to find your carcase stretched out on the prairie furnishing the coyotes a mess of carne".

In twenty minutes he was mounted and ready to leave.

"Adios boys", he said quietly. "I'm heading for the Hole in the Wall in Wyoming".

This anecdote may illustrate why Tom Ketchum became an outlaw, but obviously he did not devote himself to lawlessness simply because he though that he had been jilted. The clue to what must be the real explanation lies in the violence of the fit which seized him when he learned of his comeuppance. Ketchum's final choice, one must judge, was the natural product of his own unstable personality and improvident ways. These characteristics were manifest in his last years, with one difference: his spasms of unreasoning anger would be turned not against himself, as in the past, but against others. Yet, for all of this, it should not escape notice that there is no indication from either fact or folksay that he ever had anything further to do with women.

When Sam and Tom were not working cattle in New Mexico or enjoying themselves at trail's end, they were usually in west Texas. In the course of their several extended visits they got friendly with the Kilpatricks, who lived at The Hills, about thirty miles east of San Angelo. This family consisted of George Kilpatrick, originally from Tennessee; his wife Mary, ten years his junior, born in South Carolina; and nine children, all born in Coleman County, Texas. Mary Kilpatrick was fifteen when she gave birth to their first child, a boy whom they named William. Daniel Boone Kilpatrick was born two years later, in 1872; Benjamin in 1874; George, Junior, in 1876; Edward in 1877; and Alice in 1879. By 1885, when these hill people moved to The Hills, in Concho County, there were three more children; Felix, Ola, and Sarah. The progeny, perhaps not exceptionally large for the time and place, turned out to be an unusually vexatious one for the forces of law and order. Ben, George, Ed, and Felix became outlaws. Ma Kilpatrick, to all intents and purposes the head of the house, never disapproved of their actions. In the early nineties the older Kilpatrick boys worked around the ranches as cowpunchers and bronco tamers. The Ketchums were among their friends, and so was William Carver.

The forebears of Will Carver, like those of the Ketchums, were from Illinois. His grandfather first settled in Missouri, moving down into north Texas some years later, between 1850 and 1855. Will was born about 1869, in Bandera County. An uncle lived nearby in Uvalde County and another in Kimble County.

Nothing is known of his life prior to his appearance in Tom Green County sometime in the early 1890s. Marvin Hunter says he was just a "pretty good old country boy" until he threw in with Tom Ketchum. Carver worked for Berry Ketchum, for the Half Circle Six ranch, and a number of other cattle outfits in the San Angelo region. He was known as "a fine roper and horsemen and a crack shot with six shooters, in either hand". Perhaps through some idiosyncrasy of manner or bearing—for there must have been many punchers in that locality whose given name was William—he was sometimes referred to as "Cowboy Bill". He saved some money and married the daughter of one of Berry Ketchum's neighbors. According to what Carver later told his friends in Arizona, his wife died not long after they were married. He then took up with Laura Bullion, a local girl a few years his elder, who once described her ancestry thus: "Mother was a German. I don't know who my father was. Some say I have Injun blood in me and some say greaser, but that's a lie".

It was probably in 1894 that Sam Ketchum, like Tom, quit as a trail-driver. But Sam had at least a little money to show for his efforts.

At the age of forty he desired neither wife nor ranch. Instead, he opened a saloon and gambling house in San Angelo, taking Will Carver as his partner. They were hardly the cream of society, but they were still a long way from outlawry.

There is not a scrap of information to show how Tom Ketchum occupied himself during the time between his abrupt disappearance from the VV camp on Perico creek and his return to Tom Green County some months later. Perhaps he did go to Hole-in-the-Wall to meet old acquaintances and seek new ones. This area had been the lair of rustlers and outlaws for many years and if Tom never visited it while he and Sam were operating from Snake Valley he must have heard it talked of often enough. For want of evidence to the contrary, it has to be assumed that he was up to no serious mischief while he was in Wyoming.

There is no telling whether Tom Ketchum rode back to Texas with any fixed plan in mind, but it is clear that he had forsworn any pretension to a sense of scruple. He was not long in finding a ready adherent in David Atkins, a twenty year old cowpuncher. In the late Fall of 1895 the pair became party to a sordid and criminal intrigue which ended in murder. Sam Ketchum and Will Carver may or may not have been directly concerned in this; their reaction was such that in the long run the question of their complicity had very little bearing on their future one way or the other. From then onwards all four of them were fugitives.

Chapter Three

THREE MURDERS AND A DEAD RINGER

"John Wright gave me a brown horse to do what I did, and then he came over and took it from me. It was Wright's intention to take Old Lady Powers and leave the country with her. That was his intention... Old Man Powers was killed... There were four or five implicated in it."

In those laconic and impersonal terms, Tom Ketchum described the murder of John N. "Jap" Powers, "one of the first crimes that I was ever implicated in". There must have been a great deal more to it than that. If, as he implied, he was hired to assassinate Powers, Tom would have wanted more from Wright than the loan of a horse. Tom had never killed a man up to this time. It stands to reason that he would not have murdered Powers merely to indulge a whim or oblige a friend. Mrs. Powers certainly connived at the murder, and Dave Atkins was as deeply involved in it as Tom himself. So, according to the authorities, was a young man named Bud Upshaw, although Tom later maintained that Bud "knew nothing about it". Probably Ketchum and his fellow bushwhackers had their own reasons for wanting Powers out of the way. The man was a neighbor of the Ketchums and even if Tom and the others were paid for killing him they would hardly have accepted the commission if they had got on well with him.

Powers was shot down in his pasture, ten or eleven miles south of Knickerbocker, early on Thursday, December 12th, 1895. That morning, as usual, he left the house to catch his saddle horse. He had walked only a short distance when several men opened fire with rifles. Three bullets struck him in the back; a fourth, perhaps fired from close range, split his skull.

Mrs. Powers expressed no misgivings until late in the afternoon. This alone ought to have led to a speedy solution, for Powers had been killed so near to the house that she could not have failed to hear the shots; yet Sheriff Shields did not arrest her until May 25th. In due course a grand jury indicted Tom Ketchum, Dave Atkins, and Bud Upshaw for murder. The warrants had to be returned, each bearing the endorsement "not found".

A few weeks after the killing, Will Carver had heard that Tom Ketchum was under suspicion and was able to warn him before the law could act. That night Tom struck out for New Mexico. Atkins and Upshaw also made themselves unavailable. Both wound up in Arizona. Another suspect, W.H. Kelly, disappeared from Tom Green County at about the same time as the others.

Neither Carver nor Sam Ketchum was accused of complicity in the murder, but they may have perceived that their close association with the fugitives would tend to incriminate them, thus encouraging the officers to arrest them as accessories. Wholly innocent or not, they sold the saloon and headed west. Will Carver joined Dave Atkins in Cochise County, Arizona. Sam soon ran into his brother in the Pecos Valley country.

In the spring of 1896 the two Ketchums were engaged as line riders on the Bell ranch, near the site of Fort Bascom. Near the end of May, shortly after the beginning of the round-up, they joined the Bell wagons in San Miguel County, some miles north of where they had been riding line.

The cowhands guessed they were outlaws because "they had a great number of gold and silver watches and many bunches of keys among their effects." How the brothers came about these items is a mystery; no record has been found of any hold-up in which Tom or Sam could possibly have been implicated in the early months of 1896.

Tom Ketchum was passing as "Welsch", the name engraved upon one of the handsome gold watches he carried. Cowboys in eastern New Mexico did not usually wear pistols while out on the range; Tom never went anywhere without his. During the short time he was with the Bell, he gave some memorable displays of his dexterity with the six-shooter. Jack Culley, the range manager, recalled many years later what he had been told by the waddies:

> The fellow was an expert juggler with his six-shooter. He could twirl the big .45 round and round on the trigger finger, cocking and firing it at each turn with astonishing speed and accuracy. And he seemed fond of exhibiting his prowess.

Tom worked for the Bell for less than two weeks. One day he quarrelled with his wagon-boss, Tom Kane, collected his pay from the ranch book-keeper, and pulled out.

Sam Ketchum was working for another of the Bell wagons, a few miles further north. His name, he said, was "Steve". He refused to give any surname, and the matter was not pressed. In Culley's words, the Bell ranch was "a good place to be in... if you were wanted by the sheriff... We asked no questions, only if a man could work cattle."

Sam quit soon after Tom rode up to the wagon. For a day or so, they camped in the willow brakes of La Cinta creek, near the north fence of the Bell. On Monday, June 8th, they killed a steer "and used what meat they desired". Overnight they stole some supplies from the Bell storehouse. Tom Kane, who was a deputy sheriff, started out after them.

The Ketchums were now headed southeast across the Bell pastures. Late in the afternoon of June 10th they reached the little settlement of Liberty, where there was a store and post office operated by Levi and Morris Herzstein.

Jack Potter's story is that the Ketchums, having bought a few groceries, camped outside the store until one of the Herzsteins, seeing the stormclouds mounting overhead, invited them to spend the night indoors.

Whether or not the Ketchums took a drenching that night, they certainly looted the store some time in the small hours of Thursday. They pocketed all the money at hand, including $44.69 from the post office till, loaded their packhorse with blankets, clothing, and provisions, then made their way toward the Pecos. A few hours afterwards Levi Herzstein gathered up a posse of some three or four men and went out in pursuit. Levi, in contrast to many of those who were elected or appointed to serve as officers, really tried to overtake his quarry. It was his misfortune that he succeeded in catching up with the two thieves. The fate which befell him illustrates tellingly why most professional lawmen preferred the tactful approach.

About noon the Ketchums halted near Plaza Largo arroyo, in Guadalupe County, roughly twenty-five miles from Liberty. They were just finishing their meal as Herzstein and his companions came pounding into view.

There are a number of versions of what happened in the next few seconds. Both Thompson and Titsworth say that the Ketchums, taken off their guard, made as if to surrender; then when Herzstein's party moved closer, they stepped behind their horses, drew their guns, and started shooting before the men in the posse could do anything about it. Culley asserts that the outlaws were crouched by the horses, ready to open fire, when the pursuers saw them. One contemporary newspaper report states impartially that "a fight ensued"; another has it that the robbers began to shoot "as soon as they saw the posse". The fight, if it amounted to that, was swiftly over. When Tom and Sam stalked out into the open Levi Herzstein and Merejildo Gallegos were dead or dying and Placido Gurule was trying hard to make it look as though he were in a similar condition. The other members of the impromptu posse were streaking homewards.

Potter relates that Tom, surveying their bloody handiwork, said to his brother:

"I believe that damn Mexican lying there is not dead. I thought I saw his muscle move. I had better give him a little more lead".

"Don't waste ammunition on a dead man", Sam is supposed to have replied. "He is no doubt eating chile in hades with his compadre".

Culley tells how one of them, standing over the prostrate Herzstein, emptied his pistol into the body, snarling "You son of a bitch! You son of a bitch!" each time he fired.

Tom and Sam were unscratched, but one of their three horses was killed. They cut out the brand mark, then rode on south. Later they stole a pair of horses from the H ranch and turned towards the Staked Plains.

Gurule had been saved by his own nerve and by the apparent logic of Sam Ketchum's argument. Although wounded, he was able to mount his horse and ride home.

Tom Kane kept on the trail, albeit at a carefully regulated pace. As Culley commented:

> Tom was nervy, all right, but experienced. Unlike poor little Herzstein, he was wise to the kind of fellows he was following. I shall never doubt that from the moment he left the ranch in pursuit he was quite determined to keep one good day behind. . . . .

The outlaws had veered back, evidently determined to get down to the Pecos. At Fort Sumner Kane was joined by Deputy U.S. Marshal John B. Legg and an officer named Mike McQuaid, who declared that the man "Steve" was one Red Black, whom he had once arrested in Colorado for rustling cattle. Fred Higgins, town marshal at Roswell, joined Legg in cutting sign both east and west of the Pecos after Kane and McQuaid had retired from the hunt.

Christopher C. Perry, the sheriff of Chaves County, was in Santa Fe at this time. In fact, he had been there for nearly a month and was not thinking of going back to Roswell.

Before leaving his bailwick, "Charley" Perry had closed his account with the Bank of Roswell. Among the funds now reposing under his name in a bank at Santa Fe were the proceeds of the recent tax collection. Several weeks previously Perry's original bondsmen had withdrawn their support; so, on June 9th, he filed a second bond, nominally representing the requisite sum of twenty-five thousand dollars but actually worth little more than a quarter of that amount. The irregularities would be uncovered when the County Commissioners met in July, and the law insisted that he make settlement with the County or Territory by the tenth of that month. Charley was not worried by the prospect of the first because he had no intention of complying with the second. The sheriff, in short, was about to abscond.

If the Ketchums had not stolen money which belonged to the United States Post Office, it is unlikely that Perry would have suffered his scheme to be disrupted by their actions. But he was also a Deputy United States Marshal; and, although he had put himself out of touch with the electors of Chaves County, he could be found with the utmost ease by U.S. Marshal Edward L. Hall. When the marshal placed a couple of blank warrants in his hands and told him to try and serve them on the robbers, Perry was forced to change his plans.

First, he called at the bank to pick up all the money he had placed on deposit a few weeks earlier. He then went directly to El Paso, Texas. Near the town of Pecos he met John Legg, who had trailed the killers onto Toyah Creek, a tributary of the Pecos River. Legg was now accompanied by two officers from Eddy, New Mexico: Cal Carpenter and Dee Harkey. For some days the posse drove around Reeves and Pecos counties in a couple of hired buggies, pausing here and there to wire optimistic reports to New Mexico. The Ketchums, meanwhile, were escaping through the Davis Mountains and into the Big Bend country, south of Alpine.

On July 1st the posse learned that the police at Ojinaga, a town on the Chihuahua side of the Rio Grande, directly opposite Presidio, Texas, had arrested one Samuel Lockwood, believing him to be one of the fugitives. Legg sent a telegram from Ojinaga to notify Hall, and Perry offered to return to Santa Fe to obtain the necessary papers. But instead of going to Santa Fe, Charley headed east—all the way to South Africa. A few weeks after his exit the auditors, called in to examine the peculations of the departed sheriff, reported that he owed the Territorial Treasurer the sum of $7639.02. The money was never collected.

Nor, for that matter, were the rewards aggregating $2700, offered by Governor W.T. Thornton of New Mexico, Morris Herzstein, the United

States Post Office, and A.J. Tisdale, manager of the Bell ranch, for the arrest and delivery of "Welsch" and "Steve". Legg took Morris Herzstein. to identify Lockwood, but there were no further developments.

The description of the killers foreshadowed the controversy that would arise from a jumble of diverse claims as to the identity of "Black Jack" which, in turn, caused the operations of two entirely separate bands of outlaws to become intertwined in both the popular press and the official mind:

> Both men are over six feet in height, one being dark complexioned and stoop-shouldered, the other having light hair and blue eyes and being straight and erect in form. They are strangers in this territory, and at the Bell ranch. where they stopped for a short time, they showed a pocket-book full of finger rings and several watches, from which Marshal Hall is led to believe that they are train robbers, perhaps members of one of the gangs operating in the Indian Territory.

Some six months before this another pair of brothers had traversed eastern New Mexico, en route from the Indian Territory and the Texas Panhandle, and bound for Cochise County, Arizona. Bob Christian, the elder, was of a similar complexion to Sam Ketchum, though a much smaller man than Sam and about fifteen years younger. Will Christian, like Tom Ketchum, was very dark of complexion, powerfully built, and about six foot tall. Tom was slightly the taller, weighed rather less than Christian, and was his senior by some eight years. The two men were altogether different in temperament and manner; but both were from Texas, both worked on the range when they worked at all, and both were criminals. At the time of the murders in Guadalupe County, the Christians were ranch hands in Cochise County; but their earlier career was closely akin to the one which Marshal Hall had incorrectly predicated for the killers of Herzstein and Gallegos.

After Tom and Sam had lost posses, somewhere south of Fort Davis, they parted company.

Sam probably remained in south-west Texas for seven or eight months before entering New Mexico from the south and crossing the San Andres Mountains to reach the Jornada del Muerta.

Hardly more is known of Tom's movements during this period. Only this much is certain: he loafed around southwestern New Mexico; moved for a time into Graham County, Arizona; then resumed contact with Will Carver and Dave Atkins.

Carver had arrived in Cochise County in the summer and had gone to work as a cowboy for the Erie Cattle Company. Since there were no warrants out for him, he was using his right name. He was not without friends in that section; his brother-in-law lived near Rodeo, on the Territorial line, and an uncle of Laura Bullion was located twenty miles southeast of Bisbee, by the Mexican border. Then, too, he got acquainted with the hardy and self-sufficient crowd in Texas Canyon.

This was a secluded valley in the lower east slope of the Chiricahua Mountains, situated a few miles above the border. Jess Benton, a cattleman who found the place by chance, decided he liked it, and eventually got it for himself, left a succinct description of its setting:

> . . . a wild and beautiful locality at the south end of the range, a wooded region with a pretty spring, and a chinked log house in a clearing, one of the first such log houses in Arizona. . . . Right here were the ranch I wanted. . . .

Leonard Alverson and his partner, William Warderman, had moved into the house several years earlier, to be joined presently by one John Vinadge, or Vintage, alias John Cush. Notwithstanding the prior arrival of Alverson and Warderman, the ranch was generally referred to as "Old Cushey's place". Actually, though, none of them enjoyed title. Either through plain carelessness, or because they wished to avoid having to pay taxes on the property, they had never filed ownership on their land. A cowpuncher named Walter Hoffman helped them in the round-up. Two others who were always welcome were Tom Capehart and Henry Marshall.

Joseph "Mack" Axford, who worked with these last two during the winter of 1895-96, remembers Capehart as one of the finest "bronco stompers" on the range and Marshall as "a fair to middling cowhand, more noted for his pleasant disposition and for being a steady and hard worker". Capehart later impressed William French as one of the most capable hands he ever hired during his years as manager of W. S.

In time, all six of these men—Alverson, Warderman, Cush, Hoffman, Capehart, and Marshall—came to know Tom Ketchum rather better than was good for any of them.

During the summer and autumn of 1896 everyone in the Southwest heard a great deal of the Black Jack gang.

"Black Jack" was the nickname conferred upon Will Christian soon after his appearance in Cochise County. With his brother, now riding as "Tom Anderson", and three other retired cowpunchers, he embarked on a series of robberies which, although realizing only the feeblest of profits, sorely embarrassed two United States Marshals, many of their deputies, half a dozen sheriffs, and several Post Office inspectors. Some newspapers even blamed Black Jack and Anderson for the murders of Herzstein and Gallegos, furnishing details of the previous career of the alleged killers which corresponded so closely with what was recorded of the Christians that it is astonishing that the two fugitives from Oklahoma were not identified by their real names.

Tom Ketchum later said that he met Black Jack once, and once only. He claimed that he rode into Black Jack's camp above Deming, was invited to join the gang, and rejected the offer. Whereupon, said Ketchum, the confrontation was brusquely brought to a finish by Black Jack's "threatening attitude". No doubt there was such an encounter—probably towards the end of October, 1896—but the details as supplied by Ketchum need not be believed.

In April, 1897, Black Jack was killed in Graham County, Arizona. There was much dissension over the question of the name borne by the late outlaw; none of those who came forward to identify the body knew that the man behind the alias was William Christian. Marshal Hall accepted the statement of a man called Speck, who, in his omniscience, named the dead man as Thomas Ketchum.

Now, at this time, Tom was three hundred miles away, preparing to break out into outlawry on a scale that would make the Black Jack gang look like a bunch of scavengers. The situation was rich in humor. First of all, Tom Ketchum's crimes were being pinned upon Black Jack; and now Tom Ketchum had been appointed as tenant of Black Jack's grave. Time, with some help from Tom Ketchum himeslf, would see to it that the irony was redressed in full measure.

Chapter Four

EASY MONEY AND HARD RIDING

Sometime between December of 1896 and the following March, Tom Ketchum, Will Carver, and Dave Atkins returned to Southwest Texas. Carver had told Leonard Alverson that he was going to put a monument over the grave of his wife and did not know what he would do afterwards. Perhaps he did plant this token of remembrance; but it is nigh certain that his journey was not impelled upon him by sentiment alone. Even if the three men did not travel together all the way, the main object of the trip must have been discussed and agreed upon before they left the Chiricahuas. Through choice or circumstance, Sam Ketchum had no part in the episode which irrevocably determined the calling of all four of them. He was in New Mexico when the other three turned fo highway robbery.

They may have drawn their inspiration from an event oft talked about in the bleak and lonesome sageland along the Rio Grande, beyond the great dip which is the eastern sweep of the Big Bend.

A band of former cowboys, led by one Wellington, had stirred up much excitement by exacting a heavy toll from the Southern Pacific Railway at Samuels station, in western Val Verde County. The victim was that perennial target of highwaymen, westbound train Number 20, and the incident noteworthy in its own context as marking the very first instance where train robbers opened an express safe by blasting it with dynamite. Less well remembered by campfire raconteurs and would-be emulators was the undoing of four of the robbers—but it has always been thus. They were caught some few weeks later through the skill and tenacity of the famous trailer, Joe Sitters. Jim Flynt evaded capture only by shooting himself. The others — Wellington, Tom Field, and Jim Langford — were dealt with at Del Rio. Two of the original six did succeed in getting away with it.

Bud Newman, whose father owned a ranch twenty miles north of Comstock, was one local cowboy with ambitions to outshine the Samuels robbers. Gathering three kindred lights, professedly ordinary cowhands forced into crime by the prospect of a winter's unemployment, he held up No. 20 on Sunday night, December 20th, 1896, near Comstock. The four wishful thinkers could not open the through safe and had to be satisfied with the contents of the way safe, said to have been one gold watch and seventy dollars in cash. This masterful exploit was fittingly sealed a few days later: Rangers swooped down on the Newman ranch and took away the four miscreants, all of whom "wanted to confess at once" when presented with "circumstantial evidence of their guilt". Tom Ketchum and his two partners were in no wise deterred by the recent misfortunes of Newman's gang; some time later Tom even paid Bud Newman the compliment of springing one of his own enterprises upon Comstock station.

But, for the scene of their first venture into train robbery, the three had chosen Lozier, located on the creek of the same name just within the eastern boundary of Terrell County. There was no community here; just a tiny depot and a telegraph office, then in charge of Miss Addie Upshaw. The station was situated midway between Dryden and Langtry, two small villages thirty miles apart, and much closer to the Rio Grande than to either of these places. Ketchum and Carver, at least, were thoroughly acquainted with the terrain and the scattered ranches.

At 1.50 a.m. on Friday, May 14th, train No. 20 jerked out of Lozier station. Conductor Jim Burns caught a glimpse of two men, whom he supposed to be hoboes, running out from the depot building to swing onto the blind end of the baggage car. Just two minutes later Ketchum and Carver scrambled across the tender and into the cab. A glance at the leveled pistols was all Engineer George Freese needed for confirmation of an abrupt command to bring the train to a standstill in the cut, a mile or so west of Lozier.

Out on the crest of the hill, Atkins reached forward and snipped the telegraph wire as the train rumbled close. Then, carrying the dynamite, he made his way to the express car, where the other two were holding Freese and the fireman, Will Bochat.

One of the engine men started to bang on the express car door with a coal-pick, without evoking any response from Messenger W.H. Joyce. Engineer Freese, his ribs sore from the sporadically repeated pressure of a Winchester muzzle, earnestly requested Joyce to open up. Joyce did so when a bullet crashed through, "striking a tin wash basin on the coal box by the stove." The commotion aroused Joyce's bulldog, which "became very angry and very much excited and ran up and down the car floor growling and barking and bristles irritated to a standing point."

Ketchum brusquely ordered the messenger to chain the dog, and was clambering into the car when a voice from within cackled: "Say, who are you?"

"Hands up, hands up, or I'll fill you full of holes!" roared the bandit.

"That's only a parrot", said Joyce, indicating a cage in the corner of the car.

"Well, the damned thing almost scared me to death," mumbled Ketchum.

After the question of Joyce's traveling livestock had been attended to, Ketchum began to interview the messenger about the two safes aboard. A second bandit motioned Freese and Bochat to their engine. The third kept guard outside the express car.

Joyce explained why he could not unlock the larger safe; he had the key to the smaller safe, he added, but that one was empty. Ketchum had heard enough. He jogged the expressman's midriff with his rifle.

"I am a poor man and need money," he said, in a hollow tone. Instead of demanding the key, he produced some dynamite from the knapsack which Atkins had handed to him, placed it against the smaller safe, and touched off the fuse. He and Joyce got out of the car just ahead of the explosion.

Two of the bandits climbed into the devastated car and extracted all the money from Joyce's "empty" way safe. Freese and Bochat were then taken back and directed to shift the wreckage from around the through safe. Most of the passengers had been awakened; their curiosity was both gratified and quelled by a quick succession of rifle bullets from one of Ketchum's companions.

Tom Ketchum had plenty to learn about the finer points of his vocation: three charges were necessary before the big safe gave way. But, by 3.15 a.m. the bandits had three bulging sacks of loot to show for the work of less than two hours. The trainmen were ordered to get back into their places and the engineer given an admonition "to back the train out of bullet range". Four horses were tethered nearby. The robbers tied their booty onto one of these, then rode away to the north.

Although the bandits enjoyed a long start on the law, Captain John Hughes and his Rangers, together with several Sheriff's posses and a number of Deputy U.S. Marshals, saw to it that the chase was hard and persistent. Ketchum and his men, riding day and night, engaged in a double feint to get rid of the pursuit. First they headed for the Rio

Grande; then, just short of the river, they turned north. They crossed the Pecos River at a point about fifty miles from Lozier, but had gone no more than ten miles along the east side of the stream when their overburdened pack horse gave out. Here they stopped to eat and to divide the money.

The exhausted horse was of no further use to them and had to be killed. Before decamping they cut out and destroyed the brand. A posse which came upon the place found only the mutilated carcase, three dollars in silver, and remnants of papers burned by the gang. Shortly after the share-out the men split up and "obliterated their respective trails". None of them rode on north into New Mexico; they simply took separate routes to the east, coming to a rendezvous at or near the Berry Ketchum ranch.

Immediately after the robbery, it was announced that a hold-up had been expected for three months and that the identities of the robbers were known. Probably the first statement was true; Wells, Fargo—then almost as notorious for its parsimony as the curmudgeonly Southern Pacific—disliked hiring guards for more than a few days at a stretch. The second claim was essentially right, too: information placed in the hands of United States Marshal Richard Ware and various Sheriffs named the robbers as Tom Ketchum, Dave Atkins, and Bud Upshaw, three of the principals in the murder of Jap Powers. Tom Ketchum's connections in New Mexico were known to the officers, for when the posses noted that the Lozier robbers had crossed the Pecos they guessed that the men were headed toward New Mexico, "where...they expect to be taken care of by friends in their old haunts."

Tom Ketchum and his mates could boast of a spectacular start in their new profession. Although the booty was first reported as seven or eight thousand dollars from the through safe and two thousand from the way safe, the express company later admitted a gross loss of $42,000. Twenty-five years later W.H. Joyce, still an Express Messenger working for Wells Fargo, said that the outlaws had taken about $6,000 from the through safe, the amount "consisting mostly of Mexican silver". Joyce, a trustworthy witness in almost everything else, is not to be believed on this point. During the last ten or twelve years of the Nineteenth Century, when train robbery was commonplace, express officials in the Southwest were apt to say, disparagingly, that most of what was stolen was in Mexican currency: this reflected an aspect of the public mood, and was almost equivalent to an assertion that the coin was counterfeit. Old habits die hard; and Joyce, no doubt, was still a good company man in

1922. Actually several hundred dollars of Mexican money was taken from the safe, but the bandits had disdained to carry it away with them.

The three fugitives were detected in Knickerbocker on June 18th; or, anyway, that was the date on which their presence was reported to those who wanted them to be caught. Before any interested party could act on this intelligence, the three disappeared, traveling light.

All the indications are that most of the money, unspent, was left behind, either cached somewhere in Tom Green County or deposited for safekeeping with Berry or some other ally. Their intention may have been to lie undercover for a while; to collect the money when they deemed they could comfortably get out with it to some distant place where they were unknown. But, as the weeks passed by, nothing was more natural than for them to reflect that what they had achieved so easily at Lozier they would have no difficulty in repeating elsewhere.

Sam Ketchum was working on Eugene Rhodes' ranch in the Jornada del Muerta, north of Engle, while Tom and the others were on the run in Texas. Tom knew where to find him and and soon came for him. Sam's outlawry, incomprehensible to those who knew him, has been ascribed to his loyalty to Tom. This, or something like it, may be part of the story. But after the murders of Herzstein and Gallegos there could be little peace or security for Sam Ketchum. When Tom came up with an invitation for Sam to join him in a train robbery, Sam probably did not make much of a debate out of it.

The four men rode to Colfax County and took up residence in a secluded and heavily wooded spot called Turkey Creek Canyon (or simply Turkey Canyon), northwest of Cimarron.

The gang's camp at the far end of the canyon could be reached by two trails, both of them narrow, tortuous, and almost impassable in some places. The westerly trail wound circuitously past a massive boulder. A rivulet tumbled across this boulder and on down to the canyon floor, its waters forming a clear pool some yards below a cavern large enough to accommodate several men. The easterly entrance was a gash in the rock face, eleven miles from Cimarron. How or when the outlaws found this natural stronghold is unknown; the only surmise which readily suggests itself is that Sam or Tom stumbled onto it or were told about it sometime during their earlier wanderings.

Once in Turkey Canyon, the four men made preparations for a long stay. A corral was raised beside the cave, and logs were laid among the nearby rocks to provide additional fortification. Occasionally the gang would visit Cimarron or the much larger town of Trinidad, Colorado, but more often they rode over to Elizabethtown, a few miles west of their hideout. G.W. Moore, proprietor of the saloon there, was surprised one evening when one of a group of four strangers threw a hundred dollar bill on the counter and called upon him to serve drinks for the company. Moore had to admit that he could not change the note.

"If you have a room where we can play Poker, we will change it for you before morning", replied Tom Ketchum.

Several of the regulars accepted invitations to join what Tom promised would be "a nice honest game". To show his good faith, he stood the bill for refreshments. Everyone regarded the strangers as a bunch of good fellows.

After this the gang called at Moore's every evening for a period of several weeks, always riding away at daybreak.

The once thriving town of Elizabethtown had very few inhabitants in the 1890's but was frequented by a number of hard characters, many of them at outs with the law. One of these was "Charles Collins", a big, red-haired Texan in his late twenties, then employed as superintendent of the Aztec mine, just outside town. The occupations to which he was more accustomed were those of cowpuncher, rider, and rustler, His right name was Bruce Weaver, but his complexion assured him of the cognomen "Red". In "E-town" he swiftly gained the confidence of the Ketchum outfit—if, indeed, he was not an old acquaintance of theirs.

One evening in mid-August the foursome failed to appear for their habitual bout of Poker. Nor were they present at Moore's on the succeeding nights. Then, early in September, word came through that the southbound Gulf train had been robbed by four men at a mountain crossing in Union County.

The methods adopted by the gang were almost exactly the same as those employed at Lozier.

On the night of Friday, September 3rd, the four outlaws made camp near the tracks of the Gulf, Colorado and Santa Fe Railroad, south of the village of Folsom, which lay ten miles below the Colorado border. The country was arid and mountainous, with no settlement of any consequence between Trinidad and Clayton.

Two of the gang walked into Folsom to await the arrival of Southbound train No. 1, the Texas Flyer. At about ten o'clock that night the train ground in and the outlaws hauled themselves onto the blind baggage. As the engine started to nose cautiously into the first sharp bend at Twin

Mountains, five miles out, the bandits descended into the cab. Engineer Crowfoot and Fireman Crackley were quickly cowed by the cocked Winchesters and forced to halt the locomotive two miles further within the sweeping double curve. At once the other two outlaws started shooting over the passenger coaches, thoroughly unnerving all the occupants except Conductor Frank E. Harrington, who chafed because he had no weapon with which to resist the attack on his train.

When the train stopped Express Messenger Charles P. Drew immediately opened the door of his car, thinking they had reached Des Moines station. Before he realized anything was amiss he was covered by two guns. The men climbed into the car and ordered him to open the way safe unless he preferred to be killed.

"There's nothing in there you want", he argued.

"You lie, damn you!" snarled Sam Ketchum, as he clubbed Drew to the floor with the stock of his Winchester. Drew rose up only to be sent down again by a punch in the ribs.

One of the men repeated the threat to kill if the safe were not opened, but his companion knocked away the barrel of the gun as it was thrown down upon the dazed messenger. Drew, not caring to test their patience further, now produced the keys and the bandits confiscated the money.

Next they ordered him to unlock the through safe.

"I couldn't even if I would", he answered. This time the outlaws offered neither violence nor demurrer. They began forthwith to pack the outside of the safe with dynamite. Two unsuccessful attempts were made to blow the safe before one of the gang lost patience.

"I'll bust her", he said, placing fourteen sticks of dynamite around the obstinate steel box. A quarter of beef was lifted onto the dynamite to keep the explosion down. The safe and much of the baggage were wrecked by the blast, and the car itself was damaged so badly that eventually it had to be cut from the train and replaced by a Union Pacific freight car. The bandits extracted all the valuables and money and took their leave. An aroused Conductor Harrington ordered the train to be backed four miles, and the trainmen got out to examine the ground for clues. They found no trace of the bandits or of the direction in which they had fled.

The subsequent manhunt was spearheaded not by the Sheriff of Union County but by William Henry Reno, chief of detectives for the railroad. The posses arrested four men and a boy who may have been cattle rustlers but never even struck the trail of the four robbers.

Carver, Atkins, and the Ketchums headed northwest for a few miles, then swung southwest, to fetch up in Turkey Canyon. The proceeds of the Folsom robbery amounted to something between $2,000 and $3,500 in cash and a consignment of silver spoons — trifling remuneration compared with the sackfuls carried off from Lozier.

North-eastern New Mexico, which had not known any significant disturbance by highwaymen for fifteen years or more, was suddenly crowded with officers and detectives. Any wandering cowboy or prospector might turn out to be a lawman seeking clues to the identities and whereabouts of the Folsom robbers. For one reason or another the gang ruled out the notion of an immediate return to Texas. Carver suggested that they retreat to Cochise County, where no one would be on the lookout for them, and hold up the Southern Pacific beneath Stein's Peak, on the Arizona-New Mexico border. The others readily gave their ayes to this proposition.

Sam and Tom Ketchum, Will Carver, and Dave Atkins began the long ride down to Cochise County within a few days of their return to the camp in Turkey Canyon. Some of the money and a number of the silver spoons stayed in the Cimarron area, having passed mysteriously into the possession of the man who called himself "Charles Collins". Soon this money and these spoons were staking "Collins" at the poker tables and saloon bars, and not everyone in the locality was inclined to disown all interest in the source of the miner's new-found prosperity. The four robbers may have acted wisely in quitting Colfax County, but during the three months which followed they were dealt so harsh an education in the risks of the game that they must have wished they had kept clear of the Stein's Pass country.

Chapter Five

CROSSED TRAILS

According to Leonard Alverson, none of the Ketchum gang had visited Texas Canyon until the September of 1897, except for Will Carver, who guided the party thither a short while after the Folsom robbery. There is no great cause to dispute this, even though Alverson, in general, may have understated the extent of his acquaintance with the outlaws. Tom Ketchum and Dave Atkins had come to known much of Cochise County at sundry times during the latter part of 1896 and the first months of 1897, but many with a far more thorough knowledge of the country would not have been able to locate the canyon.

Walter Hoffman, in the autumn of 1897, was fresh from a killing. Walter, commonly described as a cowboy or "farm laborer", had fallen afoul of a ranchman named Joe Richards. Each threatened to kill the other, and one night someone tried to ambush Hoffman in Hunt Canyon. The conclusion followed swiftly. On the morning of Saturday, August 14th, Hoffman ran Richards to earth at the John Banks ranch in Horseshoe Valley, in the Swisshelm Mountains, near Bisbee. Both men were armed. Hoffman said afterwards that Richards reached for his gun with the words "I'm going to kill you."

"But I got the drop first", added Walter, "and that's all there is to it."

The probate judge found that Richards had been the aggressor and discharged Hoffman.

As Hoffman related it, their difference arose because Richards had "wrongfully accused him of carrying tales with regard to cattle brands". The real reason, or a further one, may have been that Richards had spoken rather freely of Hoffman's friendship with Black Jack Christian's old gang, the survivors of which were a migratory presence in upper Sonora and Chihuahua, southeastern Arizona, and southwestern New Mexico during the summer of 1897. United States Marshal Creighton M. Foraker claimed that the Black Jack gang were "directly responsible" for the death of Richards — an assertion which seems somewhat extravagant.

DYNAMITE AND SIX-SHOOTER

Foraker rightly discounted allegations that the Black Jack gang had committed the Folsom robbery, but he would have been surprised to hear that the authors of this latter crime were headed for the stretch of country where the Black Jack outlaws were then circulating. He did not know the names of the Folsom robbers, however; to his mind Tom Ketchum was long dead. It was merely symptomatic of the hiatus between the various law-enforcement agencies that Foraker had not been advised of Tom Ketchum's feat in rising from the grave to lead the Lozier robbers. The Texas officers, similarly, were never told of the common belief in New Mexico and Arizona that the man slain in Cole Creek Canyon was this same Tom Ketchum. By no means all of the newspaper stories on the movements of outlaw bands were rubbish; such inanities as were to be found generally owed their appearance to the hasty utterance of some officer of the law. Cowpunchers, settlers, prospectors, sheepherders—they would exchange news by word of mouth, but precious little of it ever trickled through to the officers in time for them to make good use of it.

Near the end of September one James Roberts, a cattleman from Presidio County, in southwest Texas, reported in San Antonio that the three Lozier robbers had been seen near his ranch a few days earlier. Through the months of July and August all heavy shipments of money had been guarded along the route of the Southern Pacific between San Antonio and El Paso; a tighter watch still was maintained after the warning from Roberts. But, although three intending train robbers may have dropped in on the Roberts ranch, the Ketchum gang were far away, forting themselves up in Wildcat Canyon, a mile and a half north of Cushey's place.

The best description of this hideout is Len Alverson's.

> You could not have dragged them out of there with a locomotive to say nothing of with a posse of bar-room rounders. They would cross the San Simon and strike up what is still known as the Tom Ketchum Canyon.
> At the head of the Canyon the basin widens out into what was known as the Wild Cat. This was so called because some cowpunchers once killed a beef and hung it in a tree. Every night something would come down and eat a piece. So the boys fixed a loaded gun trap and the next morning they found a wild cat shot squarely between the eyes. Above the Wild Cat was a great bluff and many, many rocks, so wild and steep that no one could possible climb from that side. Well, the outlaws would hobble their horses and leave them there, then climb up to the right and circle clear around the bluff over some almost impassable country and reach the top, almost over the Wild Cat. Here there were a series of little

caves and great boulders dividing the top of the bluff up into rooms. One of these they called the kitchen and had their cook outfit there. Then there was the parlor and the bedroom. They could go out on the bluff itself and with a glass see all over the country in all directions. They brought water up in 5 gallon cans from a spring about ¼ of a mile away.

This hide-out has been used by many outlaws, as it is very inaccessible.... Now and then some of us cowpunchers would go in and bring out a maverick. But what few cattle were in there were wild. It was pretty near out of the world.

Tom Ketchum, Alverson recalled, would help with a round-up "once in a great while—not often". The other three, more sociable and more industrious, regularly attended the round-ups. Individually they were affable, but reserved except when in the company of the few whom they felt they could really trust. As Alverson put it, "all they wanted was to be left alone.... if they got riled up they would not run from anybody but would strike and strike hard. They would not do to monkey with...."

There was a cold, hard professionalism about them which was lacking in most of the other desperadoes who had frequented the region through the years. In Tom Ketchum's own words, as Albert Thompson noted them, "we had an understanding which I guess you would call organizing". Their quiet ways, the suppressed violence in their demeanor, earned them the unflattering collective nickname of "the snaky four" among many of their cowboy and rustler associates. It was observed that each man was armed with a 30-40 caliber Winchester carbine, 1895 model. These were the first such guns seen in Cochise County, just as they had been the first to be taken into Colfax County. The 30-40 cartridge comprised a steelnosed bullet detonated by smokeless powder making this carbine a far deadlier weapon than the 30-30 Winchester then in general use as saddle-gun. Each of the four wore a Colt .45 of the most recent pattern in the single action still preferred by most Westerners, twenty years after the double action revolver had first been manufactured in quantity. This uniformity of caliber meant, of course, that all four outlaws would be dangerous as long as just one of them had a few cartridges. Well prepared as they were for a last ditch stand, they were continuously on their watch to obviate the need for it.

Despite the unenviable characteristics they showed as a group, three of them stood in high personal regard with most of their fellows. Joseph "Mack" Axford, an Erie hand in 1897, met all four of them shortly after their reappearance in Cochise County and later struck up a friendship with Atkins, whose summation of his comrades mirrored the consensus: Sam Ketchum was "as fine a man as could be", Carver was a pretty good fellow, Tom Ketchum was just no good at all. But no one was willing to damn Tom to his face and, superficially at any rate, he was a man without an enemy. Alverson, who does not seem to have liked him very much, certainly made no remonstrance when the outlaw asked him to act as barber:

> I do remember once when Tom came to the ranch. He looked as if he had not been shaved for a month. He asked me to shave him and got out an old dull razor and a cake of laundry soap which he had wrapped in a silk handkerchief. I knew it was dull by the way he twisted his face. Every now and then he would say, "Let me have that thing a minute", and he would whet it on a silk handkerchief. When I got through he said, "You are a pretty good barber. I guess I will leave the razor with you to shave me again." I still have that razor...

The Ketchum outfit were in Cochise County for no more than three or four weeks before they were evicted by a conspiracy of circumstances. In mid-October they were nearly ready to start out to Stein's Pass, fifty miles north of Texas Canyon, for a second joust with train No. 20. Then Dave Atkins went off by himself, got drunk, and told anyone who would listen all about himself, his partners, and their plans. Tom Ketchum was both disgusted and infuriated when he heard of Atkins' performance. At this time, too, further rumors that plans were ripening for a train robbery somewhere between San Antonio and El Paso had the effect of placing Rangers in each westbound express car. Wells, Fargo themselves employed guards to see the trains safely through New Mexico and Arizona.

Tom Ketchum either learned that the trains were already being guarded or assumed that word of Atkins' indiscretion would surely reach the authorities.

"It was then agreed that we should go across into Old Mexico for a while, which we did", he said later. "Upon returning to Arizona we stashed away our grub in the Swisshelm Mountains, in a canyon about three hundred and fifty yards below what is known as the old High Line ranch, and about seventy-five or eighty-five yards below a box in the canyon".

This was the truth, although not the full truth. There is some evidence that the gang may have bivouacked with the residue of the Black Jack outfit: "Tom Anderson" (Bob Christian); "Jesse Williams" (George Musgrave); Volney C. "Van" Musgrave; Theodore James; and "Sid

Moore" (Ef Hillman). In October two Texas Rangers, Robert C. Ross and John Watts, ascertained where the Musgrave brothers were holed up in northern Chihuahua state. On the fifteenth of the month, Ross wrote to Foraker, undertaking "to deliver the parties to . . . . the Santa Fe jail" if the Marshal would provide the rangers with extradition papers. Foraker at once requested further details from Ross.

There were eight in the gang, Ross stated in his second letter, all "closely located" in Chihuahua. He had "reliable authority" that Tom Ketchum was also with the gang. His letter ended:

> One other man answers the description of Chas Perry the fugetive (sic) sheriff of Roswell, but I know Charley went to South Africa, but he may have returned, these parties were friends of his in days gone by.
> The papers are saying a great deal about the present whereabouts of this gang and the work must be done quickly.

Rob Ross, in common with most men of his calling, was eminently unversed in the complexities of International Law. About the only way to restore an American renegade to his native climes was to go to Mexico and fetch him out, papers or no papers. Kosterlitzky's rurales were there to argue that it was better to have the extradition papers. Officialdom was there to see to it that the papers were granted only after protracted correspondence, if they were granted at all. No doubt Rob Ross and John Watts were aching to lay their hands on the outlaws, and Ross was anxious that the task should fall to no one but the Rangers; it made no difference—their elected overlords, mindful of earlier misunderstandings, had made it clear that the formalities must be observed. The outlaws did not have to be students of law to realize that they were absolutely safe in Mexico as long as they behaved themselves there.

This second letter ought to have made Foraker forsake his notion that Tom Ketchum was a mouldering corpse. He made no public disavowal, though, possibly because on October 16th, only two or three days before he first heard from Ross, he had reiterated his credo that Ketchum had been killed in Arizona. "The original Black Jack", he averred, "is still at large with the gang". Foraker, an energetic and zealous officer in many respects, should have been disabused of these heresies long before; but he is hardly to be reproached for not wanting to make himself look foolish by recanting immediately. In any case he was more interested in bagging Christian and the elder Musgrave than in the question of whether Ketchum was a live outlaw or a dead one. But he and Ross were beaten from the outset, and not solely by the system: a few days before Ross got in touch with the marshal, the outlaws crossed into Arizona. As usual, they had outpaced those who informed against them.

The Ketchums, Carver, and Atkins probably did share camp with the Black Jack crowd but, through incompatibility of method or personality, there was no union of the two bands. There was no truth in the report that Charley Perry, the disappearing sheriff, was in camp with the outlaws. Charley, as Ross rightly stated, had gone to South Africa, but he had gone with no thought of returning to the United States. He was killed near Johannesburg a few years after this.

George W. Titsworth, a deputy sheriff of Las Animas County, Colorado, later maintained that Tom Ketchum was the murderer of Angelo Carli, another deputy, who was shot and killed in Sopris, a mining village five miles southwest of Trinidad, the county seat. It was Titsworth's contention that witnesses, shown a photograph of Ketchum, identified him as the killer. But Carli was shot on Wednesday evening, November 3rd, 1897, and Ketchum was definitely prowling about along the border both two weeks before the murder and two weeks after it. His movements in the latter half of October and the first two weeks of November cannot be pinpointed. It would not have been physically impossible for the gang to cross and recross the whole expanse of New Mexico during this interim of some three or four weeks, but it is difficult to assign any sort of reason for a decision to head north east, especially as the Folsom robbery was of recent memory in those parts. No one was ever tried for the murder, but it seems never to have been attributed to Ketchum in his lifetime.

In the last days of October, 1897, three strangers appeared in the vicinity of Trinidad. They stole several horses and on Monday, November 1st, committed some sort of robbery at Catskill. Three days later the Trinidad *Daily Advertiser* reported the shooting of Carli:

> Angelo Carli, proprietor of the Carli saloon and bakery at Sopris, was shot down in his place of business last night by two unknown men.
> About 9 o'clock the two strangers made their appearance at Carli's place of business and shook dice for the drinks. While [they were] engaged at this two Mexicans entered the saloon, one of them leaving a saddled horse tied outside. Upon their entrance the two strangers left. Soon after the Mexicans followed and found their horse gone. They spoke to Mr. Carli about the matter and went over to another saloon to make inquiries. While they were away the

strangers passed the Carli place, one of them riding the missing horse. Mr. Carli, who is a deputy sheriff, stopped the pair and informed them they were under arrest. They asked him for his authority and replied that he would show it to them and turned and walked into his place of business, it is supposed to get his commission as a deputy. One of the men (the one who was on the ground) followed him into the room and as he turned around began shooting at him. Three shots were fired, one striking Mr. Carli in the hand and one entering the stomach.

The authorities were at once notified and Sheriff Finch and Deputy Hightower were soon at the scene of the crime. Up to a later hour this morning no trace had been found of the would-be murderers or the stolen horse.

Carli died in hospital that day. Titsworth and another deputy sheriff, Louis Kreeger, joined in the hunt, but the only thing accomplished was the routine round-up of bums, loafers, and drifters. One of the fugitives had lost his hat in the rush to get out of town. Otherwise there was no trace of the men who had been hovering around Catskill during the past few days.

Titsworth's account of the affair differs substantially from that published at the time. He said that the men were mounted when they first stopped at Carli's place, and that each was leading an unsaddled horse stolen from a Mexican rancher; the rancher followed them, entered the saloon as the dice were being rolled for the second round of drinks, and asked Carli to arrest the two strangers. The shooting occurred directly afterwards, and the men escaped through the crowd. Titsworth also gave a description of each of the pair. Both were tall and clad in cowboy outfits. The one who did the shooting, allegedly Tom Ketchum, had a black beard and mustache and wore a white hat, dark blue flannel shirt, and blue denims. The second man was clean-shaven and attired like his companion except that he wore light-colored corduroys and chaperajos. If the first man was Tom Ketchum, the other could have been Sam or Atkins. But those descriptions are vague enough to have fitted many others. No doubt those who subsequently identified Ketchum as the killer did so in good faith; it is not inconceivable that they were correct. Yet, on balance, it is easier to believe that Ketchum was not even in the United States on the day of the shooting.

Another incident in the Ketchum apocrypha took place in the same week as the murder of Carli.

On November 6th Bob Christian, George Musgrave, and Theodore James broke out of hiding to waylay a train at Grants, New Mexico.

Richer by some $90,000, the three bandits buried some of their plunder in the Malpais country before pressing on through western New Mexico and eastern Arizona, finally to cross into Sonora state. Jubilant with success, they regaled their friends with stories of the hold-up. These were picked up by the Ketchum gang, probably at second or third hand. Tom was impressed. When he got back to Cochise County he announced that he and his partners and pulled the Grants robbery. Evidently he knew that one of the bandits, while leaving the looted train, had yelled out, "Tell them that Black Jack has come to life." His own reputation as an outlaws, and his ability to recite such details of the crime as this, made it easy for his claims to be accepted.

It may be that, in the fall of 1897, Tom Ketchum saw himself as natural heir to the title of "Black Jack" and all the concomitant prestige: later, after he had been ineluctably associated with the sobriquet, he tried frantically to disown it. Lorenzo Walters, who did a fair amount of research on both Tom Ketchum and Black Jack Christian, yet pinned many of Christian's crimes on the Ketchum gang, tells of Tom riding into Bisbee one day and being mistaken for Christian:

> After explanations had been offered and accepted, Tom Ketchum, in the Brewery Gulch Saloon, declared that from that day hence he would be known as Black Jack.

Perhaps he did say that, but he was never "known as Black Jack" among those who rode with him or those who had been acquainted with the real one. Mack Axford, one of the few men living who has first-hand knowledge of both gangs, and one of those to whom Tom Ketchum "admitted" his part in the Grants robbery, says flatly: "Tom Ketchum was not Black Jack."

Nor, despite Mr. Axford's belief to the contrary, was he one of the Grants robbers. If he and his colleagues had got the ninety thousand dollars, or even one third of that sum, they would have forgotten all about their scheme to rob the Southern Pacific at Stein's Pass.

In fact, the three Grants robbers were jailed in Fronteras for disturbing the peace on Thanksgiving Day, only to bribe their way to freedom within seventy-two hours of their arrest. Marshal Foraker, stung by this last manifestation of their flair for dodging justice, publicly inveighed against the international red tape which had thwarted his efforts to have the men extradited at once. Then, with United States Marshal William M. Griffith of Arizona and officials of Wells, Fargo and the Southern Pacific, he initiated the most vigorous campaign yet mounted against the outlaw bands of the Arizona — New Mexico border. Once again, guards were hired to accompany all express messengers on the S. P. route across New Mexico and Arizona. At the same time arrangements were made for a combined posse to assemble in Cochise County.

The Ketchums, meanwhile, blithely concluded that this was the propitious moment for an assignment with Train No. 20. Their decision to reinstate this item on their program was more than a blunder. It was ruinous for three of their friends in Tex Canyon, and fatal for a certain Ed Cullen.

Chapter Six

THE STEIN'S PASS IMBROGLIO

Edwin (or Edward) H. Cullen came to Cochise County from Colorado City, Texas, where his name had been John A. Hespatch. Nothing is known of his origins, although it has been claimed that he started life as Ed Bullion, a brother of Laura.

For several years his avocation was that of range cook. While working in this capacity for the San Simon Cattle Company he had been awarded the nickname of "Shoot'em up Dick" in recognition of his feat in being bested by one of the Chinamen who were frequently the butt of revellers and who seldom dared retaliate. When a Chinese restaurant owner pressed Cullen to pay his bill, the San Simon cook solemnly assured the Oriental that he was "Shoot'em up Dick", and would brook no further argument. Thereupon the Chinese grabbed a six-shooter, intimated that he was "Shoot'em up Sam", and verily insisted upon payment.

This unfortunate reverse did not cause Ed Cullen to become a timid character. Somewhat later, when in the employ of the Erie, he tersely educated one of the Eastern owners into the democracy of the range.

One morning the man brusquely demanded a pail of water from Cullen, whom he unthinkingly addressed as "servant".

"You get it yourself, you bald-headed son of a bitch", retorted Cullen.

The deflated magnate meekly did as he was bade.

In November of 1897, Cullen was out of work and not eager for more. But he was on friendly terms with the Ketchum gang, and may have known one or two of them in Texas; in this, he thought, was the key to his future.

At the end of the month, he told Sam Hayhurst of his decision. Hayhurst vainly urged the malcontent to "steer clear of that outfit". He refused to let the obdurate Cullen ride away on an Erie horse, but said he could take one of two flea-bitten grays which had strayed across from the Mexican side of the Line. Cullen roped one of the grays, and set out from Hayhurst's camp, south of Bisbee, for Texas Canyon.

THE STEIN'S PASS IMBROGLIO

It was about this time that Jess Benton, out on a cattle buying trip, happened upon Tex Canyon:

> Smoke was coming out of the house, so I rode up to it. I were surprised to find eight outlaws there in a bunch, all from Texas, and I knew two of them, but the others I did not know. They was all wanted men and tough hombres. Some of them took part in the famous Stein's Pass train robbery. I had been among outlaws on occasion all my life and knew how to handle them. Keep your mouth shut, attend to your own business, and leave the other fellers alone, and you will get by. . . . William Downing was there. I knew him well in Pearce. A man named Cush was the owner. I bought a few cattle off him, and then I said, "you want to sell this place?"
> "Not for sale", he said.
> I knew why. It were an ideal outlaw hideaway. . . . I didn't push him. I decided just to bide my time and wait, and maybe my time would come. . . .

There is no suggestion that Benton did anything to help matters shape into what he wanted. Someone, though, was very talkative. In the first week of December, Foraker and Griffith were apprised that a train would be held up within the next ten days, at a point near the Arizona—New Mexico line. Foraker immediately traveled to Deming to organize a posse. It was arranged that the posses of Foraker, Griffith, and the Wells, Fargo Company would meet at Bowie, Arizona, because "it would be a hard ride from any other point to get into the mountains where the robbers were supposed to be located, and furthermore there was no other place to unload the horses".

Foraker's party of four arrived in Bowie on the night of December 7th, twenty-four hours ahead of the other two posses. Next day the five deputies from Arizona, the four from New Mexico, and six men supplied by Wells, Fargo made camp seven miles east of Bowie. Foraker and Griffith stayed in town. The following morning, Thursday, December 9th, the united posse was divided into two groups, each to search a section of the mountainous country along the southern part of the Territorial line. In the evening the men returned to camp to "keep watch on the movements of the gang". Shortly after nightfall they noticed what appeared to be a signal, as though from a torch, in the mountains twenty miles to the west. Fifteen minutes later, an answering light rose from the south. The signals —if they were that, for their significance was never fully explained—were repeated at similar intervals until eleven o'clock. By then the Ketchum gang had played out their hand.

Dave Atkins and Ed Cullen presented themselves at Stein's station about six o'clock in the evening. As the train was not due until 8.35 there was no call for haste. The bandits chatted awhile with the station and express agent, St. John, before going off to the post office. Here the pistols were produced and the till ransacked. The pair returned to the depot, joined Sam Ketchum, and robbed St. John. Thus far it had been a wretched night for highwaymen: they had culled two dollars from the post office, less than ten dollars from the funds of the Southern Pacific Railway, and twenty-five cents from Wells, Fargo and Company. Tom Ketchum and Will Carver, meanwhile, were cutting the telegraph wire. Tom appropriated the operator's Winchester .44 but scorned to accept a share of the $11.20 collected by his comrades. He and Carver then took the horses two miles further west and built a bonfire on either side of the track.

The three bandits at the depot waited till the headlight of the train swung into sight before they summoned St. John to the station platform and told him to turn on the red light.

Inside the express car, besides Messenger Charles J. Adair, were two guards: C.H. Jennings and Eugene Thacker—son of John N. Thacker, who was in charge of the Wells, Fargo party then encamped in the San Simon Valley. As the train toiled up the grade toward Stein's station the three were eating supper. Young Thacker, out on his first trip, was being joshed about the hazards of the road. They all kept their shotguns close to hand, should the joke turn into reality. Everyone was very conscious that in the last twelve years No. 20 had been robbed on seven or eight occasions at various points near the Pass; yet the attack came with a swiftness that caught them by surprise.

When the train halted at Stein's, Conductor Russell and the brakeman ran into the agents office for their orders, not expecting to have to take them from a bunch of robbers.

"Get your hands up and keep quiet", they were instructed.

But in a few moments they were free to do as they liked, for the three outlaws were getting acquainted with Engineer Tom North.

Only when the train pulled up between the two bonfires did Adair and the guards guess that the train was in the hands of robbers. Their impression was speedily confirmed by a tattoo of shots. They doused the lights, armed themselves, threw the doors wide open, and waited.

North was hustled out of the locomotive and ordered to uncouple the express car, which the gang intended to take a short way further west before engaging in the work of robbery. Instead of doing this he set the air brakes, so that the train could not be moved. Not knowing how to remedy the fault, or unwilling to waste time, the bandits decided to deal with the express messenger there and then. Their call for his appearance was met by a shotgun blast from the darkened car. The bandits, exposed to view by the flaring bonfires, bolted for cover. Four of the gang climbed onto the engine. Ed Cullen, more daring or more foolish than the rest, took up a position by the near corner of the express car.

The fight lasted half an hour. At close quarters the shotguns of the defenders were more effective than the rifles of the bandits, and the Wells, Fargo men were better placed than their opponents; but this hardly blunts the force of what Adair and his companions had demonstrated—that five professional gunmen could be held at bay and finally worsted by three determined novices.

Two of the outlaws were kneeling upon the tender, preparing the dynamite in between swapping shots with the men in the express car. Jennings spotted one of the gang, either Carver or Sam Ketchum, start to crawl under the train, and quickly sprayed the outlaw's rear end with loose buckshot. This put an end to any plans to blast the guards out of the car.

A number of bullets flew through the open doors, six bored through the woodwork, and two narrowly missed the mail clerk, Frank Albright —without, albeit, rousing him into any sort of action except the evasive kind. No one aboard was hit. All four bandits on the locomotive had wounds to report: Sam Ketchum's scalp was scored by two buckshot, and the other men suffered damage in various areas of the lower anatomy.

"There wasn't a word spoken by any of us in the car", Adair told a Las Angeles newspaperman some hours afterwards. The messenger's testimonial to the junior member of his team was cannily overlain with sycophancy:

"I tell you that kid, Thacker, stood up to it like a veteran. He is a worthy son of his illustrious sire, John Thacker, who has grown gray in the service of Wells, Fargo."

The passengers stayed right where they were, all but Alexander F. Stoeger, a beer salesman from St. Louis, who ran some distance down-track. There he lit a fire as a signal for the westbound Limited which followed No. 20, the Flyer.

By 9.15 Adair, Jennings, and Thacker had their shotguns loaded with the last of their ammunition. It seemed as though they would have to surrender, after all. Then, providentially, Ed Cullen reached into his belt for cartridges. As he did so he leaned forward, bringing his face close to the tip of Jennings' shotgun. Jennings promptly pulled the trigger and blew a hole in the bandit's forehead.

"Boys, I'm gone", cried Cullen, slumping back, "Boys, I'm dead". In a moment his supposition was seen to be correct. Within a few seconds the boys were gone, too. They clambered down from the engine and scooted for their horses, all fresh mounts on unofficial loan from the Erie company. Cullen's body was lifted onto the train and conveyed to San Simon. The following morning it turned up as the subject of an inquest at Lordsburg, New Mexico.

Since the gang had cut the wire in one place only, and then on the east side of Stein's station, the operator was able to send out a message to Bowie a minute or so after the seizure of the train. A courier rode out to inform the posse, seven of whom started out across the San Simon Valley for Skeleton Canyon.

Less than two hours after the defeat of the Ketchum gang the other eight possemen arrived at the scene of the shooting in a special train ordered by the two U.S. Marshals. Although the trail left by the disarrayed outlaws was easily discernible under a shimmering moon, no pursuit was essayed until daylight. As the posse got ready to move off, a raven made its descent beside the tracks and was soon enjoying the taste of a portion of Ed Cullen's brain, which was splattered upon one of the ties.

The outlaws had taken with them the horse that had been ridden by Cullen and the one on which they had intended to stow their loot, from which the posse apparently concluded that there were six men in the band. On Friday afternoon the officers came upon two abandoned horses, one of them saddled. Nothing was more obvious than that there were only four bandits to be sought, but this scarcely weighed with the posse at all. At an early stage in the hunt they had decided that if they could not catch the actual robbers, they would rope in some of the unruly and intractable crowd who regularly consorted with the outlaws. And if they could arrest more than four of them, then so much the better.

Chapter Seven

FRAMED

Besides John E. Thacker, a detective of national note, the posse called together by Foraker, Griffith, and Wells, Fargo included Jeff Milton, George Scarborough, Sam Webb, Cipriano Baca, Sam Finley, and Scott White, Sheriff of Cochise County.

Next to Thacker, Jeff Milton was the most widely known. A native of Florida, he had been strenuously on the side of law enforcement in Texas and New Mexico for seventeen years with only a few short breaks. His success as an officer sprang from a compound of courage, honesty, and shrewdness, firmly allied to skill with weapons. Milton did not permit the finer meshwork of the law to interfere with his understanding of justice. If his sense of honor was a little righteous or overbearing at times, he was respected even by most of those who had best cause to avoid him.

His close friend and associate George Scarborough was a man of curiously piebald reputation. Bellicose and fearless, Scarborough relished trouble. Born in Louisiana, he became a Ranger and later a Sheriff in Texas. In the summer of 1895, while moving among the complex underworld of El Paso, he employed the most questionable of means to lure Martin Morose from the Mexican side of the Rio Grande into a fatal ambush. Morose was a notorious thief and crook, but Scarborough's public character was gravely tarnished in the outcry that followed the affair. Nine months later he murdered Old John Selman, perhaps because he suspected that if he did not kill Selman, Old John would kill him. He moved to Deming, was engaged as detective for a cattlemen's association, and served as a Deputy United States Marshal. No one was more thorough in hunting for bank and train robbers, or more contemptuous of adverse odds. While his efficiency as a stock detective made him the hobgoblin of the rustlers, his methods and his manner were such that he was loathed by nearly everyone on the range other than the big cowmen.

These two, Milton and Scarborough, through their strategy of making the law work for them in thinning out the crop of thieves, smugglers, and abettors of outlawry, were the chief authors of the prelude to a judicial travesty.

By Sunday, December 12th, the two groups of officers had reunited. That morning they rode up to Cush's ranch and arrested Alverson, Hoffman and Warderman as three of the Stein's Pass robbers.

The three men were in an awkward predicament at once, for the trail of the bandits had led directly into Tex Canyon. To make matters far worse for them, there was a recent bullet wound in Hoffman's leg. Scarborough produced a pair of torn overalls which he had picked up along the trail, and demonstrated that the rip in the clothing corresponded with the location of the bullet hole.

In a little while Tom Capehart came up to the ranch, whereupon someone flourished the second item of evidence. This was a handkerchief mislaid at Stein's Pass by Tom Ketchum, incriminatingly marked with the initials "T. K." The posse deduced that the handkerchief must belong to "Tom Kephart" and took him in charge.

Presently Henry Marshall rode in. He was arrested for the hold-up because he and Capehart were known to be partners. Both Capehart and Marshall had seen the saddled horses of the posse in time to have turned and ridden away without being noticed, had they any motive for flight.

While this piece of mummery was being acted out, the four robbers were tucked away in the Wildcat, a mile and a half away. They had been watching the posse, but could not tell quite what was happening. Soon Milton and nine or ten others came down the canyon toward the hideout.

The story Alverson got from Tom Ketchum two years later was that the gang "ranged themselves along the rim in such a position that they could have killed two or three of the posse with one shot if necessary," and would have opened fire if they had seen any prisoners. But Milton and his party, knowing nothing of the desperadoes concealed in the crags above, jogged on by without an uneasy thought. The gang waited until they were gone, then got their horses and left. A few minutes later the remainder of the posse, headed by Sam Finley, passed through with the five prisoners lying handcuffed in a wagon.

Finley's party took the supposed robbers to San Simon while Milton and the rest searched for "Black Jack's gang". They learned of the hideout in the Wildcat and planned to storm it under cover of night. When the appointed hour came, only Milton and Scarborough would go. The gang had stored some blankets and provisions in a tree, but the officers found that these had been disturbed by a previous invader — a bear, drawn to the place by the scent of honey. Milton and Scarborough decided to search around for Cush, whom Scarborough wanted to kill so as to "get rid of a good nuisance". They split up, and it may have been fortunate for Cush that he was taken by Milton.

Griffith had agreed with Foraker that the suspects should be sent from San Simon to Silver City, but in the event he had them packed off to Tucson, where he thought they would be safer. There the guards were instructed not to divulge the names of the prisoners to the newspapers — a foolish restriction, since this information could be easily obtained from San Simon, but a fair indication of the deliberate isolation of the Texas Canyon crowd. But, despite this and other ominous signs, the men were not yet perturbed, according to Alverson's recollection.

> In order not to have any witnesses for the defense they had to implicate all of us. The only man of that posse I can speak a good word for is Jeff Milton. He acted like a man all the way through— he and [Frank] Cox the S.P. attorney. I have heard he did some big talking afterwards but I didn't pay any attention to it. I knew he was not that kind of a man and I told them if Jeff Milton had anything to say bad about me he would say it to my face. . . .
> The thing was that they were as desperate as the outlaws, there had been innumerable hold ups and robberies and no one had been caught, so they had to make an example of some one.
> Well, they brought us to Tucson and I asked them to get me a lawyer so that I might get a writ of habeas corpus, because I thought I could prove my innocence and get out. But they said I would have to wait until we got to New Mexico where the crime was committed. Then I wanted to communicate with my friends, but they would not allow that. Even then none of the three of us [Alverson, Hoffman, and Warderman] took matters too seriously, even joked about it. I remember Walter asked, as they took us from the jail in Tucson, "What do you suppose they are going to do with us", and I said, "Hang us, I guess". "Well", he answered, "I hope they leave my legs untied because I would like to kick the block off one or two of them." Guess we laughed too soon.

Foraker rushed to Tucson to demand custody of the five men. In his eagerness to secure it, he asked Washington for permission to invoke a procedure which he knew to be unusual, if not irregular:

> Laws say take before nearest [U.S.] commissioners for preliminary hearing. I think safer to take before U.S. judge. Please wire authority to do so, prisoners dangerous.

It appears, though, that the proper course was adopted, for the men were committed at their hearing and then taken before the Federal District Judge, who granted an order of removal. The five alleged bandits joined Cush in the Silver City jail a few days before Christmas.

"Politics were rotten there," Alverson charged. "President McKinley had been asked to appoint some of them (sic) to office, Frank W. Parker as Judge and W. B. Childers as U. S. District Attorney". One of these two men, he said, "was a drunken sot, in fact got to drinking so hard later that he went insane".

The grand jury for the Third Judicial District were not at all in sympathy with Alverson and his pals. On February 19th, 1898, they indicted all six for attempting to rob the United States mail car and for conspiracy to the same end. Alverson, Hoffman, and Warderman were also billed for robbing the Postmaster at Stein's; Henry Marshall, Thomas S. Capehart, and John Vinadge, alias Cush, were indicted as accessories after the fact for the latter robbery. Parker set bond at ten thousand dollars for each man. None of the defendants was able to take advantage of these terms. They lost very little liberty this way, as the ritual of selecting jurors for the trial began almost at once.

Childers naturally proceeded with the first indictment. He subpoenaed more than forty witnesses; James S. Fielder, the defense counsel, could call upon a mere handful. Yet it was Childers who was soon floundering in an almost untenable situation. In a letter to the United States Attorney, written a few weeks afterwards, he complained bitterly about the structure of the laws—forgetting, perhaps, that these were the laws he had ungrudgingly sworn to uphold:

> . . . the territorial laws applicable to summoning and empannelling (sic) juries cover United States cases in this Territory, and . . . the statute on that subject provides that the Territory shall have three challenges, the first named defendant five and each additional defendant two additional challenges, so that in this case the United States had three peremptory challenges and the detendants fifteen. . . .

Fielder made the most of these provisions. Several special venires had to be issued before the defense was satisfied with the jury.

The first witnesses were heard on Friday, February 25th. T. W. North, the engineer, was altogether sure about it: Hoffman and Alverson were two of the men who had boarded his engine. Other members of the train crew thought they could identify Hoffman, Alverson, and Warderman as three of the robbers. Various of the posse described how the trail of the bandits had been followed right into Texas Canyon, where the officers found "dynamite, fuses, ammunition and other articles such as would naturally be used in outlawry of the kind tried." Testimony was also introduced to show that Cullen had been with the defendants just before the hold-up.

Fielder called a few alibi witnesses and obtained evidence that Cullen "had stated that he was about to join the Black Jack gang of border bandits." The explanation as to how Walter Hoffman came by the bullet hole in his leg was wonderfully improbable; but since Alverson and Hoffman, in relating the circumstances, made admissions which were not in their own best interests, it may well have been the truth. Their story was that they had held up a man near the border and robbed him of ten gallons of mescal. In the evening, while Hoffman, in a drunken daze, was squatting beside the campfire, Alverson was lurching about in the brush nearby. Alverson, for some undisclosed reason, had drawn his pistol. When Alverson tripped up, the gun went off, "the ball ranging up through the calf of Walter's leg, coming out just below his boot top." Contrary to Alverson's assertion, a shot fired from an express car would not necessarily have ranged down through the leg of anyone who happened to be in way, for the bandits were perched on the engine and tender most of the time. Even so, none of the bandits could have acquired a wound such as Walter's unless he had been kneeling or crouching in an absurd posture, back turned toward the express car.

Childers maintained that "a complete case had been made out against at least five" of the six defendants. Fielder argued that the culprits were the Black Jack gang, that the explosives cached near the ranch were theirs, and that the defendants "dared not offend these outlaws and were of necessity aware of what was going on but could only remain quiet."

On Wednesday, March 8th, the jurors retired, stayed out long enough for a smoke, then confounded Childers' calculations by returning a verdict of not guilty.

Parker, beside himself with rage, assailed the jury with blame for the "worst disgrace in a courtroom" he had ever seen, and threatened never again to hold court in Silver City.

Childers was by no means through. The men went back to jail while the District Attorney thought about what to do next. His letter to the Attorney General, dated March 28th, he represented as a "special report and explanation of the case," but it is more than faintly redolent of self justification and prompts more questions than it answers:

> ... I am fully satisfied that the jury in the case was tampered with, and that we will be able to discover before the next term of court how it was done and possibly have indictments found against

the guilty parties.

I am also fully satisfied that the next trial for robbery of the Post Office will result in a conviction of almost (sic), if not all, of the defendants. . . .

It is possible that they may be tried in the Territorial court for violation of the Territorial statute against train robbing, but I am very much afraid that the Territory will not be able to succeed in getting the witnesses necessary for a conviction. . . .

I desire if possible, to secure a conviction of these men as I am fully satisfied of their guilt, and if they were discharged it would have a very bad effect upon the element from which train robbers are recruited in this section of the country. . . . .

First, the newspapers reported that the jury needed less than half an hour to reach its verdict. (Len Alverson said their deliberations occupied only eleven minutes, and this, at worst, could not have been far from the truth) Did the defense bribe all twelve of the jurors? And why was nothing more heard of Childers' expressed determination to take action against the alleged "guilty parties"?

Second, what made Childers feel so sure of reaping his convictions if the men were tried for the robbery of the Post Office? Although the emphasis placed upon the relevance of the various items of testimony would be different from before, the witnesses would be the same.

The District Attorney's reluctance to make way for a prosecution by the Territory obviously owed nothing to logic and could not have been based on the reasons he advanced. It is manifest that a prosecution for attempted robbery of a passenger train would require exactly the same evidence and exactly the same witnesses as a prosecution for attempted robbery of the mail car attached to that train.

If, as he pretended, his one concern was to see train robbers punished with a severity which would keep other men off the outlaw trail, Childers ought to have been delighted to yield to the Territory. Twelve years imprisonment was the heaviest sentence that could be imposed for armed interference with the United States mails. But under the Compiled Laws of 1897, Section 1151, the death penalty was mandatory for anyone convicted in a Territorial court of "assault upon any railroad train, railroad cars, or railroad locomotive."

At length Childers dropped the lesser charges still outstanding against Capehart, Marshall, and Vinadge. Something must have happened to the confident belief that he could make out a complete case against five out of the six. One consequence of this was that, since only Alverson, Hoffman, and Warderman would be on trial, the defense would be entitled to only nine peremptory challenges.

A Territorial charge was laid against Capehart, Marshall and Vinadge but dismissed in December, 1898. Tom Capehart, however, had already taken the lesson to heart. After his release he began to associate more closely with the outlaws, and soon became a professional bandit himself.

Childers had the case against the three remaining defendants transferred to Las Cruces. The second trial was held in the fall term of court and resulted in the conviction of all three. Alverson claimed that Pat Garrett, Sheriff of Dona Ana County, "had the jury packed with some of his professional jurymen:"

> They were the most damnable looking lot of men you ever saw on a jury, a number of them the most ignorant kind of Mexicans, dirty and shod with pieces of leather with strings coming between the toes for shoes. Two were not even citizens. When the trial was over the Judge said, "Leonard Alverson, stand up. You are found guilty by twelve of your *superiors!*"
> . . . Cox, the Southern Pacific lawyer, though he was supposed to be against us, was so disgusted when he saw how they were railroading the case that he threw up the whole thing. . . .

On September 28th, 1898, the three men began serving their ten-year terms as Federal prisoners in the Territorial Penitentiary at Santa Fe.

One other associate of the Ketchums was journeying through the courts during the greater part of 1898. This was Bruce Weaver, alias Charles Collins, the Elizabethtown miner who had come by a wad of the money stolen from the train at Folsom.

Collins began to spend the money soon after the robbery, but the bills were torn and so attracted unfavorable notice. Eventually he sent the money to Washington for exchange, on the advice of a Dr. Schuler, of Raton. Schuler, however, could not swallow the man's explanation that the notes had been chewed by rats. He reported his suspicions to Reno, who got in touch with the Treasury. A check on the serial numbers of the damaged bills showed the money to be part of the Folsom loot.

Collins was traced to Cochise County, arrested in Bisbee, and returned to Springer on the last day of March. A week later the Commissioner at Clayton bound him over to await the action of the United States grand jury. Four days after this the grand jury indicted him at Las Vegas for interference with the free passage of the United States mails. He was held for safekeeping in the Territorial Penitentiary pending trial, which opened on November 23rd and ended with his acquittal. The officials of Union County held him on the Territorial charge of train robbery, but on January

7th, 1899, a grand jury at Clayton found there was no case for him to answer. His story was that he had won the money from Tom Ketchum in a poker game at Trinidad. It was no more true than the one he had tried out on Dr. Schuler, for Ketchum had not visited Trinidad at any time since the robbery. On the other hand, there was not a sliver of evidence to support the charge that the defendant was one of the robbers.

After his acquittal Collins made for southwestern New Mexico, where he reassumed his right name of Weaver and again fell in with the Ketchums.

Alverson, Hoffman, and Warderman served a little more than half of the terms to which they had been sentenced. In the spring of 1901, it was predicted that the three would shortly be released, but only after a change in the Administration and the passage of three more years was a presidential pardon forthcoming.

For all of Alverson's denials in his later years, it is plain that the three men were accessory both before and after the fact; so much was implied in their defense at the trials. Whether they were in treaty with the bandits through inclination or as a matter of prudence is of small account, for they were arrested, charged, indicted, and convicted not as accessories but as robbers. Lawlessness cannot be remedied by legalized persecution of the innocent, but it would be unfair to assert that all of those responsible for the ultimate conviction of these men knew them to be innocent of the principal charges, or that some were not acting — however misguidedly—in pursuit of some notion of rough justice. The conclusion, however, bears of no genuflection to charity. It is that the conviction of Alverson, Hoffman, and Warderman was callously engineered by men who, in the main, neither knew nor cared whether the three were innocent or guilty and had no regard for the letter of the law, for justice as an abstract, or indeed for anything except their own political future and personal well-being.

Chapter Eight

DYNAMITE AND SIX - SHOOTER

Through the three months that followed their discomfiture at Stein's Pass, the Snaky Four lingered in and around Cochise County. They hid out mostly in the Swisshelm Mountains or in the Wildcat. Outwardly, at least, they were still welcome with the cowpunchers, prospectors, and small ranchers.

The one man whom they regarded as a menace was John Slaughter, owner of the San Bernardino ranch and sometime sheriff. One day, while the gang were passing the time of day at a cabin near Mud Springs, in Sulphur Springs Valley, the conversation touched upon Slaughter. Tom Ketchum glared balefully.

"Let's go down and kill that little rat-headed son of a bitch", he proposed to the other three.

But before they had made up their minds what to do, Slaughter himself drove up in his buggy. Seeing the four badmen lounging outside the house, he handed the reins to Mrs Slaughter and ostentatiously rested his shotgun across his knees. As he passed by he looked them over, as if to dare them to made trouble. The outlaws said nothing until the rig was out of sight. Finally one of them remarked drily: "Well, there he is, fellers; if you want him, go get him".

Tom Ketchum, it developed, did not want him all that badly, after all.

Slaughter apart, those who really objected to the Ketchums were too afraid of them to think about laying information against the outfit; since, however, the local officers were cordially disliked and mistrusted, few people wanted dealings with the law anyway. Events after the Stein's Pass hold-up had afforded a vivid lesson of what was liable to happen in Cochise County when lawmen came looking for outlaws. The Ketchums, for their part, were wise enough after this not to imperil themselves by holding up another train in the neighborhood; to provoke a further incursion of deputies into western Cochise County might be to overstretch the tolerance of the inhabitants for the Ketchums and their like. Flat broke as they were, and confirmed in their outlawry, only one course was open to the four bandits.

With the coming of spring they pulled out of Arizona, crossed New Mexico, and rode down into Val Verde County, Texas. Two of the places they visited may be plotted with fair certainty: Old Man Lusk's spread at Chimney Wells and the Berry Ketchum ranch. Once again they had plans for train No. 20 of the Southern Pacific. In order to fulfil them, they had ridden five hundred miles to Comstock, where the Newman gang had robbed the train some sixteen months before.

The proceedings of Thursday night, April 28th, 1898, were true in every detail to the well-tried formula which made up the so called "regulation style" for train robbers in the 1890s.

As the train drew away from Comstock station two of the band started to crawl across the coals towards the locomotive cab. They made the engineer stop the train, uncouple the express car, and pull ahead until their two partners standing by the tracks gave the signal for a second halt by firing off their pistols. All four of the bandits then approached the open door of the express car, prodding the engineer before them.

Messenger R. H. Hayes later pictured himself as a figure of splendid defiance, frustrated first by a rifle which hung fire and then by the concern for the safety of the engineer which kept him from taking on the desperadoes with his revolver. When one of the robbers climbed into the car and demanded the keys to the way safe Hayes, according to his own story, denied having any key. Dynamite and fuse were then applied to the through safe, the while Hayes vacillated from assurance that the safe was empty to entreaty for it not to be blown up. Everyone ducked away as the fuse was lit, and soon an almighty explosion rent the still night air, tearing "a hole as big as a barrel" through the roof of the car and splintering one side "into kindling wood." The bandits rummaged through the remnants of the car, denuded the shelves of the riven safe, then "walked round the engine and disappeared in the darkness."

The express company, too, honored precedent. Their officials alleged that no booty had been obtained "except one small package of money destined to San Diego, Cal.," They explained, most unconvincingly, that they had "discontinued shipping by that route" several months previously "on account of the frequency of hold-ups in the vicinity of Comstock." Hayes stoutly averred that the leader of the robbers had remarked that the messenger was right in saying there was no money to be had. Newspapermen in El Paso, disregarding all of this, took it upon themselves to decide that the robbers had borne away twenty thousand dollars. Of course the express people were lying and the newspapers guessing, as was usual on such occasions.

On their flight northwards through the Devil's River country of Val Verde and Crockett Counties, the Ketchums, Carver, and Atkins were untroubled by any posse. Fresh horses were secured from a ranch near Ozona, along with a saddle which was to turn up in New Mexico more than a year afterwards. A hundred miles north of Ozona, and twice that distance from Comstock, lay the Berry Ketchum ranch, where the outlaws could tarry safely, for all that everyone from the Sheriff on down knew them to be the four most desperate men in the Southwest. While they were there Will Carver would certainly have spent some time with Laura Bullion. Some or all of them also have called on the Kilpatricks and other friends in Concho County. Their precipitate departure, early in June, followed no indiscretion of their own.

Just before the Comstock robbery another bunch of outlaws had quit Val Verde County. These men were Bud Newman, Pierce Keaton, and two brothers named Taylor. They had stopped at Sonora, in Sutton County, to buy dynamite, then headed north-east to Coleman, no more than sixty miles from San Angelo. There, on the night of June 9th, they held up a Santa Fe train. Two passengers opened fire on the band, who decamped without having enriched themselves in anything but experience. Little enough notice might have been taken of all this had not the fireman been killed. Rumors charging the Ketchums with this affray, together with the direction of the pursuit, were enough to hasten the outlaws away from Tom Green County.

No matter whether they had brought back twenty thousand dollars from Val Verde County, or merely two thousand, Tom Ketchum and his comrades could scarcely have spent all of the booty within a couple of months. They seem to have had little real use for money, seldom purchasing anything they might borrow or steal. Never once did they venture into the large cities, and now they dared not be seen in the cow-towns. If Sam and Tom asked Berry to hold on to their share of the stolen money until they were ready to give up outlawry, they were deluding themselves, perhaps in more ways than one. But whatever the motivation, they had determined to rob another train before they left the State.

Andy Jones, owner of a ranch in Sterling County, furnished them with a change of horses. They continued directly northwest to the tracks of the Texas & Pacific Railway, finally to make camp by Mustang Creek, five miles out of Stanton, and "one of the most desolate spots on the line."

DYNAMITE AND SIX-SHOOTER

At about ten o'clock on the night of Friday, July 1st, westbound train No. 3 was brought to a standstill near the Mustang Creek crossing, the engineer having whistled down brakes for the red light glowing ahead which told him that the switch had been thrown. Instantly three of the gang rushed the engineer and fireman and cut loose the express car, which was then hauled down the spur track, well beyond the stranded passenger coaches. Confronted by a messenger who insisted upon keeping the door between the bandits and himself, they settled the dispute by breaching the car with a charge of dynamite. After the way safe had been cleared of its contents they set about the through safe. This second explosion turned the car into a most spectacular wreck. Nearly all of it now littered the track and the surrounding prairie. The safe had been blasted into fragments, its contents strewn about what was left of the floor. Evidently the outlaws were well satisfied with the outcome, for when they rode away to the southwest a number of ten-dollar bills and some jewelry still lay there amid the debris. Officials of the Pacific Express Company maintained an obdurate silence on the extent of the haul; even hearsay could do no better than to place it somewhere between $10,000 and 50,000.

Posses went into the field from Martin, Midland, and Howard Counties. Sheriff John Y. Lovell, of Reeves County, far to the southwest, even started out with a special train loaded with deputies. No sightings were recorded. Whenever the outlaws wanted a change of horses, they simply took the best of those they could find in the great pastures of the Circle Dot and Quien Sabe. Unhampered by purposeful pursuit, the bandits got away into New Mexico. Public interest was unaroused: even in West Texas, talk of the Stanton robbery made dull fare compared with news of the siege of Santiago.

Nothing is known for sure of the movements of the outlaws during the next three or four months. The firmest conjecture would be that they went first to Turkey Creek, where after a while they split up. Probably Carver went on north, perhaps as far as Hole-in-the-Wall or even further. Atkins may have accompanied him. This is no evidence of what Sam or Tom did or where they went, until one day in October or early November, 1898, when they came in for food at the WS ranch near Alma, in western Socorro County, New Mexico. Sometime in the night the brothers stole down to the stable and led out Rattler, the favorite saddle horse of William French, the manager, who was then on vacation in the Near East. Next, their eyes fell covetously on a pair of horses in the pasture. These were French's buggy team. Major, the better of the two, was quickly secured; but his mate broke through the loop of the rope and would not be caught. Sam and Tom gave up trying and fled north. Major was ridden into the ground and was in such bad shape when found several days later that he had to be destroyed. Rattler, French's pet gray, was still in sound condition when the Ketchums rode into Hole-in-the-Wall.

Here they may have rejoined Carver and Atkins. It is altogether certain that they now met two other notables, though perhaps not for the first time. One, called "Butch", was George L. Parker, alias Cassidy. The other, usually addressed as "Elza", was William Ellsworth Lay.

"Elza" Lay was born about 1865 in Coles County, Illinois. There is nothing to give substance to the story that he had been through college, other than that he was intelligent and well-spoken. In the 1880s, he went to Colorado, got into some sort of trouble, and became a fugitive. Possibly he first met one or both of the Ketchums during these years of wandering the rangelands and hold-outs of Wyoming, Colorado and Utah. In 1896 he fell in with Cassidy, a bank robber and convicted rustler. Cassidy and Lay were associated in robberies at Montpelier, Idaho, and Castle Gate, Utah. By the fall of 1898 they were ready to fade out for country where, for a while, they could pose as ordinary cowpunchers.

Subsequent events indicate that they must have struck up an understanding with Carver and the Ketchums at this time. Nor could it have been random chance which directed Cassidy and Lay to Cochise County. It was not usually a simple matter for a cowhand to find work during the winter months, but the two outlaws were hired at once by the Erie outfit. Cassidy was traveling as "Jim Lowe" and Lay as "Will McGinnis." Before the close of the winter of 1898-99 they and three other Erie hands— Mack Axford, Jim James, and Clay McGonegal—had moved on to the WS, in response to a letter from Perry Tucker, who had just returned to his old position as foreman there. Tom Capehart and Bruce Weaver joined at about the same time. William French had cut short his overseas vacation on learning that larcenous neighbours were steadily trimming the WS herds. In short order he had dismissed his foreman and most of the other employees, persuaded Tucker to leave the Erie, and drafted a crew of men who could be relied upon to dampen the activities of the local rustlers. His trust was not misplaced.

French was furious with the Ketchums for having stolen and maltreated two of his best horses, and neither they nor Carver were so tactless as to be seen near the house. Naturally this did not prevent them from holding regular meetings with Cassidy, Lay, and Weaver to discuss their plans for the future. Elza Lay agreed to throw in with the Ketchums; Butch Cassidy, however, had definite ideas of his own, and wanted to go back to Wyoming.

But, in the spring of 1899, Tom Ketchum had about run his course as leader of a band of outlaws.

Friction had been mounting for some time, with the traits of meanness and surliness in Tom Ketchum's uneven temperament the prime source of it. Dave Atkins was the first to quit. Tom still bore rancor towards Atkins because he had let liquor loosen his tongue while they were planning the Stein's Pass robbery; moreover, he thought of him as a coward. The truth may be that Atkins lacked the depressive fatalism which steeled the others to fight against desperate odds. At length, somewhere in Cochise County, there was a flare-up between the two men and Atkins left.

Despite the tensions, the other three, mounted on horses stolen from the Erie, set out together across New Mexico. Only two of them were to keep their appointment with Elza Lay.

Chapter Nine

SEPARATE WAYS

On or about May 3rd, 1899, one of the three men was seen on the LX pastures, some thirty miles east of Roswell. His partners must have been close at hand for, barely a day later, three mounts were stolen from the nearby LFD horse camp, and the three Erie animals left in their place. Then, on May 6th, the outlaws swapped the LFD horses for three from the A—V ranch of the Cass Land and Cattle Company, north of Roswell. W. G. Urton, manager and partowner of the company, and a former employer of the Ketchums, was particularly incensed because the thieves had killed one of his horses: when caught, it broke away with the rope and the outlaw, in a fit of irrational fury, had shot the animal. Sheriff Fred Higgins and his deputy, Will Rainbolt, were reported to have trailed the thieves closely; but they were never close enough to be seen by them.

This is the last occasion on which the three outlaws were together. Very soon afterwards Tom Ketchum was either thrown out or deserted by the others. His sullen moods, charged with sudden paroxysms of savage rage, had become intolerable to them; even to Sam, who knew him best. Will Carver and Sam Ketchum were outlaws and desperadoes; if either of them were pressed to the point where he felt he had to kill a man, he would kill him and suffer few qualms or none. But neither would kill upon impulse, and neither was inclined to destructive tantrums. . . .

Dave Atkins was done with outlawry, but he did meet Carver in Cochise County, months later. Atkins remained in Arizona until late in 1899. Sometimes he would visit Mack Axford and Charlie Mowbry, who were working a copper claim in the Swisshelms; once he told Axford that the gang had broken up because of Tom Ketchum's "brutal ways". Presently he informed them that he was going off to Idaho, in the hope of making a better life. He did go, only to be arrested in Montana a few months later.

After parting company with Tom Ketchum, Sam and Carver headed for Turkey Canyon to await the arrival of Elza Lay. Every so often they would visit Cimarron or Elizabethtown to pick up a few supplies, take a few drinks, or play a few hands of Poker. James K. Hunt, the postmaster and principal merchant of Cimarron, first saw them in town during the latter part of May.

It was probably during the first days of that month that Lay told William French he was leaving the WS, his pretext being that there were no more horses to be broken "and he did not much care for any other class of employment." Red Weaver quit at the same time. They traveled from Magdalena to Springer with a trainload of cattle destined for the northern pastures of the WS, by the Vermejo. This was their last service for French, and it fitted in well with their plans.

Weaver decided to laze about on the ranch for a while. Lay went directly back into Springer, stopping there until about the seventh of June, and then proceeding to Cimarron. According to George Crocker, he put up at the St. James Hotel. Postmaster Hunt saw him shortly after he came into Cimarron, and kept him in mind. Red, meanwhile, had contracted smallpox, and had been hauled into Springer and placed in the ramshackle structure which served as the local pest-house. Evidently he had fully recovered by the twelfth of June, for he and Lay were seen together in Cimarron on or about that day. Soon after this, Lay went to the house of Agapito Duran. He boarded there for a week or so. He dealt Monte at Charretta's saloon but otherwise appeared to be inactive.

No one in Cimarron ever saw "McGinnis" or "the Red man" in the company of the other two strangers until one day near the end of June, when Lay returned to Duran's place, bringing Carver with him. During the preceding week, presumably, the gang had got together for a meeting in Turkey Canyon or somewhere in the vicinity of Ponil Park.

Carver, giving his name as "G. W. Franks" and his address as "Simerone," wrote to James Correy, a storekeeper in Springer, ordering two forty-inch rifle scabbards and enclosing a five-dollar bill in payment. He also wrote to Denver for certain other essentials: one 30-40 carbine and one thousand rounds of 30-40 ammunition. There were duly shipped to him by those dependable agents, Wells, Fargo and Company. The gun was for Lay. After a stay of four or five nights the two outlaws rode away from Duran's.

Only two men in Cimarron seem to have been suspicious of or perturbed by the comings and goings of the strangers. One was James H. Morgan, a cowboy who wanted to play detective. The other was the watchful postmaster, Jim Hunt: he thought they meant to rob his store.

In the meantime, officials in newly-formed Otero County had other, and lesser, outlaws to deal with. Three of them, led by Ernest Gentry, had robbed the paymaster's office of the Alamogordo Lumber Company on April 10th. Then a posse from Eddy County, headed by Sheriff Cicero Stewart and including Constable Dee Harkey, caught up with another band of five men on May 2, in western Otero County, and captured four of them. By mischief or mischance, one of them was at first identified as Tom Ketchum. The four were Volney C. Musgrave; Dan Johnson, an uncle of the Musgrave boys; Sam Morrow, the one errant member of a well-respected family; and, last and worst, James Knight, alias Jim Jones, alias Jack Underwood, alias Charles Ware, one of Bill Dalton's gang in the bank robbery at Longview, Texas, an old acquaintance of Will and Bob Christian in the Indian Nations, but now on the run from the Texas penitentiary. Hill Loftus, alias Tom Ross, who in north Texas and the Nations had enjoyed the dubious benefit of having much the same circle of friends as Jim Knight, was the one that got away. All four of those taken by Stewart's posse were on the loose again within a short time.

Tom Ketchum himself was now more dangerous and more elusive than ever before. His statement, nearly two years later, that he was somewhere in the Sacramento Mountains during this time was, no doubt, a characteristic half truth: he might indeed have traversed the Tularosa country at least once in the spring of 1899, but he did not loiter there overlong. The next misdeed attributable to him was, on the face of it, one of the most outrageous crimes enacted in the Southwest of the 1890s. It took place in Yavapai County, Arizona, two hundred miles from any point where Ketchum is known to have been at any time previously.

R. M. "Mack" Rogers, a native of Arkansas, had lived in Texas for some years before joining relatives in the Verde Valley of central Arizona. In 1898 he went into partnership with Clinton D. Wingfield to purchase the old sutler's store at the former cavalry post called Camp Verde. Rogers was then a little over thirty, several years older than Clint Wingfield. Although good natured, and well-liked in and around Camp Verde, the two young merchants showed themselves to be grasping and unscrupulous in transactions with certain others who lived further afield. Rogers made another enemy in the spring of 1899 when he helped the authorities to build up a case against Oscar Wade, an alleged horse-thief. After the jury had voted him free, Wade "made threats of getting even" with Rogers. Wade, who was well known in Camp Verde, did not try to carry out his declared intentions; and the question of whether he seriously meant to seek revenge was nullified by the intervention of someone else whose designs appear to have been similar.

As twilight settled into nightfall on Sunday, July 2nd, 1899, Rogers and the clerk, Lon Turner, went out onto the porch to chat with the mail carrier and Captain John Boyd, a retired cavalry officer. Wingfield was in a bedroom, working on some papers. Somewhat after eight o'clock a man stepped up to the porch, walking so softly that the others saw him before they heard him. After the latecomer had exchanged a few commonplace remarks with Boyd and the mail carrier, Rogers got to his feet. He may or may not have asked the man whether he wanted supplies; he certainly recognized him. As the storekeeper sprang through the doorway and ran for his six-shooter, the other man was no more than a pace or two behind him.

"That won't do, Mack!" he called out, just before he shot Rogers in the back.

Wingfield started to his feet and rushed out to investigate. It occurred to him that the discharge might have come from a firecracker. A moment later a revolver bullet tore through his stomach and smashed his spine.

Without pausing to loot the place, the killer dashed out onto the porch and told the onlookers to scatter. Boyd, a cripple, moved too slowly to satisfy the gunman, who sent a shot after him. The old man was wounded slightly in the leg, probably from a ricochet. Then the killer hastened on foot to the stream, a mile from the store, stopping on the way only to eject the shells from his pistol and to reload.

Wingfield lived for about two hours after he was shot. In that time he warned his younger brother, Frank, not to go out after the killer. The death of Rogers had been instantaneous. Both were buried on the Fourth.

Not unnaturally, Frank Wingfield ignored the advice of his dying brother; if anything he was all too prominent in the manhunt, antagonizing possemen and settlers by his headstrong and domineering manner. Although the search was lengthy and extensive, it was an ill-organized, harum-scarum effort during its first vital days. Almost at once the Camp Verde party ascertained that the killer was fleeing on an unshod horse, which had been tethered by some willows. For a while the trail was clear; then, some distance east of the village, it was lost amidst the tracks of a herd of wild horses. Presently the pursuers found sign again, or thought they had found it. This led them north. On the Mogollon Plateau the posse, now headed by Sheriff James Munds of Yavapai

County, arrested Robert Lee Cutbirth (or Cuthbert) and William Cameron.

Suspicion had fastened on one Charley Bishop, but he knew it and kept well ahead of the posse. Bishop was innocent of the killings; since, however, he did own the barefoot horse ridden by the murderer, he may have been an accomplice—wittingly or not. Cutbirth and Cameron had helped Bishop to get away, though they did not admit this until after their release. That horse had been left near Bishop's cabin, presumably by the killer, who obtained a remount either from Bishop, or from John Merritt, a neighbor.

Munds, with a handful of possemen, followed their quarry southeast, through Springerville, and across the New Mexico line before the trail disappeared near the Plains of San Augustin. There was little to guide them except a fair general description of the killer, his horse, and his saddle—and reports that he was toting a blanket of a very distinctive and unusual design—but they continued to look for a fresh lead in western New Mexico.

During these weeks a motley of discreditable (and mostly scurrilous) stories about Rogers and Clint Wingfield gave rise to or were inspired by all manner of surmise. Gossip dies hard, and the tales circulating about the valley were not stifled when, in mid-August, Sheriff Munds produced what he regarded as good evidence that the much-sought assassin was Thomas E. Ketchum. Whether Ketchum made the journey to Camp Verde especially to kill Rogers, whether he expected a friendly reception and started shooting only because Rogers tried to arm himself, or even whether two old enemies had been unexpectedly brought face to face by some trick of fate, are questions that rest unresolved. It seems plain that robbery was never contemplated. Possibly the secret underlying the bloody work of those few seconds in hidden somewhere in whatever past Mack Rogers left behind him in Texas.

As to the murder of Wingfield, the fact that he was ruthlessly shot down when unarmed—whereas the three bystanders, who could just as well have been killed too, were instead merely ordered to make themselves scarce—does not begin to prove that the killer carried a grudge against him or even knew him. Wingfield had startled the killer by bursting into the room; so he was shot, without any hesitation and probably without very much thought.

Two motives were open to the killer, although it is unlikely that he would have had time to formulate either. One was that, for all he knew,

Wingfield might well have been armed; and the safest way of settling that problem would be to kill him as soon as he showed. The other was the need to eliminate a witness who was about to confront him in a lighted room.

Recently the premise that Tom Ketchum was the author of the Camp Verde killings has been disputed. Yet, in the late summer and autumn of 1899, officials in Prescott and Phoenix were strongly of the belief that he was the man they wanted. The following anecdote, from Albert Thompson's manuscript, has an authentic ring but, for want of corroboration, must be taken as standing somewhere betwixt hearsay and evidence.

> A posse was formed at Camp Verde and the trail of the suspected assailant of Rogers and Wingate (sic) followed. The posse stumbled onto the camping place of the murderer. Here they found scrawled with a lead pencil: "Boys, I know you are after me. I'll be back in two or three hours and if not I'll be four miles north gathering bees". "How did you happen to write that, Tom?" asked District Attorney Leahy afterwards, in Clayton. "Oh, hell, I thought I'd like to have 'em know which way I'd gone so, when I left the place where I camped that night, I wrote a few lines on a cracker box for whoever might find it".

It was through no lack of effort on their part that the Arizona courts were denied their right to decide whether or not he was the guilty party. Ketchum's future was unaffected. An Arizona rope, after all, would not have differed overmuch from the one that they were measuring him for in New Mexico.

Chapter Ten

ANOTHER INCIDENT AT TWIN MOUNTAINS

By the end of the first week of July, 1899, Sam Ketchum and party were almost ready to leave Cimarron. On Friday, the seventh, Sam and Carver bought supplies at Jim Hunt's store and stashed them away in Turkey Creek Canyon. Lay and Weaver spent Friday night at Duran's and whiled away Saturday forenoon in the bar of "Lambert's saloon" — the name commonly given to the St James Hotel. Early in the afternoon Weaver settled up with Duran and rode off northeast. He had told Duran that he was going to pick up his traps from the WS ranch, but did not call there. Lay left at the same time, heading northwest for Ponil Park.

No sooner had they gone than the cowboy, James Morgan, reported his suspicions to Marshal Foraker (though not to Robert Campbell, the sheriff of Colfax County) and tried to get on the trail of the gang. He was too slow: on the night of the 11th, train No. 1 of the Colorado and Southern was held up and robbed by three or four men. The robbery occurred at almost the same place as the hold-up in September of 1897 and was accomplished in almost the same fashion.

Among the passengers were two sheriffs: Fred Higgins of Chaves County and Saturnino Pinard of Union County. Frank E. Harrington was the conductor.

A good many railroad men were held up by robbers more than once. At the annual conventions they liked to fill the notebooks of the reporters with facetious and light-hearted recountals of their adventures with the bandits. Harrington was not at all of this way of thinking. It still rankled with him that he had been unable to intervene on the earlier occasion. The proceedings on the night of this second Tuesday in July did nothing to make him a happier man.

It was 10:10 P.M. when two of the gang slipped aboard the blind baggage while the engine was being replenished at Folsom tank. Just as the locomotive was crossing the south switch, a little way beyond the station, Elza Lay stepped into the left hand side of the cab and pressed his six-shooter against Fireman Howard.

"Don't make any bad breaks," advised the outlaw. As the engineer, J. A. Tubbs, began to turn his head towards the disturbance he felt the barrel of a revolver touch his cheek. He took a quick look behind him and saw Sam Ketchum standing there.

Because "the engine was rocking some" and "the fellow was trying to steady himself", Tubbs at first took Sam to be "a drunken tramp who was trying to run a sandy." About the revolver he was under no misapprehension at all.

"Go ahead. I'll tell you where to stop," bellowed Sam, jabbing the gun into the engineer's ribs.

Five miles out of Folsom, as the train was gathering momentum for the grade at the great double-horseshoe bend through Twin Mountains, Sam issued a further command:

"Stop where the last hold-up was."

"I don't know where the last hold-up was," Tubbs protested.

"There'll be a fire on the left hand side of the track," Sam replied, "Stop there."

Nearly two miles further into the curve, they saw the fire. Carver, lying behind a rock a dozen feet away from the fire, already had the train covered. Three horses were tied to a snow fence on the other side of the track; somewhere nearby was a fourth horse, and probably a fourth man, Weaver. Less than a quarter of a mile away was the scene of the first Folsom robbery.

"I intended to fall out the window after bringing the train to a standstill," Tubbs declared, somewhat later; but when the time came to jump, he concluded that it might be safer to stay where he was. Sam then motioned the two trainmen to step down ahead of him on the left hand side. Lay quickly crossed the cab and alighted from the right hand side.

By now Carver had got his voice and his carbine into action. "Come out of there, God damn you," he bawled at the unseen messenger. He fired a shot or two into the express car, yelling: "Open up! Come out of there!"

Sam marched Tubbs and Howard to the express car "to protect the robbers in case the messenger should do a little shooting." Just to make sure that he did not, the trainmen hollered out for him to hold his fire.

Shots were ringing out from both sides of the train as Messenger Hamel P. Scott hurriedly unlocked the way safe and flung most of the currency among some merchandise: there was a far greater sum in the through safe, which he could not open. Then he unbarred the doors of his car and got out. One of the robbers took his place and ordered the bag containing the "giant" (dynamite) to be handed up to him. Lay, as Scott recalled it, "was helping to make us step around as they pleased" while the bandit in the car was preparing the explosives.

When the train stopped Fred Higgins had asked Harrington to turn out all the lights in the coaches. Each of the sheriffs was wearing a pistol, and between them they had fourteen cartridges. Sagely enough, they pointed out to the indignant conductor that a couple of six-shooters would be no match for an uncounted number of rifles. Their fellow passengers agreed with this. Harrington himself was armed with nothing save anger and determination. He at once proposed that they steal out of the coach, find the horses, and cut the hitching ropes. The three men were still discussing strategy when the robbers touched off the fuse. A few seconds later a vast explosion cleft the big safe and heaved chunks of wreckage in all directions. When Harrington examined the express car, some hours later, he saw that "the big safe had a hole in it about as big as a common soup bowl.... it was blown down like someone had thrust a pile through it." The roof of the car, he observed, "was pulled back just like you peel a banana."

The outlaws removed every box and package from the safe and dumped them on the ground. They missed nothing except the money which Scott had taken from the small local safe. Even a consignment of pears was found amid the shambles and shared out between all hands, including the train men. Later a carton of peaches was similarly doled out. Then, as Tubbs related it, one of the gang proffered a flask of whiskey and asked him to drink to their health. This, said Tubbs, he declined to do; so they told him that it made no difference, and drank to themselves. Irritated by the delay, Carver started to curse his companions and told them they "didn't know enough to rob an ox train." Finally Tubbs, Howard, and Scott were escorted to the locomotive and ordered to pull out.

While the outlaws were looting the express car, Harrington and the two Sheriffs crept nearer to the horses. They were still thirty yards short when the bandits started towards them. Fred Higgins made the most of this unusually good vantage point by taking careful note of everything the robbers did. In narrating his experiences to a newspaperman he seems to have remembered everything except the part played by Sheriff Pinard as a fellow-spectator:

... "The robbers' horses were hitched near the track, and with the conductor I crawled to the place and made as close an examination of the horses, saddles, etc., as the darkness would permit, and remained near the spot until the robbers returned. They seemed to have a great many packages and bundles and were some time getting them tied on their saddles. There were three horses, and I think I recognized all three of the parties. I was armed only with a pistol and could not afford to fire in the open, exposing myself and the conductor to the guns of the gang. The passengers were badly frightened, and asked me not to shoot from the car, which would have been useless, as I could not see the robbers from that position . . . ."

Doubtless he and his companions were undecided whether they should feel relief at being unnoticed by the gang or mortification at finding themselves in a situation not altogether dissimilar to that in which they had hoped to place the outlaws. Fortunately for their sense of well-being, Tubbs soon stopped the train because the displaced roof of the express car was dragging and had to be hacked away.

Those "packages and bundles" carried away by the gang had contained a large sum of money—no less, probably, than the $70,000 reported to Governor Otero and at least $50,000, the figure mentioned in one contemporary account.

Company officials blandly explained that the messenger had concealed all the money before the robbers entered the car to blow the safe, and that nothing had been stolen except a saddle tree. As an attempt at evasion, this was sublimely inept, even for an express company. Hamel Scott really had hidden the money from the small safe; the one blasted to pieces by the outlaws was the through safe, which could be unlocked only by certain station agents.

Reports of the affair were riddled with contradictory statements, as was usual after a highway robbery carried out under cover of darkness.

Most onlookers stated there were four of the robbers, and the posses certainly picked up the trail of four horses. Higgins, Pinard, and Harrington had seen only three horses and three bandits. Engineer Tubbs—unwilling to belittle the perils which had beset him—first swore that there were ten in the gang; some months later, though, he admitted in court that he had seen no more than three. Others said that one of the horses was carrying double as the men rode off. Someone else was reported as having noticed but two horses. Juan C. Martinez, who lived near the scene of the hold-up, soon came forward with the statement that at 6.00 A.M. on the day of the robbery he had seen three mounted men, one of them leading an extra horse, traveling east, toward the railroad. Three hours later, Martinez added, he seen them camped on a hill half a mile from the tracks. At eleven o'clock, it developed, Juan Maria Apodoca, another local man, had ridden past the camp; he saw four horses, but only two men. He had stopped by to make enquiries about some strayed livestock of his own. Although, in due course, he was to identify Lay as one of this pair, it is much more likely that the two men were Carver and Weaver. The outlaws, at this time, had "one roan horse and three dark-colored horses."

Probably the first of the two men were to board the locomotive at Folsom had been set down afoot before the party was encountered by Martinez. The second man must have left in mid-morning, meeting the other not far from Folsom station. Some hours later Carver had ridden down from camp, leading two of the other horses, and had built the fire beside the tracks. Weaver may have remained on the hill as a lookout. Later, presumably, he must have gone down on foot to join the others; this, at least, would explain the statement that one of the horses was carrying two men.

The outlaws, having recovered the fourth horse, had fled directly west. Just north of Springer, near the WS ranch, Weaver left the party. He planned to take a train for Silver City, and then make his way to Alma. The other three went on to Turkey Creek Canyon, twenty miles further west. They still had four horses; but now these comprised a roan, two bays, and a gray. The men have intended to hole up in the canyon for a day or two and then to ride down to Alma. None of them guessed that at least two people in Cimarron—Jim Morgan and Jim Hunt —had studied them over a period of several weeks, had at once connected them with the train robbery, and were more than ready to place their information in the hands of the authorities.

Sheriff Pinard gathered a posse of four men to go out after the gang, but soon gave up the pursuit. John Thacker was sent out from San Francisco to investigate the case for Wells, Fargo. He, too, made little headway. In practice almost the entire onus fell upon the railroad company and the Federal officers.

United States Marshal Foraker at once wired through a formal request to Washington for authority to send out a posse; but, since his impatience with the methods of bureaucracy matched his exasperation at the laxity and torpor of the Territorial officers, he organized the posse without waiting for permission. In point of fact, it was not a very large posse, to begin with: it consisted of Wilson N. "Memphis" Elliott. He was called a Deputy United States Marshal, but this was just a sort of courtesy title, since he was only sworn in as a posseman, and not given a regular commission.

The Colorado and Southern Railway reacted even more swiftly. A force of sixteen men was mustered overnight and taken to Folsom on a special train. Among the sixteen, all of whom were from Colorado, were Sheriff Edward J. Farr, of Huerfano County, and Deputy Sheriff George W. Titsworth, of Las Animas County. None of the men enjoyed any official standing in New Mexico; but the railway was looking after all expenses, which meant that their Special Agent, Reno, was nominally in command. A few days later Reno and several of his party were to join Foraker. Hardly less violent or dramatic than the battle which ensued when seven of the officers sprang an ambush upon the outlaws in Turkey Canyon was the barrage of accusation and recrimination afterwards hurled back and forth among the possemen themselves. Swept aside by the flood of sensation and controversy was the question of how the posse came to locate the gang that Sunday afternoon, July 16th, 1899.

Chapter Eleven

BULLETS IN TURKEY CREEK CANYON

Reno and his men soon found that the bandits had retreated in a westerly direction. For a while the trail was blotted out because "there had been sheep all over the country" but presently it was picked up again, clearly marked and still pointing west. The posses, Sheriff Pinard's and the railroad's, had followed it for nearly twenty miles when a driving rain set in, obliterating all sign and persuading them back to Folsom. Most of the men from Colorado now voted to go home; only Farr, Titsworth, and Hugo Pfalmer stayed in the hunt with Reno. An allegation that "information was furnished by an ex-member of the gang which was considered of sufficient importance to act upon" was then relayed by Associated Press to show how wise the C & S manhunters had been in returning to Folsom. In fact the informant was Juan Martinez, one of the men who had seen the gang some hours prior to the robbery; he had guided Titsworth and Pfalmer to the place where the outlaws had camped, and Titsworth picked up a torn envelope which, when pieced together, provided a substantial clue: the package bore a Springer postmark, about a fortnight old, was addressed to "G. W. Franks", and had been collected from the Cimarron post office.

Reno, Farr, and Titsworth, for some reason — perhaps tactical, perhaps merely domestic — then went back home for a day or two. But on Saturday afternoon they returned to Springer for a meeting with John Thacker. Titsworth and Thacker stayed at Springer overnight; Reno and Farr, having made some inquiries in town, went on to Cimarron to interview Postmaster Jim Hunt. As the storekeeper had been keeping careful scrutiny of the men and their equipment even before "Franks" had shown up for the package, and was about the only person in Cimarron whose peace of mind was disturbed by their presence, he was delighted to help Reno.

Marshal Foraker now arrived in Cimarron to assume control of the pursuit; to his field deputy, Wilson Elliott, would go the honor of riding out at the head of the posse. Elliott was a Texas man who made his living from whatever form of law-enforcement work he could find, wherever he could find it; when he could not find it at all, he would take just about any kind of job that was going. There must have been hundreds like him.

Four nights after the robbery the officers learned the whereabouts of Ketchum, Carver, and Lay.

One of the official versions told of a teamster coming in to report that he had encountered three horsemen in Cimarron Canyon and had seen them turn into Turkey Canyon. No doubt; but there are signs that the officers may have had a second and surer source of information.

From testimony later given in court, it is evident that the "teamster" about whose identity the officers were so reticent was James Morgan — whose livelihood came from shipping freight, as well as from ranch work and occasional spying for the law. There was no casual sighting of the fugitives by a man with a freight wagon; Morgan spent several hours "out in the mountains" on horseback, reported to Foraker in Cimarron, and rode out again next morning with Elliott. Assuredly the marshal's men could not have tracked the gang all the way to the hideout, because that posse came through that tangle of mountains and canyons to the right spot in the right canyon hardly more than four hours after their departure from Cimarron.

Most curiously, among the thousands of words spilled out to the Press by various officers about the Turkey Canyon fight, there is not a single allusion to the fourth man supposedly present at the robbery and certainly in company with the others just beforehand; and only one diffidently vague and indirect reference to a man whose recent past corresponded exactly with that of Red Weaver. Then, after a further week or so, and enwrapped in the most ambiguous and mysterious of terms, some report of the fellow did come to figure in the published developments. Foraker did get some information out of Weaver at some stage: how much, and how willingly imparted, are open to guess. Nor are there any indications as to just when or how the deal was accomplished, because Foraker told his superiors in Washington absolutely nothing about the negotiations—thereby keeping faith with his expressed policy that it was right for the utmost discretion to be observed in such matters. It is probable that Weaver did not deliberately set about betraying his partners—although there would have been a most compelling motive for his taking this course, as will become apparent.

Whoever their informant, the officers did know for sure that the robbers were in Turkey Canyon. In the morning, while Elliott and Morgan were away, Foraker had raised a small posse. Its members were Elliott, Farr, Reno, Morgan, Henry M. Love, Perfecto Cordoba, Santiago Serna (or Silva), and F. H. Smith. Serna and Cordoba were local men, enrolled by Reno as special officers of the railroad. F. H. Smith, a young man from New York who had been staying with his friends, the ranchers Garrett and McCormick, could have had no real notion of the desperate character of the men he had volunteered to help run down. Love, originally from Illinois, was a cowboy in the employ of Charles Springer. He had been engaged in skinning the carcasses of cattle afflicted with blackleg, and the infected knife was still in his pocket when he joined the posse. Notwithstanding some reports to the contrary, Thacker was not among the men who rode out with Wilson Elliott. Technically, Reno and the others were posse under Elliott, sworn to aid in the arrest of parties suspected of interfering with the free passage of the United States mails. But if Farr and Reno were not actually in charge, they behaved at times as though they were.

Sometimes bunched in twos and threes, strung out in single file wherever the trail was narrow, and with Elliott and Farr alternating in the lead, the posse rode to a point nearly three miles north of Cimarron, followed Cimarron Canyon for a further three miles, then swung into Turkey Canyon. One man, Serna, either dropped out or was sent home. The others pressed on.

At a few minutes before a quarter past five in the evening the posse emerged from a patch of scrub oak to the crest of a steep hillock. Elliott, who was in front, turned in the saddle and motioned the rest of the party to dismount. He had seen smoke curling up from out of the brush on the high ground across the glade.

Elliott's instructions were for the posse to open fire straight away if the suspects did not surrender at the first command. Farr also issued a directive, which Elliott and Morgan later denied that they had heard: "As soon as you see a man, shoot him down as quick as you can, as we have no chances to take if we kill them."

A distance of just 240 yards lay between that campfire and the place where the posse had halted. The officers were as much forearmed by the carelessness of the bandits in leaving the approach to the camp unguarded as they had been forewarned by the rising smoke.

Reno, Farr, and Smith moved off to the left, keeping to the ridge; it was their purpose to gain a position from which they could look down upon the camp and enjoy a clear field of fire. Elliott and the others were to set up a crossfire by converging upon the camp from the lower ground, to their right; when they had reached the far side of the little valley they headed for a gulch which ran along the downward slope of the hill where the bandits were encamped. By following this gulch as it twisted up and around, Elliott and his men could creep up onto the outlaws from behind.

But before any of the officers had reached their intended positions, Elza Lay, deshevelled and not fully dressed, came into view. He was carrying a canteen but no rifle. As he made his way through the pines and brush to a pool in the rocks beside the dry creek, he was untroubled by any sense of alarm. Sam Ketchum and Will Carver were standing near the campfire, not far from the cave. Perfecto Cordoba caught sight of them at about the same time as the other possemen noticed Lay.

Lay was about halfway between the camp and the creek when Reno urged his two companions to charge. They were more than one hundred yards from the outlaw, almost directly ahead of him but high above, and he did not see them. Farr and Reno may have ordered him to surrender; if they did, no more than a very few seconds were given him to think it over before they started shooting at him. Elliott, who was sixty-five yards from Lay and walking in roughly the same direction, also took aim at the outlaw and may or may not have shouted to him. The two sections of the posse were separated by something between fifty and seventy yards; Carver and Ketchum were less than thirty yards from Lay when the shooting started, but at this time were seen by Cordoba only.

The first shot, Lay afterwards related, "just kind of dropped me, just the same as if I had been hit with a club." It was fired by Farr, or by one of the two men near him, and struck the outlaw in the left shoulder. A bullet from someone in Elliott's party then ripped into his back and knocked him down.

"I tried to move," Lay said later, "and I could not move. I felt just as if I had been cut in two from where the bullet struck me first; then the next sensation was just like my feet was turning back over my head. There was several shots fired . . . I think all the first volley was fired at me."

A man in a white shirt, believed to be Morgan, was heard to exclaim: "We've got one of the sons of bitches, anyway."

The outlaws' four horses were standing near the fallen man, and Elliott could make out the—V brand on one of them. He opened up on the horses and hit one.

Perfecto Cordoba had joined the posse, in his own candid words, because "I thought we would not find anything." (Although he did not say so, the certainty that he would be paid for making the trip whether anything was found or not must have been another weighty consideration.) Perfecto found plenty. He saw the two men by the campfire; the smaller of them seemed to bear a resemblance to "McGinnis", whom he had seen in Cimarron more than once. Actually the two men were Ketchum and Carver. But before Cordoba could make any movement of tongue or trigger, shooting broke out from others in the posse.

Sam Ketchum grabbed his rifle, fired a shot or two towards Farr, and shambled off in search of a suitably sturdy and well-sited pine tree. Carver at once tumbled onto his face, but in a moment he was on his feet again, now clasping his Winchester. He had not been hit; none of the shots had been directed at him or Ketchum, anyway. But he had located Farr, Reno, and Smith, and he did not lose another second in heading for a place where he would be safer from them than they would be from him.

Cordoba, seeing Sam Ketchum running towards him, rushed back to where Elliott was standing.

"Look out! There's one of them right at you!" he yelled, "Look out, he'll shoot you!"

"Show me where he is at," Elliott rather naturally requested.

"I can't see him now," was the unhelpful reply.

"You ought to have shot when you did see him," Elliott chided.

"I didn't have time," Cordoba argued.

Long before the conclusion of this unfruitful conversation, Sam Ketchum had stationed himself behind a tree less than forty yards from Elliott.

Both Elliott and Cordoba caught glimpses of the top of Carver's head as he scurried, hatless, through the brush and up the slope. Even though he was far away, they assumed that he was the man seen by Cordoba less than a minute before. Elliott snapped a couple of shots at him, but it was a waste of good cartridges. Soon Carver was pouring lead at what little he could see of Farr, Reno, and Smith, who were nearly two hundred yards across the canyon from the rocky knoll where he had taken his stand.

The sheriff and the tenderfoot, Smith, had jumped behind one tree; it lacked the girth to conceal the persons of both and, soon after Carver had started to direct his fire at them, down went Smith with a wound "through the fleshy part of the calf of the left leg." A number of Carver's shots flew too high to do more than curb the rasher impulses of Farr and Reno; he was placed just above the officers, and had not yet found the right trajectory. But a screen of bushes, and the almost smokeless powder of the 30-40 cartridge, made it impossible for the officers to locate him.

The possemen either could not see Lay, or did not think of watching out for him after he had been shot. But, although hurt, bleeding, dazed, and shocked, and unarmed besides, he was not out of the fight. Within two or three minutes, the numbness in his legs and shoulder had started to ease away. Traveling mostly on all fours, he began to make his way back towards camp. He kept raising himself upright, but collapsed each time just as he tried to walk. He got his rifle and crawled downcreek until he found satisfactory cover. Then, when he was fifty or sixty yards below Carver, he fainted. Perhaps ten minutes passed before he was conscious again. During that time Sam Ketchum was put out of action and Carver, for awhile, had to take on the entire posse.

From his tree, no more than a hundred feet or so from Elliott's group, Sam had opened fire on Cordoba, then turned his attention to Farr, who was about on a level with him and more than a hundred and fifty yards away. At one point, he raised his voice to invite the possemen to "come down here." Numerous shots were aimed at him by Elliott, Love, Cordoba, and Morgan. Sam returned their fire until his active interest in the fight was ended by a bullet from Elliott which broke his left arm just below the shoulder. It had been a good shot, or a lucky one, for Elliott knew that the bullets from his 40-82 Marlin lacked the punch to penetrate the tree trunk which kept nearly all of Sam out of sight for nearly all of the time; he had borrowed Morgan's gun, which fired a steel-nosed cartridge, and had reloaded it, before he realized that the outlaw was already finished.

About then, Carver widened his arc of fire to cover both flanks. Elliott's section were rather more than two hundred yards away, but clearly visible. Elliott and Morgan soon scrambled for safety behind a ledge of rocks and stones; they could not see the marksman, and hoped that he could no longer see them. Cordoba and Love each stayed close to his own tree.

This was the situation when Lay revived. He quickly selected Sheriff Farr as his first target.

Farr was peering around his tree in the hope of spotting Carver when a bullet creased his right arm near the wrist. He drew back sharply. While wrapping the wound he called across to ask Reno whether he had seen the man who was shooting at them from across the canyon.

Angry because the sheriff had moved just as he was pulling the trigger for his first shot — which had been destined for the officer's protruding rear — Lay deliberately shifted his aim to the center of the tree trunk.

"You son of bitch, I'll get you this time," he muttered, just before he "blew splinters clear through the officer."

Farr, a big, brawny man, fell across the prostrate Smith. The sheriff had been shot through the chest, near the heart, and died within a minute or two. Lay fainted again shortly afterwards, and took no further part in the fray; but that one shot was probably decisive in turning the fight against the possemen. Now it was they who were on the defensive. Carver, unaided but occupying an excellent firing position, harassed and finally routed them. First he silenced Reno, whose equanimity had already been ruffled by several bullets whistling only a few inches wide of him. One ball cut through the detective's trousers and coat-tails, severing a Winchester cartridge. This convinced him that he was anything but master of the situation. An hour or so later, long after the shooting had died away, Reno was a badly frightened man as he laid his hand on the cold forehead of the dead sheriff and saw from close quarters how little protection a pine tree afforded against steel-nosed bullets from the 30-40 rifle. He had no idea of what had happened to Elliott's men. He freed Smith, who had been trapped under the much bulkier form of the slain sheriff; then, because he was "apprehensive for Mr. Elliott and his men," and because Smith asked him to go for help, he slipped away from the scene.

With Farr dead, Smith wounded, and Reno intimidated, Carver had been able to concentrate his fire on the four men, led by Elliott, who were spread below him on the other side. His most telling shot accounted for Henry Love: the bullet slammed into the cowboy's thighbone, smashing the infected knife and driving the poisoned blades deep into the flesh.

For some time, until the dead weight of Ed Farr's body was dragged by Reno off Smith's wounded and crippled leg, the young New Yorker was groaning loudly. Elliott and Morgan heard the groans, thought that the sufferer was Farr, and were not emboldened. The two shots which ended the fight were fired by Carver, at about six o'clock.

It had been a clear but cloudy afternoon. Early in the evening, a quarter of an hour or so after the last shots were heard, the rain began to come down. Keenly aware of their failure, and not daring to move or shoot, Elliott and his men waited for nightfall. About all they could do in the meantime was to crouch under the rocky overhang and watch the rain soaking the ground beside them. Love's condition was deteriorating. He begged for a "little fire" to be built beside him but they could not grant him this.

Elza Lay had recovered consciousness at dusk to see Carver standing over him. Despite the two wounds he got to his feet and went over with Carver to Sam Ketchum, who was lying among some rocks. As darkness settled they prepared to ride away; but Sam was prevented from mounting by his broken arm. After he had made a number of ineffectual attempts to stay in the saddle he urged the others to go on without him. This they refused to do. At length the three men moved slowly out of the canyon, with Ketchum supported on his horse between Carver and Lay. Even then, the pain was too much for him; so they decided to rest at the cabin of Ed McBride, near the junction of Cimarron and Ute Creeks. Here Sam told his companions that he could go no further. Carver, by now, was too anxious to get away to argue with this. But Lay wanted to stay and fight. He began to pile sacks of flour against the windows. Finally Sam and Carver convinced him that it was of no use and prevailed upon him to leave.

McBride came in later. He had been out hunting for strayed horses when the outlaws reached the ranch, but he had been friendly towards them in the past and they believed they could trust him.

Back in Turkey Canyon, the outlaws had left a box containing thirty or forty sticks of dynamite, a saddle and bridle, a saddle tree (the one taken from the express car), a bloodied hat and slicker, a wounded horse, a large agateware coffeepot, the tin-cans which had served them as cups, and sundry provisions and cooking utensils. Twenty-three shells were scattered about the place recently vacated by Carver. Somewhere nearby they had buried Sam's rifle and ammunition, probably because these were of no further use to him and he would be less conspicuous without them. They also cached the stolen money, or most of it. . . .

An hour or more after the rain had set in, Elliott and Morgan deemed it safe for them to walk over to where Farr, Reno, and Smith had last been heard from. Here the situation was even worse than they had feared. They found the dead Farr, the wounded Smith, and no Reno at all.

Reno had watched the horses of the band, he explained afterwards, till it was too dark for him to see the sights of his rifle. Then he had crossed to where Farr lay, ten feet distant, to tell Smith that he would go for help. He left his rifle and pistol on the ground and struck off on foot.

For some hours he stumbled blindly across the mountains. In the end he trudged into Cimarron at seven o'clock on Monday morning. Foraker, rather unfairly, berated him for desert and cowardice. Reno next incensed the marshal by ignoring a request "not to wire the story until all of the facts had been ascertained." Since there was no telegraph office at Cimarron, he started for Springer, twenty miles away. Inexplicably, he chose to go on foot. Nearly half of the road was behind him before he encountered any vehicle.

William French had hired a rig in Springer and was driving out to visit a Cimarron rancher, Bud Nash, when his attention was seized "by a man coming along the prairie parallel to the road." French had just heard about the train robbery and had been greatly taken aback by the talk in Springer which held that one of the bandits was "Will McGinnis," whom he always regarded as "a paladin among cowpunchers." He did not at first connect this news with the stranger, "a small man, of what might be termed insignificant stature, with very fair hair and light eyebrows," who raced towards him, hatless and "gesticulating wildly."

"For God's sake, take me in to Springer," panted Reno. After some demur French agreed to go back and the detective climbed into the buggy. When Reno had given him an account of the fight, French glanced at the torn coat-tail and made an uncharitable remark to the effect that if Reno had not run away from the bullet so swiftly he would be sitting less comfortably now. Reno offered no rejoinder, according to French, other than a black look.

The detective sent out his messages and returned to Cimarron to find himself at the wrong end of a controversy. In fact, however, his showing was better than of Wilson Elliott, whose party, although it included two men experienced in gunplay and law-enforcement work—Morgan and Elliott himself — had given up the fight and had made no move to get assistance.

Elliott and the remnants of his posse had camped by their horses and spent the night in Turkey Canyon. Shortly after daybreak they had set out for Cimarron, leaving Farr's body in the mountains. They got into town soon after Foraker had ridden out with a search party.

Foraker did not go right into the canyon; striking the trail of some four or five horses, he decided to follow it, although he did not know whether he was on the track of robbers or possemen.

In the meantime, Elliott and Morgan, having stopped in town just long enough to feed themselves, had started back to collect the remains of Ed Farr, taking with them Jim Hunt, Bud Nash, and one or two others from the locality. Evidently Marshal Foraker must have found the longest route between the two points, for the tracks which he picked up were those made by Elliott's new group as they were returning to Cimarron with the body. And in Cimarron, some jackass of a reporter assumed the body of the sheriff to be that of an outlaw "known by the names of William McGinnis and G. W. Franks." It was also alleged, and later found not to be true, that the bandits had been firing explosive bullets.

Henry Love, the wounded cowboy, died on Thursday afternoon, four days after the fight. He was the second fatality, but not the last.

After the departure of Carver and Lay, Sam moved into the granary because, he said, he did not want to bring trouble to the house. The McBrides bandaged his wounds and gave him food and blankets. They also made up their minds to betray him; in truth, they could hardly risk doing anything else. On Tuesday their son, Jim, rode into Cimarron and went straight to W.H. Reno. Young McBride and three others were immediately designated Special Officers of the railroad and the party drove out at once.

When they reached the ranch they devised a stratagem by which Ketchum could be disarmed. Reno knew that the outlaw had only a six-shooter and was in a weakening condition; but he, Reno, "had come up against such men before." Among the force of "special officers" was Earl Clause, the McBrides' hired hand. Clause and one of the young McBrides took a cup of coffee to the wounded man, and Clause asked Sam if he could borrow the revolver for a few moments so that the boy could see what a fine gun it was. Sam allowed him to do this. All at once the shed was full of armed men.

Reno, in a fury because the prisoner seemed disinclined to get up, kicked and cursed him until restrained by Ed McBride. Ketchum was placed in a spring wagon and hauled into Cimarron. The captors were so eager to tell everyone what they had done that they left Sam unattended with one of their rifles lying within a few feet of him. He was about to move for the gun when George Crocker noticed him and wrested it away.

Sam admitted his identity when questioned by Jim Hunt. Pointing to Clause, who was standing nearby, he said: "There's a meaner man than I am. If he hadn't worked it the way he did and got my gun, I'd have had his hide hanging on the fence."

The outlaw spent the night in the St. James Hotel. In the morning he was bound over by a Justice of the Peace for the murder of Farr. He was then taken to Springer to face a charge of mail robbery. He waived the right to a preliminary examination and his bond was set at $10,000. This amount, naturally, was not forthcoming; but he could not have been bailed out on the murder charge, anyway. Foraker, Thacker, and the route agent for Wells, Fargo escorted him to Santa Fe, where he could be given proper medical treatment while the Territorial and United States authorities were reaching agreement as to which of them would try him. On the evening of July 20th Sam was booked into the Territorial Penitentiary as Number 129.

By this time the ground was crawling with fresh posses from Walsenburg, Trinidad, and elsewhere, but Carver and Lay had vanished. One story has the outlaws hiding out for several weeks on a ranch, a few miles south of Elizabethtown, where a local man with some knowledge of medicine tended Lay's wounds. They may have rested up near Elizabethtown, and Lay certainly needed attention, but they did not stay in the neighborhood for more than a few days. Tom Capehart, who had left the WS at about the same time as Lay, met them soon after their escape from Turkey Canyon. All three of them then rode down into Texas.

Jim Hunt established himself as Reno's most willing assistant. He accompanied Reno to Bowie, Arizona, where they picked up a man thought to be "G. W. Franks." The journey was a wasted one, but Hunt did not lose his appetite for detective work or for the concomitant publicity.

Shortly before this, Red Weaver slipped in and out of the picture. On July 17th one of the officers, probably Reno, told a reporter in Cimarron that among the robbers was "a man well known here, who was indicted for train robbery about the same place some time ago, and was acquitted at Las Vegas". He would say nothing more; but the stated circumstances fitted only one man.

Nearly a week passed before, on the 23rd, it was announced that a man suspected of complicity in the robbery had been arrested at Springer. Through some freak of miscalculation or misreporting his name was first given out as "David Carver." Foraker released him and the following day Weaver bought a ticket to Santa Fe (where, of course, the Marshal's office was situated), but shipped his saddle to Silver City. To a press correspondent who interviewed him he said: "Just such arrests as this make train robbers. I have been arrested before for train robbery. Just because I came up here from Silver City with McGinnis is no evidence that I belong to this gang." The reporter, evidently knowing that Weaver had been discharged from the pesthouse some time before the robbery, was mystified by the whole affair:

> It is not known why Wheeler (sic) was released, for he was in continual company with McGinnis and Franks while they were at Springer and at Cimarron, after Wheeler was released from the pesthouse. . . .

That meeting at Springer between Foraker and Weaver may not have been their first since the robbery. If it was not, the "arrest" could have been prearranged to still conjecture as to why the officers should allow Weaver to come and go as he pleased. But if Weaver, like many another bandit, had traded a full confession for a promise of immunity from the courts, it is improbable that Foraker would have let him slip away so quickly. It is more likely that Red told a smooth story, gave a certain amount of information, and perhaps even promised to keep in touch with the marshal's office.

While the tussle in Turkey Creek Canyon was a heavy tactical and moral defeat for the posse, it was in the longer term a kind of victory for them; there would be no Ketchum gang afterwards, whether led by Tom or Sam.

In a way, one man fashioned the course of events simply by having no part in them. If Tom Ketchum had been with the gang there might have been no incriminating envelope, no unguarded camp for a posse to surround at leisure, no battle in Turkey Canyon, and no Red Weaver.

This is one of the Four photographs taken of Tom Ketchum in San Rafael Hospital, Trinidad, Colorado, by Deputy Sheriff George W. Titsworth, on August 21st, 1899.

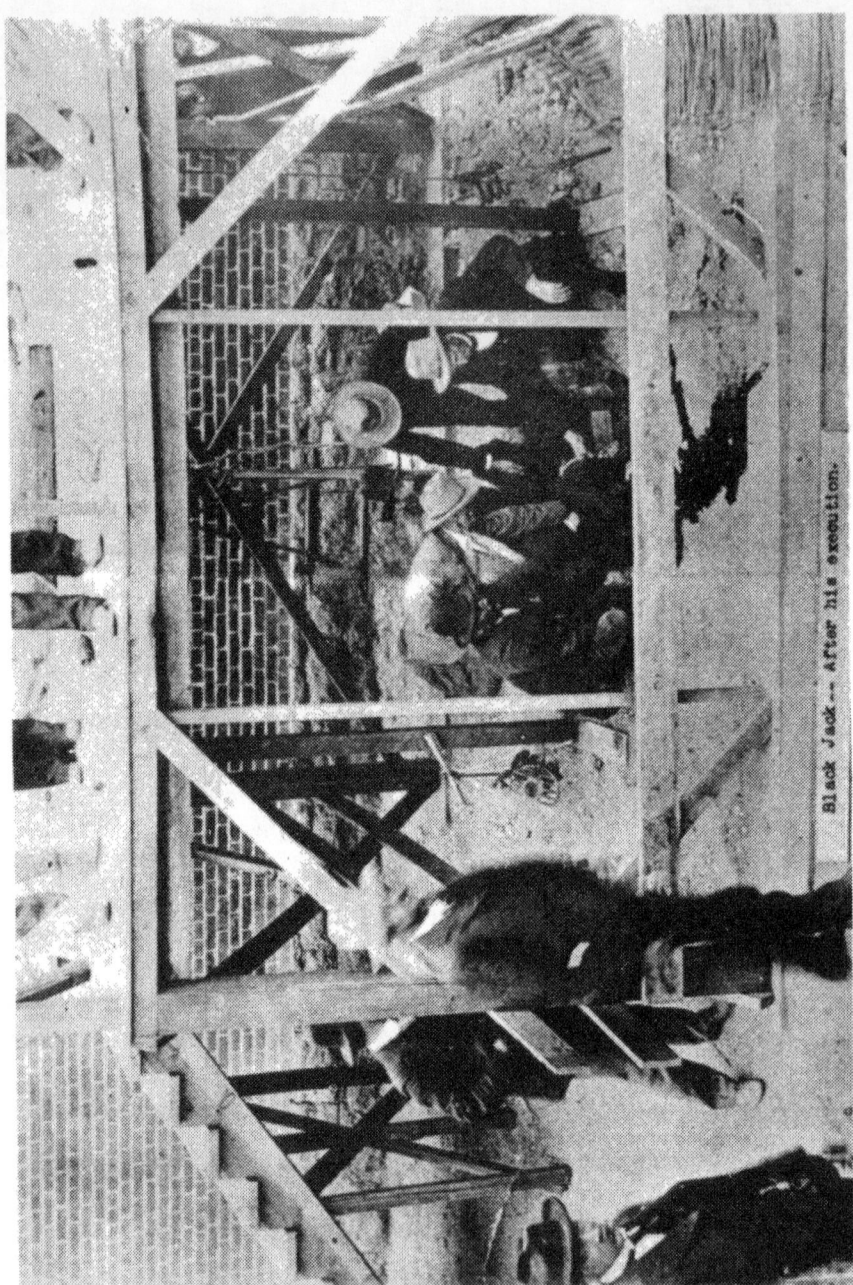

Arizona Pioneers Historical Society.

Black Jack --- After his execution.

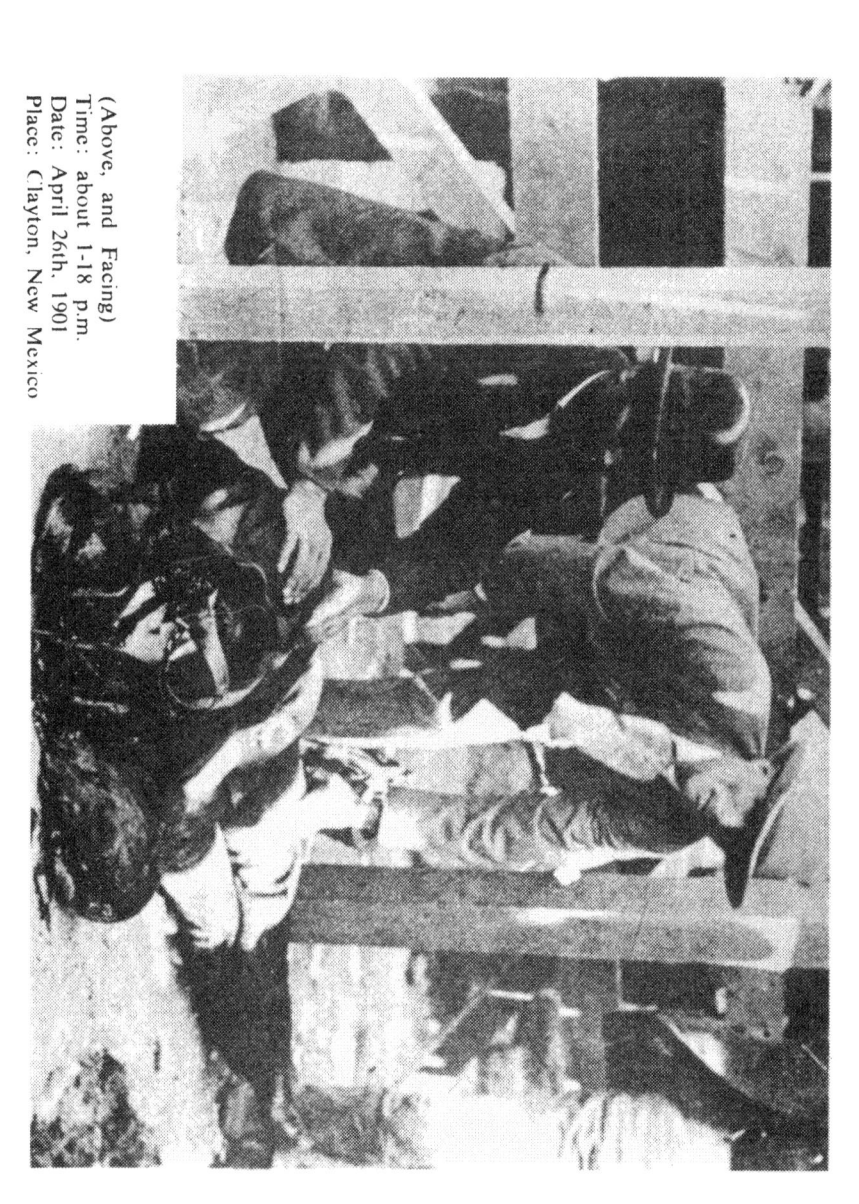

(Above, and Facing)
Time: about 1-18 p.m.
Date: April 26th, 1901
Place: Clayton, New Mexico

Tom Gray, Deputy Sheriff of Union County at the time of the execution, stands on the right.

The scaffold for Ketchum's execution was built directly in front of the building shown in the center of this photograph.

ɔm Ketchum's grave.
3oth of the pictures on this
ge were taken in 1969).

Carl W. Breihan.

William T. "Will" Christian, known as "Black Jack". The nickname "Black Jack" was later misapplied to Tom Ketchum, although he tried to repudiate it. William and Robert F. "Bob" Christian were outlaws in the Indian Nations and Oklahoma Territory, and later pursued a similar course in New Mexico and Arizona. This photograph was taken in Clifton, Arizona, shortly before Christian's death in 1897.

Chapter Twelve

THE SIXTEENTH OF AUGUST

Sam Ketchum had little information for the law. He stated that he had been the first of the men to be wounded in the Turkey Canyon fight, would not name his companions, and maintained that he had made his way alone to the ranch on Ute Creek.

His wound, although very painful, was a small one which would not have proved serious if it could have been attended to promptly. But gangrene had set in before he was captured. By the time he reached Santa Fe his condition was critical.

"I guess I can stand a little thing like that", he remarked, as a doctor began to probe for the bullet; but afterwards he averred that his swollen arm "seemed to weigh 300 pounds". When told he would die unless the arm were amputated he refused to allow the surgeon to operate and calmly awaited death. The Territory, he knew, hoped to keep him alive only because they wanted him to stand trial for a capital offense. He now declared that he had fired the shot which killed Ed Farr. On at least three occasions he spoke of the Stein's Pass hold-up, saying that he, his brother Tom, and their partners were responsible for the crime and that Hoffman, Alverson, and Warderman were innocent. His allusion to the misunderstanding over the identity of Black Jack fell upon barren ground: he affirmed that he was a brother of Tom Ketchum, and that "the original Black Jack" was dead. One correspondent construed this as an attempt at misleading everyone into the belief that Tom Ketchum had been killed; another elected to make it intelligible by applying a few deft touches of revision which transformed the outlaw's words into an avowal that he was "a brother of Tom Ketchum, the original Black Jack."

"The other fellows will tell all about it", Sam replied when pressed to make a detailed confession. At 8 a.m. on Monday, July 24th, he died. Three days later Berry Ketchum and Sheriff Shields arrived in Santa Fe. Berry declined to speak upon the subject of Sam's outlawry, although he did allege that "he had neither seen nor heard from his brother for many years". After arranging with Undertaker Wagner for the body to be interred in the Odd Fellows cemetery, Berry and the Sheriff returned to San Angelo. The *New Mexican* reported that the scene had been a touching one.

As Berry rode the train homeward, he could hardly have guessed that Will Carver, with the two strangers, Tom Capehart and Elza Lay, would turn up in Tom Green County almost as he and Shields were alighting at San Angelo.

That Lay could have traveled two hundred and fifty miles on horseback in not more than five or six days affords striking evidence of his powers of endurance and recuperation. There were no slugs to be extracted: his wounds were "through and through". Yet, weakened as he was by loss of blood, shock, and exposure, it is still little short of astonishing that he was ready to saddle up and leave within a week of going to ground at Elizabethtown and undertake the long, hard ride into Texas. For, on July 28th, three men, riding horses owned by a rancher at Sterling — that crossways for the gang on their journeyings between Texas and New Mexico—were seen near Knickerbocker and identified as the last three members of the Black Jack gang. An allegation that Tom Ketchum was one of them was unfounded; had he been there at this time, he would have heard of Sam's death, and he knew nothing of this until mid-August.

There was to be no respite for them in Tom Green County. A call went out for the Rangers, some deputy United States marshals talked over plans to trap the fugitives, and various corporations affered to advance money for expenses. Nevertheless, on Sunday, July 30th, the trio appeared in San Angelo and "rode through town two or three times, defying the authorities". Next day Shields' posse and the Rangers moved in to arrest them, but the three were already riding west.

For a period of about ten days in the early part of August they were encamped somewhere in the southeast corner of New Mexico or the adjacent section of Texas. Capehart later told William French that it had been his intention to find employment on a ranch in the locality until such time as Lay was fully recovered. It was subsequently claimed in Carlsbad that two of them visited the town on four consecutive days during this time, allegedly to size up the possibilities of robbing the bank. If this is true, the two were most likely Carver and Capehart since, by Capehart's story, Lay was resting. If seems improbable, though, that they entertained serious thoughts of trying their hands at bank robbery just then.

At Chimney Wells V.H. Lusk and his men were waiting for someone to claim the three Erie horses which had drifted down onto Lusk's range. He knew, of course, which bunch of outlaws had turned the animals loose; it was the outfit who had stopped by his place a number of times in the last two or three years to exchange their jaded mounts for horses they had left to fatten on his range perhaps months earlier. Hence, he knew more or less whom to expect. By the summer of 1899, Lusk said, he was beginning to suspect that these men were horse-thieves. He must have been strangely myopic before this, since the Ketchums had been widely known as cowpunchers in the Pecos Valley long before they became the most notorious professional robbers in the whole of the Southwest. Anyway, he had agreed to send word to Sheriff Cicero Stewart when the wanted men finally came into camp at Chimney Wells.

On Tuesday evening, August 15th, Carver and Lay came up to the Lusk house from the east, riding two gaunt ponies and leading a third. Lusk, amenable as usual, gave them straight answers. Yes, the horses they wanted were on his range, although one of them, a gray, was running with Lusk's own remuda away in the salt-grass flat. He suggested they wait until morning before looking for the gray, and invited them to stay the night under his roof. They replied that they would rather sleep out, where there was better grazing for their ponies. Besides, they had lost a good many horses, and were anxious to start looking for those that were loose. Before the men went they told Lusk they would return in the morning for breakfast.

Lusk was worried lest something in his manner had put the outlaws on their guard. Reassured when he saw their campfire glowing through the dusk from a high hill to the north of the house, he mounted his best horse and rode in to Carlsbad.

Cicero Stewart could not afford to use up time by raising a large posse. He enlisted the help of Rufus Thomas and John D. Cantrell and got ready to leave at once. Thomas, having no rifle with him, borrowed one from Silas T. Bitting's store, thinking little of a bystander's warning that the gun was liable to hang fire. At about four o'clock in the morning they swung down from their exhausted mounts by Lusk's camp, where they hoped to trap the fugitives. John Lusk, the young son of the rancher, hobbled the horses of the posse in a dip, so that they would not be seen by the two incoming guests. He then cut the Erie gray from the herd and corraled the remainder. A tarpaulin was thrown over the saddles and equipment of the posse, who stationed themselves in a dry tank, encircled by barbed wire. Some two hundred yards from this tank was pitched a tent, which served as Lusk's camp headquarters.

Carver and Lay had rounded up two of the Erie horses and another, branded 8D Connected, which had been abandoned just over a year earlier, when the gang were fleeing across New Mexico after their raid on the Texas & Pacific. They were still determined to pick up the gray, however, and after a futile search Lay proposed that he and Carver take their breakfast by turns; while one man ate, the other would scour the prairie for the elusive pony, at the same time keeping watch for the approach of any unwanted stranger.

Mounted on the 8D horse and leading one of the Erie animals, Lay jogged down from the hill and into Lusk's Camp. After dismounting, he surveyed the horizon through his field glasses, apparently uneasy because Carver had vanished from the skyline. Lusk, afraid that the newcomer might discover the posse before they were ready to act, then stepped up and, with a good imitation of a hearty welcome, called the outlaw to go inside for breakfast. Lay tied the two horses to a wagon and followed Lusk into the tent. The wagon was a good deal closer to the tent than to the tank, but the horses were tethered on the side nearer to the officers.

Somewhere inside the tent Stewart had concealed a rifle. The stratagem was for Lusk to show himself at the entrance of the tent as soon as he had located the weapon; then, while the posse was charging across the open ground, the rancher was to seize the rifle and hold the men under guard. There were only two flaws in this plan: it was based on the assumption that the outlaws would ride into camp together, and it presupposed that Lusk would have no trouble in finding the gun. The second miscalculation would have been obviated if Stewart had shown the rancher where he had hidden the weapon, instead of merely telling him.

While Lay was gulping down his breakfast, Lusk shambled around the tent, hoping to chance upon the rifle. Thus preoccupied, he forgot about the prearranged signal and blundered into the opening of the tent. Immediately the posse scrambled over the barbed-wire fence and rushed toward the wagon. Lay heard the commotion, rose in alarm, and glanced outside. At once he rounded upon Lusk.

"Did *you* do this?" he growled. But there was no time to settle the matter just then. In a desperate effort to get to his horses and rifle before the posse could reach them, he sprang through the opening and ran.

Rufus Thomas almost beat him there but he ignored the posseman's levelled rifle and was deaf to his command to surrender. Drawing his pistol, he dodged under the wagon. Thomas kept squeezing the trigger, but each time the gun misfired.

With Stewart and Cantrell now joining the fight, Lay retreated toward the tent. He caught sight of Lusk, who, still unarmed, was trying to duck away from the line of fire.

"You old son of a bitch, you're the cause of this!" he bawled. Lusk instinctively turned to run as the bandit took aim. The bullet plowed along the rancher's wrist and forearm but did not hamper his flight.

Belatedly, Thomas remembered the advice should to him as he was riding out of town. Then he was knocked almost off his feet as Lay's second bullet scorched through his left arm and thudded beneath the shoulder blade.

Lay fired twice more, then ran behind the tent. Stewart and Cantrell stayed right where they were and kept shooting through the canvas. After about one minute of this Stewart saw Lay standing by the corner of the tent. In another moment a bullet from the sheriff's rifle sent the outlaw tumbling face downwards into the grass.

Though stunned for an instant by the slug at it whipped past his forehead, Lay had worked out his next move before the possemen came up close to him. First he made a studied pretense of examining his revolver, although he knew it to be empty. Then he raised his hands and started to get to his feet. Cantrell, nervous or suspicious, would have shot to kill, but Stewart restrained him.

"He's wounded, I guess, he's fallen again," the sheriff remarked, as Lay allowed himself to keel over for a second time.

Stewart ordered the outlaw to rise and walk forward, and told Cantrell to "set his gun down against this stone here" before undertaking a search of the prisoner.

"Look here, Cis," said Cantrell, indicating a belt loaded with 30-40 cartridges which the bandit was wearing under what were described as his pantaloons. Cantrell had already taken possession of Lay's six-shooter. Stewart then came up, jerked open Lay's pants, and told his companion to unbuckle the cartridge belt.

As Cantrell walked away, carrying the belt and pistol, the sheriff dropped his eye off the prisoner. Immediately Lay's clenched left hand flew towards Stewart's jaw; his right darted for the officer's holstered revolver.

"Look out, he'll get your gun," yelled Cantrell.

Stewart was looking out. He partially deflected the blow with his arm, felled Lay with a single punch, drew his gun, and beat the outlaw over the head with it.

"By God, Cis, let's kill him," urged Cantrell.

"No, John, we won't kill him," replied Stewart, "I suppose we ought to kill him, but he says he wants to give up and I won't kill him."

"No, don't kill me," Lay is alleged to have added, "You can't blame a man for scuffling a little."

Cantrell got a rope and Stewart hog-tied the glowering outlaw.

Lay's wounds had burst open in the tussle but he was less concerned by this than he was infuriated by the pistol-whipping.

"I may never get out of this," he told Stewart, "but if ever I do you had better leave New Mexico, for I'm coming after you."

Will Carver had seen the gray horse while Lay was riding into Lusk's camp. He roped the animal and left him hobbled on the prairie, returning to the crest of the hill after the posse had closed in on Lay. For a while he surveyed the scene, three quarters of a mile away, through his field glasses. When he saw Lay sprawled out on the ground he thought him dead. He went back for the gray; then, waving his hat derisively, he galloped out of sight of the glaring posse. Stewart did not give chase. Carver was next seen at Dagger Draw. After that nothing was heard of him for some time, although he was known to have headed southwest.

A few hours after the arrest of Lay, Capehart rode into Lusk's camp with provisions he had purchased for the ride to Arizona. Lusk, in describing what had happened to the others, modified some of the details and omitted to mention that the sheriff had found the men only because the Lusks had told him where they were. As Capehart understood it, Lay would not have been captured had he not run out of ammunition. Without doubting anything he heard, he set out in the same general direction as Carver had taken.

Sheriff Stewart's prisoner was not communicative. At different times he gave his name as John Thompson and Tom Johnson. His weapons and equipment were closely inspected. "The Winchester," observed one correspondent, "is a new gun, having seen little use"; the scabbard "was marked in plain gothic letters JO YOUNWA, the 'N' inverted and indistinct". The saddle was the one that the gang had obtained from Sam Murray, of Ozona, just after the Comstock robbery. Sheriff Stewart was more interested in the man's wounds. When he saw them he felt pretty sure he had "Will McGinnis". But more startling developments elsewhere precluded any immediate confirmation of this.

While Lay was making ready for his first night in a prison cell, Tom Ketchum was plodding along the Colorado and Southern right-of-way in the direction of Folsom.

For three months he had avoided all but the loneliest of trails, visiting no one except a few settlers whose homes were remote from any town or village. The killings at Camp Verde had aroused an energetic if ineffectual pursuit, but so far his name had not been connected with the affair.

Plans for a second train hold-up in north eastern New Mexico had been discussed before the quarrel which led to his banishment from the gang. Late in July he made up his mind to seek a reconciliation with his brother and Carver. He rode to Wagon Mound, thinking that they might be in camp there. The place was deserted; there was no one to tell him about the recent robbery at Folsom or the fight in Turkey Canyon. He decided to hold up the Atchison, Topeka and Santa Fe train near Wagon Mound. One night, the 10th or 11th of August, he walked up to the station. When the southbound express pulled in, he strolled casually alongside the coaches and toward the locomotive. As he passed the open door of the express car he glanced inside and at once recognized George Titsworth, who had been hired as a guard. Titsworth saw him but did not know him and suspected nothing. Desperate as he was, Tom had no intention of holding up a train which he knew to be guarded. He walked on past the blind baggage, past the engine, and into the darkness. After this he did what must have seemed the easiest and most natural thing. He headed for Folsom, seventy miles further north and east. If he had heard about the hold-up there, scarcely a month earlier, and about its aftermath, he might well have kept as much ground as he possibly could between Twin Mountains and himself.

Southbound train No. 1 chugged out of Folsom at about 10.20 p.m. on Wednesday, August 16th. Conductor Frank Harrington was about to experience a hold-up for the third time—but now he would not be taken unprepared. Since the second robbery he had never gone on duty without a double-barreled shotgun, which he had borrowed from a friend. He had resolved to do his best to ensure that any third similar occurrence would be the last exploit of some train robber.

In the express car was Messenger Charles P. "Scotty" Drew, who had been beaten up by Sam Ketchum during the first robbery. Fred Bartlett was the mail clerk, Joseph H. Kirchgrabber the engineer, Tom Scanlon the fireman, and Robert B. Hawkins the brakeman.

They had proceeded just over a mile out of Folsom when Tom Ketchum slipped into the cab and nudged Kirchgrabber with his Winchester rifle. In compliance with the bandit's orders, Kirchgrabber stopped the train at a point some four miles south of Folsom. The wheels came to rest upon a curve in the track, two miles short of the bonfire which marked Ketchum's camp.

Ketchum had cached a gunny sack containing a large stock of dynamite, caps, and fuses under a cattle guard, at a safe distance from his signal fire. He intended to have the coaches uncoupled from the express car and locomotive; afterwards the engine could be run up to his camp and the express box blown without any risk of interference. When this was done, he reflected, he would get out of New Mexico and sail for South America, even if he found no more than five hundred dollars. It was learned, much later, that there was rather more — perhaps a great deal more—than five thousand dollars' worth of express matter in Drew's through safe that night.

From the beginning, the scheme would not unroll smoothly for Tom Ketchum. First of all, the engineer refused to get down from the locomotive.

"You son of a bitch, I'll kill you," snarled Ketchum, poking the rifle into Kirchgrabber's armpit. "I'll shoot if you don't."

"Shoot away," was the stolid rejoinder.

Beaten for the moment, Ketchum turned upon the fireman, who stepped down without argument. With a rifle at his back, Scanlon raised his coalpick and banged on the door of the express car. Drew awoke with a start; he assumed — as he had assumed at the time of the first Folsom hold-up—that the train had reached Des Moines station. He was halfway to the door when he was hailed by the fireman: "Hi, Scotty!"

He opened the door.

"Fall out of there god-damn quick," snapped Tom Ketchum, and Drew did exactly as he was told. He was then ordered to hold out a lantern while Scanlon tried to unfasten the drawheads of the couplings. Ketchum did not realize that the "Miller hook," the coupling device then in general use, was certain to bind whenever a train was halted on a curve. It would then be almost impossible to unlock the drawheads. Scanlon, however, set about the couplings as well as he knew how.

Every now and again, Drew would take a hurried look at the bandit.

THE SIXTEENTH OF AUGUST

He could not but notice that Ketchum was "nursing" his gun "very tenderly."

Distracted for a moment when Bartlett craned forward from the mail car to see what was going on, Ketchum shouted at him to "get back in there." To give point to his instructions, he threw a warning shot which glanced off a steel brace on the side of the car and through Bartlett's jaw, knocking out two double teeth, spinning him right around and felling him face downwards to the floor. Scanlon redoubled his efforts to break the couplings. Presently he said that he had unhooked the cars. Ketchum made the messenger and fireman walk ahead of him back to the engine. They all climbed into the cab and Kirchgrabber was ordered to pull ahead. He tried, but the train would not budge. Scanlon had succeeded only in cutting the air hose, thus sealing the brakes on all the coaches behind the express car. Ketchum guessed what had happened. By now he was past the stage where a railroad engineer could safely bandy words with him.

"If you won't come back there I'll kill you," he stormed, between curses. "I want you to cut the baggage car off."

Kirchgrabber, this time, went along quietly. He bent down over the couplings and strove to loosen them while Ketchum shuffled around impatiently, urging him to "hurry up."

"I'm going to shoot to kill now, pretty soon," he muttered.

"Well now, partner, don't be in a hurry," said Kirchgrabber, "We can't do these things all at once." But he sent the fireman back to the engine to fetch a jack bar or pinch bar—a rod about three feet in length, with which it might be just possible to prise the drawheads apart. Nearly twenty minutes had elapsed since the robber had first appeared in the locomotive cab, and Kirchgrabber knew that the man's temper was right on edge.

Frank Harrington, unlike Drew, guessed at once just why the train had stopped. He and the brakeman, Hawkins, had got out of the train and gone up front to investigate. Discerning a group of men hovering about the express car, Harrington thought there were three or four robbers. Undeterred, he went back for his shotgun, unpacked it from his box, assembled it, then walked down through the train to the combination mail car and smoker. There lay Bartlett, moaning that he was "bleeding to death." Harrington left him in the care of the brakeman. Stealthily he began to open the end door. The four men were standing below him, from ten to fifteen away. Now he could recognize three of them: the

DYNAMITE AND SIX-SHOOTER

fourth, the one with the rifle, was facing him but was partially blocked from view by the form of Charles Drew. Harrington's chance came when the messenger moved, as if to help Kirchgrabber, who was sweating over the stubborn couplings. Drew still holding the lantern, and Harrington had a clear target. At once he threw the door wide open and fired from the hip. Ketchum looked up and, quick as light, switched his rifle from Drew toward the buttons glinting from Harrington's uniform. Eleven buckshot struck Ketchum just above the right elbow, an instant before the rifle bullet flicked Harrington's left sleeve.

"I wanted to hit the bandit in the heart," Harrington explained, afterwards, "but in the dim light I misjudged. It had to be done quickly. I knew that as soon as I opened the door my appearance would be noticed by the robber who faced me and I aimed the best I could."

Tom Ketchum had this to say about it: "His buckshot jiggled my aim. I'd have killed him if he'd waited a fraction of a second. I had a bead on his heart but he jiggled my aim."

Ketchum fell, then reeled across the front of the locomotive and away into the night. Kirchgrabber and Scanlon fled in different directions. Drew stayed put, still hanging on to the lantern. Then, having crossed the tracks, Ketchum took a couple of pot-shots at the glimmering flame, each bullet puncturing the side of the mailcar, and the lamp was instantly turned out. After that, there was no more shooting. Harrington's wound was dressed and the train resumed its run, thirty-five minutes after it had been stopped. From the next station, and from various other points during the few hours that followed, word was sent out of what had happened, along with advice for the officers to look out for a badly-wounded man near the scene of the hold-up.

Tom Ketchum had collapsed about a hundred yards north of the tracks. Some time in the night, he picked himself up and lurched toward his camp, where his two horses were staked out. But now he was assailed by the hopelessness which had swept over his brother just one month earlier.

"I tried a dozen times to mount my horse but was too weak to do it," he told Albert Thompson later. Exhausted, and dizzy with pain, he sank down by the track to wait for the posse.

At eight o'clock next morning, the 17th, he saw a northbound freight train lumbering slowly towards the place where he had attempted the robbery. He stuck his hat on the end of his rifle and waved feebly. Perched on the roof of the cab was the front brakeman, John W.

Mercer. He noticed the signal and the train ground to a standstill. Sheriff Saturnino Pinard, who had boarded the freight at Clayton, got out and followed the crew to the water hole, some three hundred yards away, beside which the outlaw was huddled, "his legs kind of cramped up, sitting on his feet."

Mercer and the engineer, Chris Waller, who were in the lead, halted some few paces from the wounded man. They eyed the rifle, which seemed to be "buckled up under him."

"The distance is the same from here to there as it is from there to here," the outlaw called out. "You'll have to come down and get me." Then, almost casually, he lifted his canteen and took a sip of water. But as the men gingerly moved closer, he put aside the canteen and raised his six-shooter — smeared with blood, like his clothing and the patch of muddy ground in which he lay.

"You wouldn't call a man out here to shoot him, would you?" quavered Waller.

"No, I guess not," replied Tom, after giving the question due thought. "I'll die anyway and the buzzards will eat me."

He let go of the pistol, only to reach for his rifle as the man edged still closer.

"Partner, don't do that," remonstrated Mercer, and Ketchum was persuaded. He allowed Mercer to pick up his rifle and six-shooter, but protested when the brakeman, searching for a second revolver, touched his wounded arm:

"I haven't any other . . . Don't do that, it hurts me."

"How did you get that done?" Mercer asked, looking at the bloodied arm.

"Somebody shot me out of the baggage car last night when I was trying to hold up the train. I wish the son of a bitch had shot me through the head or heart and then this would have been over with. I hadn't done anything to him and I don't see what the son of a bitch wanted to shoot me for. If it hadn't been he shot my right arm off that I had my gun in, I'd have fixed the son of a bitch, all right."

Ketchum turned his eyes onto three other men who were walking toward him. Two of them were in uniform: they were the conductor, Clarke, and the rear brakeman, Robbins. The third man carried a rifle.

"Who is that son of a bitch with a gun there?" Ketchum wanted to know.

"It's the sheriff from Clayton," Waller replied.

"If I had that gun I could shoot the son of a bitch's heart out," Tom remarked, with a regretful glance towards the rifle he had just lost.

"Yes," said Mercer, "but you haven't got your gun."

"I suppose I'm under arrest?" Tom asked Pinard.

"Yes, I'm the sheriff and you are my prisoner," responded Pinard. "Can you walk?"

"I wouldn't be here if I could," retorted Ketchum.

A wire stretcher was brought out.

"I'm so weak if I got on my feet I'd faint," Tom said to Clarke; but as they lifted him onto the stretcher he must have been feeling troubled for having let himself be taken without putting up a fight.

"If I could use my gun with my left hand, we'd have had a little fun," he declared, offering the best excuse he could think of.

He was placed in the caboose and the freight sped north. For awhile the outlaw talked to Robbins, the brakeman. He gave his name as "George Stevens" and said that he had "a brother and sister in the Panhandle country whom he would like to send word to, and if he did not die, why, he did not want them to know it." The hold-up, he asserted, was his first attempt, "and a damned poor attempt I made." At Folsom the shattered arm was bandaged by Doctor Harry Lutemann, a railroad physician, and a posse from Colorado boarded the train. Superintendent Webb and Special Agent Reno were at the head of the party and were to take the outlaw into Trinidad: Present, too, were the town hot-heads. When one of the Folsom men started to make some talk about getting a rope, a member of the posse, Harry D. Lewis, was quick to intervene.

"There will be nothing of that kind go on here," he told the ringleaders, "not so long as I have got these guns on me."

For this he received scant thanks from Ketchum, who was not so ill as to miss an opportunity for a sly dig at the possemen. As the men were getting ready to leave on a hunt for his supposed confederates, Tom addressed Lewis.

"I wouldn't go if I were you, pal," he advised the officer, "I wouldn't go out with those fellows, pal, because them other fellows can shoot and you can't." But the posse left and spent two or three hours chasing nothing.

Webb and Reno serenely took charge of the prisoner. Ketchum and his escort arrived in Trinidad just as a special train, containing a further load of officers, was about to steam out. The party rushed to San Rafael

Hospital, an institution run by the Sisters of Mercy, where the most notorious desperado in the Southwest modestly introduced himself by his impromptu alias of "George Stevens."

Chapter Thirteen

DEAD TO RIGHTS

The removal of Thomas Edward Ketchum from Union County, New Mexico, to the most easily accessible hospital—which happened to be in Colorado—did not spring spontaneously from the exercise of a little plain common sense.

Sheriff Pinard had intended to wait at Folsom for the arrival of a special train which would convey the prisoner and himself south to Clayton. But when the freight reached Folsom, the sheriff had found Webb and Reno there ahead of him, all ready to pounce on the wounded outlaw. They exhibited a piece of paper which gave them authority to take the prisoner to Trinidad for interrogation. It also started that a Deputy United States Marshal was on his way from Albuquerque to take official charge of the outlaw. This order was signed by Jeremiah Leahy, District Attorney of Colfax and Union counties, and Chief Justice William J. Mills, of the Fourth Judicial District. Pinard, disgusted by this jiggery pokery, had then struck off with the Colorado officers in search of the bandit's horses, dynamite, and presumed companions. United States Marshal Foraker, whose efforts during the last two years had been directed almost entirely toward the extirpation of the various bands of outlaws, was obliged to travel into Colorado to question a man who had been arrested in New Mexico. But at least the would-be train robber had been given the best chance to pull through and so become available for disposal by the courts.

Ketchum still maintained that he was George Stevens, formerly a cowboy, more recently a miner; that he was not a regular train robber; that he had resorted to crime this once only because he had been down on his luck. Now, however, he was insisting that he had made the attempt alone — though the detectives continued to believe that there had been two other robbers, who had fled at the sound of the shots.

"Did you ever hear of a man robbing a train alone?" he asked Webb. "I have. I'd have got away with that, partner, if we hadn't stopped on that curve."

DEAD TO RIGHTS

They tried to loosen his tongue further by telling him that he was near the point of death. Far from gratifying their hopes of a confession, Tom began to curse Kirchgrabber and Harrington, discursing fervently upon what he ought to have done to them and what he would do yet if he should ever get the chance. (Twenty months later he was still damning them, and by then their names had been joined by others in his litany of unsettled grudges.) Conversely, he expressed regret at having shot Bartlett, now his fellow-patient in San Rafael Hospital: he had warned the mail clerk three times, he explained, and had fired only to warn him away. This may well have been true, but Bartlett was not mollified, and in any case he did not believe it: his feelings toward Tom Ketchum were much the same as those of Tom Ketchum toward Kirchgrabber and Harrington.

For almost a week Ketchum would admit to no other name than that of "George Stevens." But the officials guessed from the beginning that they had Tom Ketchum; and nothing would ever dissuade them from their belief that Tom Ketchum was "Black Jack", the rascal who had made life so uncomfortable for postmasters and others during the fall of '96. It looked very much, too, as though they would soon be given the opportunity to pay for the outlaw's funeral, for his hold on life was a precarious one and he seemed determined to do nothing to improve his chances of recovery. Dr John R. Espey had advised him to agree to amputation of the mangled arm. Tom allowed the doctor to extract the buckshot but, like his brother before him, stolidly refused to undergo an operation. This did not deter one press correspondent from dashing off a garish package of mendacity in which the bandit was portrayed as contemptuously declining an anesthetic and watching nonchalantly as Espey chopped off the putrefied member.

Weak as he was, he was closely guarded. In the daytime he was under the eye of Harry Lewis; the night watch was assigned to George Titsworth. Ketchum talked a great deal to his keepers, and they to him. Once, apparently in jest, Lewis told him that there was eighty or eighty-five thousand dollars aboard the train he had failed to rob. It was no joke to Tom.

"If I hadn't bad luck, and got the money, they would never have seen my dust," he answered.

He wanted to know from Titsworth whether the charge of attempted train robbery would take precedence to that of the murder for which he was wanted in Texas. It is not clear which of these two charges he feared the most, but, as Titsworth informed him, he would first be tried in the courts of the party by whom he was being detained: this, technically, was the United States Government.

On another occasion Ketchum told Titsworth that the gold fountain pen found in his coat had been used to compile a history of his outlawry; the manuscript, he assured the deputy, was three hundred pages long. He also said that, notwithstanding his earlier denial, two other men really had been involved in the attempted robbery. When Titsworth asked him why he had not tried to rob a train on the Santa Fe line, Tom answered, "I seen you there," and went on to relate the story of how nearly they had met at Wagon Mound.

Foraker and Reno were anxious to go down to Carlsbad for a formal introduction to "McGinnis." As it was thought likely that Cicero Stewart might be able to identify "Stevens", Titsworth was shown how to operate a camera and was instructed to take photographs of the prisoner. On the morning of the 21st, "after considerable coaxing" by Titsworth, Ketchum agreed to face the camera. After Titsworth had taken his first picture, the outlaw's beard was shaven off; he had protested so vehemently when the razor was applied to his upper lip that he was permitted to keep the mustache. This touch of vanity may have expedited his identification. He would not pose for a second picture until someone handed him a revolver — after the cylinder had been emptied. Altogether, four pictures were taken of Ketchum.

Some few hours afterwards Tom was told of the arrest of McGinnis, whereupon he "became very restless and ugly and begged the officer (Titsworth) for a gun that he might kill himself." Later, thinking Titsworth asleep, he "removed the bandage from his arm, tied it around his neck and placing his foot in a loop at the end tried to commit suicide by strangulation." Titsworth, through half-closed eyes, watched the macabre performance for a few moments before he jumped up to "put a stop to the game."

In the meantime, Reno and Foraker, no longer openly warring with one another, were traveling to Carlsbad. With them was Jefferson D. Farr, who had been appointed to succeed his brother as sheriff of Huerfano County, and the omnipresent postmaster, Jim Hunt. They had no hesitation in identifying the man in the Eddy County Jail as the train robber "McGinnis"; so far no one in authority had connected this alias with the personage of Elza Lay. Reno then produced prints of the photographs taken in San Rafael Hospital, telling Stewart that he believed "George Stevens" to be none other than Black Jack. Stewart dissented vigorously.

DEAD TO RIGHTS

The face staring out of the snapshots did not belong to Black Jack; it was the familiar one of Tom Ketchum, whom Stewart had met on many a round-up in the Pecos Valley. Paradoxically enough, Stewart's opinion served as proof positive for Reno and Foraker; so far as they were concerned, Tom Ketchum and Black Jack were one and the same.

As Stewart wanted to see Ketchum, it was arranged that he would accompany the other officers to Trinidad; "McGinnis" would go, too, there to be lodged in the Las Animas County Jail until the time came for him and Ketchum to be put on the train for Santa Fe. A. F. Codington, one of Foraker's office deputies, joined the train somewhere en route. The party reached Trinidad at about six o'clock on the morning of August 23rd and, once Lay had been put safely under lock and key, Stewart headed for the hospital.

"Hello, Tom!" he called, as he entered the room in which the outlaw was confined.

For the first time since his arrest, Ketchum was visibly agitated. He could only stammer out that he did not know the visitor, although he might have seen him somewhere before. When Stewart pressed him to think back to his days as a cowpuncher in the Pecos country, Ketchum shook his head, scowled morosely, and clammed up. Jim Hunt, who seemed to grow more and more knowledgeable with each passing day, was on hand to corroborate Stewart.

The train in which the two prisoners were to be taken to Santa Fe was due to leave Trinidad at 10.30 a.m. Everyone in town seemed to know this, and a throng of more than eight hundred was milling in the street and around the depot as the outlaws were driven to the A.T. & S.F. depot. Lay rode inside a closed carriage and was not bothered by the sightseers. Ketchum, reclining in an open spring wagon with a big white hat pulled down over his features, was almost drowned in a sea of bobbing faces. Badgered by the crowd because he kept his face hidden, Ketchum told Stewart that he undertook to remove the hat if the crowd would give him five dollars. Even this hold-up failed; so the hat stayed where it was.

At the depot a reporter "endeavored to draw McGinnis into conversation but he politely declined to talk, other than to say that he was not wounded by the sheriff's posse near Carlsbad".

"They hit me a few licks on the head with their guns", he remarked, "but no damage was done except breaking the skin on my forehead".

By way of clarification he tilted the brim of his hat so that the spectators could stare at the large bump which darkened his brow.

"Several dimes and quarters were handed to him by those who sized him up", noted the *Chronicle-News* reporter. "McGinnis stood the searching gaze of the crowd without flinching in the least, but refused to be Kodaked".

Ketchum was feeling sick and "asked for a cantaloupe" just as the train was ready to pull out. Realizing the futility of denying his identity further, he talked quite freely to Stewart and Foraker during the journey. He spoke of the several phases of his life, touched upon various incidents in his outlaw career, told Foraker that he would not have essayed a hold-up at Folsom had he known of the recent robbery, but dismissed their news of the capture and demise of his brother as an artifice to beguile him into divulging more than he wanted.

Next day Thomas E. Ketchum was committed for safekeeping into the penitentiary at Santa Fe as Number 130. William E. Lay gave his name as "William K. McGinnis" and was received as Number 131. Before he was carried into the prison hospital, Ketchum urged Stewart to call on him some time later, vouching that, if in the meantime he had not died from blood-poisoning, he would make an important disclosure. That night the outlaw's temperature was recorded as 103F, which seemed to suggest that his chances of pulling through were as poor as he thought they were. He appeared indifferent until he was handed a photograph of Sam, taken shortly after death. The sight of it destroyed his composure.

"When you're through with me," he said resignedly, "just plant me alongside Sam."

Both prisoners were bound over on the charge of interfering with the United States mails, the hearing being held at the penitentiary on the 25th. The authorities in Arizona were already taking steps to have Ketchum extradited to face trial for the Camp Verde murders. His saddle—"high-forked, center-fire, full-stamped, with twenty-eight inch tapaderos and buckskin pockets"—his elaborately-woven Navajo blanket, and his own physical appearance matched the descriptions furnished by those who had encountered the killer as he fled across Arizona. An order of requisition was laid before Governor Otero on the 26th. Two days later he rejected it, on the grounds that the Federal authorities were proceeding with their charge against Ketchum. Sheriff Munds, who was ferreting for clues in the Datil Mountain Country of Socorro County nevertheless made ready to go to Santa Fe.

Meanwhile, on the 28th, Ketchum had entertained visitors from San Angelo.

"How are you getting along?" inquired Gerome Shields, as he and Bige Duncan greeted the outlaw. This, according to Shields, was his first meeting with Tom Ketchum for six or seven years.

"Very well, I'm sorry to say," was the cool reply.

Shields and Duncan had "a long talk" with the prisoner, during which he vowed he "would never be hung . . . he would make a dash for liberty first and be shot down." Before the visit was over, though, he "broke down and cried like a child."

In Trinidad, where he and Duncan had to change trains, Shields offered to "bet a box of cigars with every officer in Las Animas County that the outlaw would not stretch hemp." Duncan "choked up several times" and "controlled his feelings and kept back the tears" only with difficulty. Shields, on the other hand, was most expansive.

"Tom Ketchum has great nerve, though I think his brother Sam had better," he declared. McGinnis, he opined, was a 'ringer'; maybe "a safe cracker or some general all-around crook." Bige managed to mumble that "the relatives were all broken up over the downfall of the boys."

Quite suddenly, the outlaw appeared to regain the will to live, perhaps because he could see some hope of escaping from the penitentiary. He told the doctors that he now wanted them to amputate. The operation was performed on September 3rd, and Tom surprised the surgeon by refusing to take a drink after the sunderance of the rotting limb.

Sheriff Munds added his name to the visitors' list on the day of the operation. When he left he was satisfied that he had at last found the slayer of Rogers and Wingfield; some time later he stated that Ketchum openly admitted having killed the two men. Then, on September 5th, John Boyd—the witness with best cause to remember the killer—put the finger on Ketchum. Yavapai County, it seemed, could present an unassailable case against him; but Governor Otero was anxious to find a way to keep Yavapai County from getting him. Otero wanted to demonstrate that the Territory was capable of dealing with its own outlaws. People were saying that New Mexico was an outlaw paradise, totally unfit for Statehood; worse, they could count off an embarrassingly long list of cases in which the Territory had most signally failed to bring its desperados to account. Thomas Ketchum might be of help in mitigating this deplorable impression. First, though, "William K. McGinnis" had to be tried for the murder of Farr. Chief Justice W. J. Mills and District Attorney Jeremiah Leahy would dispose of this issue while Tom Ketchum was convalescing in the prison hospital.

Chapter Fourteen

POINTS OF LAW

District Attorney Leahy was assisted by Lewis C. Fort and Elisha V. Long in the preparation of the case against "William H. McGinnis." Leahy and Fort were two of the ablest and most energetic prosecutors in the Territory. Moreover, they and Chief Justice Mills were of one mind: "Ezra Lay McGinnis," as some of the newspapers would soon begin to miscall him, was an outlaw, a train robber, and a salutary example was going to be made of him.

The trial was due to start at Raton, seat of Colfax County, on Monday, October 2nd. Mills had invited Governor Otero to attend the proceedings. Presumably the judge was counting on bestowal of the seal of approbation by the chief executive of New Mexico; or he may have been extending a simple courtesy. Otero was present throughout. In due course of time he would castigate Mills for having grossly mishandled the trial and would turn out to be about the best friend Elza Lay ever made.

Lay was represented by Edwin B. Franks and Andrieus A. Jones. As far as is apparent from the record, very little play was made of the fact that the surname of one of the outlaw's attorneys was the same as the alias used by William Carver.

Franks and Jones tried hard to secure a continuance. In a sworn affidavit, Lay told the story of the Turkey Canyon fight in the words which, assertedly, the fugitive "G. W. Franks" would use were he to testify. Into this extraordinary document went an address for the missing witness: "In or near the town of Geronimo, Arizona Territory, to wit: at a place known as Freezeout Creek, in Nantac Mountain; the same being a distance of sixty miles north of said town of Geronimo." It is quite possible that Carver really was in the Gila Mountain country of Arizona: he had friends scattered all over the eastern half of that Territory, from Flagstaff to the Border. Lay promised, in his affidavit, to procure Carver's attendance, or failing that, his deposition, if the trial was held over for the next term of court. But the Territory of New Mexico, for its own reasons, would have liked very much for Carver to be in Raton for the current term.

Next, lawyer Franks sent a telegram to E. A. Cunningham, of Mogollon, New Mexico, who had made friends with Lay while the outlaw was working on the Socorro County ranch of the WS. Cunningham and Lay's other cowpunching pals, perhaps abetted by the attorney, claimed that they would not be able to make up a fund for the defense until they had located William French and secured the wages due to them. The Territory had no trouble in procuring three counter affidavits. One of these was given by Wilson Elliott, who was "personally acquainted" with French. The other depositions were made by James Morgan and a man named W.G. Hughes, both of whom had worked for French in Colfax County. All stated that the WS cowboys were paid by the foreman of the ranch concerned, and not by French himself.

These and all other moves by Lay's attorneys to gain a continuance having been rejected, the trial opened on the date originally set. Not until the Wednesday were twelve jurors empanelled from the seventy-five men examined by counsel. There were seven Anglos on that jury, and five Spanish Americans.

In his opening address, Leahy described the movements of McGinnis, Sam Ketchum, and G. W. Franks in Colfax and Union counties during the preceding summer. He dwelt lengthily upon the train robbery, contended that the first shots in the Turkey Canyon engagement had been fired by the defendant, and told the jury he expected them to return a verdict of guilty of murder in the first degree.

No sooner had the Territory's first witness, James Hunt, taken the oath than Ed Franks jumped up to state the defense's objection to the introduction of any testimony at all: there was no "legal indictment upon which to try the defendant," said Franks, and "no issue joined between the Territory and the defendant; therefore no issue of fact to go before the jury."

"Is there no issue joined?" the court queried mildly, "Does the record show the defendant has pled not guilty?"

The clerk confirmed that the plea had been entered, the motion was formally turned down, and the ruling of the court excepted to by Franks. Fort now got on with his examination of Hunt.

Four of the Territory's witnesses were heard before court was adjourned. Their testimony dealt mainly with the actions of the defendant and his three companions during the period just prior to the robbery.

Numerous other witnesses were called on the next day, Thursday. All of them, like those who had gone before, offered evidence bearing in some way upon the defendant's participation in the train hold-up. They included Conductor Harrington, Engineer Tubbs, and Express Messenger Scott. The pattern for this stage of the trial had been set very early in the examination of Jim Hunt. This witness had testified that he had first seen McGinnis in Cimarron "about the 7th of June, — along the fore part of June," and was just going to respond to Fort's question as to how long the defendant had remained in the neighborhood, when Jones intervened:

"Judging from the statement made by counsel for the Territory, I presume we might as well object now to this line of testimony. I cannot imagine the purpose of it, — we desire to enter our objection to it, because it is irrelevant and immaterial and does not tend to prove any of the issues in this case."

"I will overrule your objection," replied the court. Jones and Franks reserved exception to this.

Scenes like this, with variations, were enacted on more than a score of occasions during the first two days of the trial. Once, while Agapito Duran was on the stand, a long argument was waged between Jones on one side and Fort and Long on the other, with the court joining in at one point, before the defense's motion was overruled. From beginning to end, in fact, very few of the defense's objections were sustained. Briefly stated, it was the contention of Leahy and his associates — and in this they were very largely upheld by the trial judge—that nearly everything Lay did, or was thought to have done, from the day of his appearance in Colfax County, to the moment he was put inside the Eddy County Jail, was related in some wise to the murder charge on which he was being tried. The attitude of the defense was, naturally, quite different. Franks and Jones intended to show that their client had not murdered Farr, or even shot at him, but that he would have been entitled to kill him to protect his own life; in their submission, all consideration save these were extraneous. A layman's view might be that the Territory was seeking to have the defendant informally convicted of train robbery in order to justify the indictment for murder in the first degree. But the wording of the statutes which defined the three degrees of murder left some scope for learned argument (statutes aften do) on the interpretation of sundry provisions and their application to this particular case.

Ironically, the defendant's most valuable ally was the man seated next to Chief Justice Mills. In his reminiscences, written many years later with the help of his former secretary, Otero recorded some instructive comments on the trial:

> Public opinion was aroused to a high pitch against all persons connected with train robberies, and the courts were determined to stop this crime which gave New Mexico such a bad name for lawlessness, even though all points of law were not adhered to literally. Personally, I believe that all courts should be impartial and just at all times. Sometimes, however, popular clamor and political ambitions combine to banish the calm and careful consideration due to justice . . . I noticed that every (sic) ruling in the case went against the defendant . . . it seemed to me that he was convicted before he was tried . . .

A recondite element was introduced with the testimony of William A. Chapman, superintendent of schools for Colfax County and a surveyor, who had been sent into Turkey Canyon to prepare a topographical map of the ground on which the fight had occurred. When Jones asked to see Chapman's memorandum book, the witness pointed out that is was "very hard for anyone to make out a surveyor's memoranda." Jones modestly allowed that he knew a little bit about surveying, himself, and maybe he could understand the notes. But in the end both sides of the courtroom seem to have been willing to accept that Chapman had drawn a pretty good map, and to let it go at that. (The court stenographer, plainly, knew less than nothing of the surveyor's craft: he consistently rendered the word "topography" as "typography.")

After Chapman had stepped down, the Territory recalled H.P. Scott, the express messenger. The next witness, and the fifteenth, was W.H. Reno. He had told of his part in the investigation of the train robbery, and had described how the posse was assembled in Cimarron, when Fort concluded his examination:

"That is all for the present with this witness. I will recall him later."

Jones, to his subsequent regret, was quite satisfied with this.

"If he is to be recalled we will wait for cross examination until he is recalled," he told the court.

The first testimony to be heard which dealt directly with the fight itself was Wilson Elliott's. Under examination by Fort, he gave a fairly clear and straightforward account of the events in Turkey Canyon. Andrieus Jones' cross examination was both thorough and incisive. Sometimes, too, it was sharpened by sarcasm.

Jones began by making Elliott recite the entire story of his variegated career over the past twelve years. . . .

Q. And you did nothing in New Mexico as an occupation except to prospect prior to the time you went to Trinidad.
A. Most of the time I prospected. I ran a rock outfit down here on the road for awhile.
Q. When was that.
A. That was in 1892.
Q. What kind of a rock outfit was that.
A. I had charge of an outfit that was getting out rock for the coke ovens.
Q. Where was that.
A. South of Cerrillos.
Q. How long were you engaged in that business.
A. I expect a month or so.
Q. Did you do any other work in New Mexico besides prospect and that rock work.
A. No sir, not to amount to anything.
Q. Well, what was it if it did not amount to anything.
A. I prospected most of the times and worked in the mines a few days. . . .
Q. What were you doing there (El Moro, Colorado).
A. Running an outfit, building some coke ovens.
Q. How long were you engaged in that job.
A. I don't remember, I think I moved to Trinidad in October 1893.
Q. Were you building those coke ovens all the time up to the time you moved to Trinidad.
A. I believe so, I don't remember.
Q. Did you do anything else at El Moro.
A. No sir.
Q. What business did you engage in after moving to Trinidad.
A. I was Constable of that Precinct in the town there. . . .
Q. What did you do in Trinidad from 1893 to 1895.
A. I just rested around.
Q. That job of building coke ovens was a pretty hard one.
A. No, I did not work very hard.
Q. Well, it took you a good while to get rested.
A. I am not rested yet. I am tired now. . . .

And thus the interrogation was carried along for some little while. More recently, and for about a year, until June of 1899, witness had been employed by Wells, Fargo as an express guard; he had quit working regularly for the company because the pay was not high enough to suit him, but he still made the occasional run for them. When pressed, he admitted having known that, some time before the second Folsom robbery, the company had placed a standing reward of $1,000 each for "a man named Sam Ketchum, Tom Ketchum, William Carver, Dave Atkins and two or three others" of the outlaw gang. As he understood it, the bounties would be paid whether the men were brought in dead or alive, although the company's offer was not worded quite in that fashion.

Elliott was forced to concede, under persistent questioning, that he had not actually received a commission from Foraker. Strictly speaking, then, Jones concluded, Elliott was not a deputy marshal at all — he had been merely a deputized posseman in charge of other deputized possemen. Apparently, Elliott was nettled by this disclosure; but the real damage was yet to come.

Jones now tackled the subject of the fight, and by the time he had finished with Elliott the witness had been shown to be untrustworthy, besides having been made to look foolish now and again. He got more and more confused, contradicted himself in places, and had to admit more than once that he had forgotten his answer to this question or that one of a few minutes earlier. Fort's re-examination retrieved little or none of the lost ground, and Jones let the witness go.

Perfecto Cordoba (spelled "Cordova" in the record) was the next witness. Although he spoke and understood English well, he was served by an interpreter. This must have given him the opportunity to think twice before he answered any question. His performance was even more lamentable than Elliott's had been.

Cordoba, when examined by Jerry Leahy, said that he thought McGinnis had been armed at the time he was shot, but was no more positive than this; he stated, however, that the defendant had certainly done some shooting in the later stages of the battle. In this he was not mistaken; it was just as well for the outlaw that Perfecto's evidence was at fault or equivocal in other respects.

It was common knowledge in Cimarron that Cordoba had told a number of people — Miguel Lopez, Patricio Montoya, a man named Strivens, and others—that the man called McGinnis had been shot down whilst unarmed. Edwin Franks, in cross examining the witness, reminded him of all this. Cordoba wilted a little, but maintained that his words had been misunderstood. Nor would he knowingly change the sense of the story which he had just given to Leahy, although Franks did manage to expose some of its inconsistencies. Moreover, since it had been established that the bullet which killed Farr had ranged upwards, Franks succeeded in weakening or muddling the Territory's case by drawing from Cordoba the statement (almost surely an incorrect one) that the sheriff's position had been roughly level with or just above that occupied by Carver.

In his re-examination, conducted by Fort, Cordoba reiterated that the posse had been fired upon by all three of the fugitives. Jones, who put the witness through re-cross examination, seems to have been the first of the four lawyers to grasp what ought to have been clear all along: that the defendant had not been one of the two men whom Cordoba had seen at the beginning of the fight. Fort realized what Jones was getting at, and asked leave of the court to have the witness explain further what he had seen of the movements of the man whom he "took to be McGinnis." Nothing was clarified by this, or needed to be; it must have been obvious by now that Cordoba had been describing the actions of Carver, not those of the defendant. Nearly forty years afterwards, Otero had this to say of Cordoba's testimony:

> I do not pretend to know what changed Perfecto Cordoba, but any person who heard his testimony could tell that he was following instructions. In fact, after the trial, he admitted to several that he had been mistaken about McGinnis firing his gun.

In truth, though, Cordoba had not been wrong about this; it was just that he *thought* he had been wrong.

James Morgan had appeared on the stand, early in the trial, to describe how he had observed the movements of Ketchum, Carver, the man known as "Red" or "Wheeler" (Weaver), and the defendant before the train robbery. Now, after the dismissal of Cordoba, he was recalled to give testimony on the fight. His answers were far more helpful to the defense than to the prosecution: as nearly as he could tell, all the shots fired at the posse had come from Ketchum and Carver, or from the direction of the places from which these two were shooting. He was certain that McGinnis had not been carrying a rifle when the bullets started to fly.

Morgan was followed by David E. Farr, who had gone into Turkey Canyon with George Titsworth and others shortly after the fight. Dave Farr's testimony was mostly concerned with the firing positions taken by the three outlaws and with the nature of his brother's wounds. His findings tended to show that the defendant must have been the man who had shot Ed Farr; but such testimony as his, now matter how impartially and with what precision it was delivered, probably would have struck that jury much less forcibly than the testimony — and manner — of the eye witnesses.

M.C. (Cicero) Stewart was called next. He told the jury how the arrest of McGinnis had been accomplished. Then, during cross examination, he produced the clothing taken from the prisoner. The pants, the old grayish vest, the yellowish shirt which was really only an undershirt, were the garments which the outlaw had been wearing in Turkey Canyon. The vest and the bloodstained shirt, each with two bullet holes on the left hand side, were held up for the inspection of the jurors.

"I believe the Territory will rest here," announced Fort, when Jones had concluded his cross examination.

This came as an utter surprise to Franks and Jones, who evidently were very anxious indeed to listen to Reno's version of the shooting. Jones protested that it was incumbent on the prosecution to examine Reno "as to the facts and circumstances occurring at the time of this homicide or alleged homicide." He had a fair point; Farr and Reno were so close to one another when the battle started that they could very nearly have shaken hands had they reached out.

"We do not desire to call Mr. Reno. We claim that we can call any witness we choose," Fort responded curtly.

Jones renewed his objections, contending that it was "a rule of law" that the prosecution produce all witnesses who were within its power; the record showed, he added, that Reno had "already been upon the stand as to a preliminary matter."

It was no good; his motion to have Reno put upon the stand was overruled. The other material witness, F.H. Smith, had returned to the East and had not been summoned back to give evidence.

This is, unfortunately, nothing to indicate just when or by whom it was decided that Reno should not be recalled. But in the light of the contradictory and sometimes highly suspect nature of the testimony already heard, as well as the notorious ill-feeling between Reno and the U.S. Marshal's office, a reasonable theory might be that counsel for the Territory were heeding the principle of the lesser risk; their case would stand in greater jeopardy from Reno's exposure to cross examination than from their conspicuous failure to call the principal eye witness. Reno's thoughts on the matter, and those of his employers at the chief office of the railroad company, are unknown and beyond sensible conjecture; from all the different factors, he might equally have been anxious to testify or anxious not to testify.

Edwin Franks chose not to make an opening statement for the defense. He was to call only two witnesses: Miguel Lopez, who had been subpoenaed to attend, and McGinnis himself. His intention was to use Lopez to complete the demolition of Elliott and Cordoba, each of whom had already discredited himself, and the other, from the stand.

Several days previously, Lopez and the man Strivens had visited Franks in his room at the Palace Hotel and had related the story of the fight as they had heard it from Cordoba. When he took the stand, though, Lopez was not too willing to confirm the accuracy of what Franks had scribbled in his notebook during the meeting at the hotel. Early in the examination the Territory was sustained in an objection to the defense's impeaching its own witness. But Lopez did say that Cordoba had told him that he (Cordoba) was not sure whether McGinnis was in Turkey Canyon at the time of the fight, and that, even if he had been present, Cordoba did not know whether or not he was carrying a rifle. He recollected, too, having been told by Cordoba that Elliott and Farr, upon locating the outlaw camp, had agreed to divide the posse into two sections —an assertion totally contrary to Elliott's testimony, in which it was stated that Farr, Reno, and Smith had slipped away unseen and unheard by the titular leader of the posse.

Elliott's name was not brought into Fort's cross examination. Fort tried, but failed, to persuade the witness that he simply could not remember what Cordoba had said about his doubts as to the presence of McGinnis in Turkey Canyon and about his inability to say truthfully whether or not the defendant could have been armed at the time.

The defendant then stood up to testify for himself, his manner so frank and fearless that Otero erroneously believed that he spoke the unalloyed truth. Indeed, he did not tell very many direct lies: as far as he possibly could, he simply avoided mention of any facts injurious to himself or to his associates in crime. Naturally, Edwin Frank's examination was not calculated to bring out any such facts.

Towards the end of his evidence in chief, McGinnis paraded before the jury the scars from his wounds, accompanying the demonstration with a brief descriptive commentary. Presently, after Long—who, thus far, had taken little visible part in the proceedings—had risen to cross examine, there were theatricals of another kind. It is at once plain that the authorities were still quite ignorant of the true identity of the defendant; he was even accused of being Carver!

Q. What do you say your name is.
A. William McGinnis.
Q. Has that always been your name.
A. Yes sir.
Q. Ever go by the name of Carver.
A. No sir.

Q. Where were you born.
A. I was born in the East.
Q. Where.
A. In Illinois.
Q. What place in Illinois.
   (WITNESS) Well, if the court please, I am here tried for murder. I understand there is other charges against me,— for train robbery, — I have been put on trial without any chance to get my witnesses.
   (The Court) Don't make any address to the jury, Mr McGinnis, your lawyers will do that. What do you want to say? Don't you want to give an account of your life?
   (WITNESS) What I mean to say is this,—I have got no way to protect myself and I positively refuse to answer any questions except concerning this fight and I will not under any circumstances answer any.
   (The Court) Very well.
Q. You put yourself in this attitude, do you, that you decline to answer any questions with relation to your past life?
A. I decline to answer any questions except concerning this fight.
Q. Do you decline to answer any questions which relate to your past life up to the time this occurrence happened? Answer Yes or No.
A. Yes, I decline to answer any except about this fight.
Q. Except on this particular occasion.
A. Yes sir.
Q. Where were you on the 11th day of July 1899.
A. I was at this camp on Turkey Creek.
Q. I don't believe you understand my question, I said the 11th of July.
   (Mr Jones) If the court please, I submit that is not proper cross examination of this witness.
   (The Court) Judge Long, the witness has declined to answer and I don't believe you ought to go into it.
   (E.V. Long) Well, all right McGinnis. . . .

Most of the questions that were asked of him about his companions he declined to answer. He denied having known that one of them was named Ketchum; this man was always called "Red," he declared, but sometimes was referred to as "the old man." Now Sam Ketchum had been of ruddy complexion, and his hair had been reddish blond; but the nickname "Red" had already been assigned in evidence to its proper place: to the identity of the man whose real name was thought to be Wheeler—and he, quite certainly, was nowhere near Turkey Canyon when the posse got there. It seems that the defendant seized upon a mild coincidence—the general similarity in stature and complexion of Ketchum and Weaver—to thicken the confusion. Anyway, Long designated Sam Ketchum as "Red" in his subsequent questions to the witness.

McGinnis continued to insist that he had been shot first by someone in Farr's group, then, moments later, by someone in the Elliott party, and that he himself had been unarmed from start to finish. At no time did Long look like shaking him. His cross examination was aggressive, sometimes crafty, but never shrewd.

Fort, for the Territory, then took the maladroit step of calling upon Elliott to make a rebuttal of the defendant's testimony. The credibility of Wilson Elliott, in the context of this case, is well conveyed in the closing exchanges of his cross examination by Jones:

> Q. Didn't you state the first shot you fired was at the horses?
> A. I perhaps did. I believe I shot the first shot at the horses. I don't know. I am not sure now. I don't know whether I fired the first shot at the horses or the first shot at this man up here.
> Q. Well, didn't you so state in your previous examination, that the first shot you fired was at the horses?
> A. I don't know whether I did or not.

After the testimony, the closing speeches. E.V. Long, in his speech, made a flagrant attempt to browbeat the jury. The defendant, declared Long, had every opportunity to have a fair trial; if the jury were to make any mistake in bringing in a verdict against the defendant which was not warranted by the evidence in the case (he meant any verdict that did not suit the prosecution), the court would set the verdict aside. The defense objected strongly to this, and Mills, perhaps embarrassed by the implications, commented:

"The court has a right to set aside such verdict, but I do not know whether such verdict would be set aside or not."

The defense were to find fault with this, too.

Mills received from the prosecution twenty-five requests for instructions to the jury, but allowed only seven of them. The defense made fifteen requests, of which four were allowed. His own instructions were nineteen in number. In essence, this was the proposition put to the jury: if they accepted that Farr and his companions, whether a legally-constituted posse or not, had proper grounds for believing that McGinnis and the two men with him were in flight from the recent train robbery, and provided that the evidence showed that the suspects had been given a chance to surrender before any shots were fired at them, McGinnis should be found guilty of murder; and for this, in these circumstances, it did not have to be proved that he himself had fired the fatal shot. If, on these premises, the jury were not satisfied that the defendant, personally, had killed Farr, or were satisfied that one of the defendant's companions was the actual killer, the verdict would be returned as guilty of murder in the second degree. If, however, they believed that Farr was killed by the defendant himself, they would assess guilt in the first or the second degree, depending upon whether, in their view, the killing was part of a premeditated plan or common design, or whether it had been an act "perpetrated in the heat of passion." It was, of course, also open to the jury to find the defendant guilty of murder in the third degree or to acquit him. What Mills did not make plain to the jurors was the verdict they should find if they believed that Farr and those with him had reasonable cause to arrest or detain McGinnis and the others but had fired on them without having first given them an opportunity to surrender.

Before the trial, Mills had told a newspaperman in Raton that he expected the case to be over with by Saturday night. On the Thursday, and again on the Friday, court had remained in session until eleven o'clock at night. It was now well into the evening of Saturday. He informed, or reminded, the jury that if they had not found a verdict by eight o'clock in the morning they would have to stay in the jury room for another twenty-four hours. A train for Las Vegas was due to pull out of Raton shortly after eight o'clock on Sunday morning, and Mills intended to be on that train. He would be back in Raton on Monday.

As the jurors were about to retire to consider a verdict, counsel for the defense came forward to object and except, separately, "to each and every instruction given by the court upon own motion or upon the request of the plaintiff, and also, . . . to the refusal of the court to give each and every instruction asked for by the defendant." Franks and Jones were given until Tuesday to file specific objections and exceptions.

It took the jury about three hours to agree upon a verdict that McGinnis was guilty of murder in the second degree. This was punishable by imprisonment "for any period of time not less than three years." The defendant's attorneys then gave notice of a motion for a new trial.

On Tuesday, October 10th, Mills overruled all the defense's objections and exceptions and denied the motion for a new trial. Then he passed sentence:

"It is therefore considered and adjudged by the court that the defendant, William H. McGinnis, be and hereby is sentenced to imprisonment for the full term of his natural life at the penitentiary situated at Santa Fe, Territory of New Mexico."

So, on the 13th. the fallen "paladin" of the range again entered within the gates of the penitentiary, this time as Prisoner Number 1348. Mills had granted him leave to appeal to the Supreme Court, and the cause was heard in January 1900 before Justices J.W. Crumpacker, John R. McFie, and Frank W. Parker.

Crumpacker began with a statement of what he called the "important facts in the case." Most of Crumpacker's "facts" on the shooting were items taken without reservation or qualification from Wilson Elliott's testimony. The trusting judge even repeated Elliott's assertion that the shooting had not lasted for more than ten minutes; Cordoba and Morgan had testified (and, incidentally, Reno had stated outside the courtroom) that the fighting had gone on for three quarters of an hour or so. No vital issue turned upon this question as to the duration of the shooting; the significant point is that Crumpacker permitted himself to be guided solely by what the man Elliott had said.

Appellant's argument that the killing of Farr could not have been "traceable directly to the conspiracy to rob the train" because the two events were separated by a period of five days and seventy miles was, remarked Crumpacker, "more ingenious than helpful in the case at bar." The judge commented at some length on such matters as how the basis for "common design" was constituted or could be constituted and on the question of "mixed law and fact" through which it had to be determined whether the posse had been actuated by "good faith and honest purpose" and had "acted as reasonable men would have acted in like situation." His opinion ruled against the appellant on every issue, and—with McFie and Parker concurring—the sentence of the District Court was affirmed.

In an empirical sense, the verdict in the case against Lay, alias McGinnis, was the right one; he had killed Farr—although he must have been the only man in that courtroom who knew it—and undoubtedly the outlaws would have fought or run even if the posse had tried to take them alive, rather than dead. The sentence was much severer than the evidence, alone, would warrant: obviously Mills was influenced by factors which did not belong to the case at all. The judges of the Supreme Court preferred to accept the testimony most unfavorable to the defendant and stood by the doctrine which had governed Mills' conduct of the trial.

According to Charlie Siringo, the ex-cowboy author and detective, the outlaw's attorneys were paid out of the loot from the bank robbery at Winnemucca, Nevada. If this be true, they had to wait almost a year for their money.

About the first news Lay heard when he entered the penitentiary as

No. 1348 was that Tom Ketchum had already manifested very definite signs of unrest.

After his operation, Ketchum had swiftly regained his strength, and with it much of his old defiance. Despite the loss of the arm, and the vigilance enjoined upon the guards by Superintendent Holm O. Bursum, he evolved and brought near to fruition an implausible yet ingenious scheme to escape from the prison hospital. His confederate was Prisoner Number 1208, Frank Attlebury, who was serving a three-year sentence for robbing a store in Colfax County and who was under treatment for "consumption." Their apparatus comprised one block of wood, one clockspring, and some tinfoil. The wood was painstakingly fashioned into a replica of a Colt's six-shooter and then encased in tinfoil; in uncertain light it would look most realistic to a guard if thrust suddenly into his face. The clockspring was cleverly improvised into a saw. In a field half a mile away a white pony was grazing, easily visible from the hospital and as elusive as a mirage to the imprisoned outlaws.

Ketchum and Attlebury planned to overpower their attendant and cut through the bars of the window. Next, they would waylay the watchman as he was making his rounds; they would hold him up with their wooden pistol, disarm him and knock him senseless. If they got clear of the prison, Attlebury would catch the white pony, which would have to carry double until the men could find fresh horses.

It can hardly be credited that Ketchum, seriously handicapped and highly conspicuous as he was, could have expected to get very far away. Yet, in the last days of September, his spirits were buoyant, his manner seasoned with bravado. He gained further stimulus from the visit of Cicero Stewart, who displayed an amazing lack of sagacity in believing that the oultaw really meant to make some important revelation to him. But Tom acted rather like the cheat who is so gratified by his own artfulness that he cannot resist letting his prospective victims into the secret.

In response to the sheriff's query, Ketchum jovially said:

"I'm getting fat so that when they hang me they can eat me if they want to".

Then, adopting a confidential tone, he directed Stewart to the location of a certain juniper tree in Texas Canyon, the gang's old hideout in the Chiricahuas. Buried at the roots of the tree, he said, was the sum of $1,800 in gold. Stewart swallowed the whole story and hied away to uncover the hoarded treasure. An official named Martin was more perceptive. Sensing from Ketchum's jaunty banter that the outlaw was planning to escape, he reported to Bursum. It was not long before the dummy pistol was found in the hospital water-closet. An examination of Ketchum's person brought forth the clockspring, wound around the outlaw's body and tucked into the bandage. The two convalescents were hustled away into cells. Ketchum "broke down with emotion" at the discovery of the scheme; but, only a short time later, a prisoner named William Hall was surprised to see the one-armed desperado dancing a jig.

"I'll learn that fellow to punch cows with me and then come to Trinidad to identify me!" chortled Ketchum. "If he goes into that canyon, and the gang happens to be there, they'll fill his hide full of lead!"

For some days afterwards, Ketchum eagerly scanned the papers for news of Stewart's death. His disappointment owed nothing to any special precautions on the part of the Sheriff.

Stewart was gullible enough—or greedy enough—to fall for Ketchum's tale. He went straight to Cochise County and rode out to Texas Canyon with Steve Roup, a Deputy Sheriff from Bisbee. They found everything exactly as described by the bandit, except the money. Fortunately for them, there were no outlaws, either. But matters might easily have turned out as Ketchum had hoped. During that autumn Will Carver was roving about southeast Arizona and southwest New Mexico, together with Tom Capehart and others, including one or two of the Kilpatricks. Butch Cassidy and Red Weaver were back in Alma, and in touch with Carver and the rest.

For Tom Ketchum there would be no further opportunity either to escape or to seek revenge, although, in a way, Governor Otero was zealous in his efforts to protect him from the Arizona courts. On November 9th, United States District Attorney Childers acceded to the request of the Arizona authorities by waiving the Federal charge against Ketchum "on the understanding that should he be acquitted or sentenced only to a term of years he should be brought back to be tried on the charges that the United States has brought against him". This duly led to a second requisition from the Governor of Arizona, and on the 11th Sheriff Munds reappeared in Santa Fe, flourishing the papers which wanted only the signature of Governor Otero to make Tom Ketchum the responsibility of Yavapai County. But Governor Otero was not going to append his signature, so Munds was again sent empty away.

Otero was unalterably determined that Tom Ketchum was to die by the rope and that the job was to be done in New Mexico. This, it was hoped, would purge the Territory both of highway robbers and its ill repute. More; it would proclaim that, at last, the celebrated "Black Jack" had been brought to the end which awaits all outlaws. There was said to be little chance of securing evidence to prove Ketchum guilty of the murders of Herzstein and Gallegos. Hence the way was clear for him to be thrown before the bar of justice on the capital charge of assaulting a railroad train. In spite of his disapproval of the means by which Lay, or McGinnis, had been dealt with, Otero was anxious to support Jeremiah Leahy in the matter of Thomas E. Ketchum.

After the second requisition from Arizona had been turned down, the United States proceeded with its own charges. Ketchum was taken to Las Vegas where, on November 15th, he pleaded guilty to delaying the United States Mails. Leonard Alverson maintained later that the Federal officers had agreed to hoodwink Ketchum into entering a plea of guilty so as to facilitate conviction on the capital charge:

> They said, "Now, Tom, there is a Federal charge against you which bears a maximum sentence of ten years. If you will plead guilty to that we will give you ten years. Meanwhile you can get your friends to working getting things fixed for the other charge and also toward getting a pardon." Well, he pleaded guilty but they sentenced him to only six months. . . .

Alverson, it should be noted, was anything but an objective reporter; no man who has been hounded into prison on charges of which he is innocent ever can be an enthusiastic advocate for the cause of law and order. He was mistaken in saying that Ketchum was given a six-month term in the U.S. court; actually, sentence was suspended to enable the Territory to dispose of its charges against him. This tends to show that Alverson's story may well be true in its essence. But if Ketchum was tricked in this way, he was as foolish as Cicero Stewart had been in believing the outlaw's own fiction of a few weeks earlier.

As Ketchum was driven to Las Vegas station after the trial, he was besieged by shoals of curiosity-seekers. His reactions were much the same as those he had evidenced in Trinidad.

"What in the hell is the idea of this crowd?" he demanded. Given the anticipated reply, he exclaimed: "To hell with them!" With that he drew his vest and shirt over his face. If the gathering would make up a purse of $25, he would let them see his face. The offer provoked "a lot of good-natured raillery"; but no hands shot moneywards.

Nearly a year dragged by before Union County was ready to set in motion the legal machinery which, few doubted, would ceremoniously accomplish the removal of Tom Ketchum into the death-cell.

On the morning of Monday, September 3rd, 1900, Ketchum was escorted from the penitentiary by Deputy U.S. Marshal Frank W. Hall and Sheriff H.C. Kinsell. At Trinidad, where they were to stay overnight, they were met by W.H. Reno, who was in charge of arrangements for the second leg of the journey. Upon the morrow the town of Clayton turned out in force to gaze upon the doomed outlaw. The special train bearing Ketchum, six guards, and a whole convention of railroad and express company men, arrived at Clayton depot at 12.30 p.m. Tom was in a reminiscent mood. This was very much the same town as the one he remembered so well from his trail-driving days. He spoke ruminatively of the places and people he had known—eight, ten years ago. The march ended at the Union County Jail. As Hall unlocked the shackles, Ketchum delivered himself of sentiments less amiable:

"Hall, you are the first man that ever put shackles on me. One of these days I'll do the same thing to you and I'll take you way off on the prairie and leave you."

Turning to survey the cells, he allowed that "these is right smart pleasant quarters."

"But I'd a heap rather be out on the Perico eating dinner at the chuck wagon," he mused.

Court was called to order at two o'clock. At 2.40 the outlaw, "looking rather nervous," was brought into the crammed courtroom to hear and answer to the three indictments. William J. Mills was presiding; the prosecution was being handled by Leahy and Fort. Before Leahy started to read the indictments, Ketchum asked and was granted leave to speak to Reno.

The first indictment dealt with his felonious assault upon a railroad train. Perhaps contemptuous of the legal jargon, Ketchum "seemed impatient" and ran his eye the faces of the spectators "as if seeking a friend somewhere." When Leahy had paused to clear his throat before turning to the second indictment, Ketchum rendered a plea of guilty. Mills refused to accept the plea; since the crime for which the indictment had been found was punishable by death, he told Ketchum, the only admissible plea was one of not guilty. The clerk was instructed accordingly. To each of the other indictments, wherein he was charged with the wounding of Harrington and Drew, he pleaded not guilty. Since the defendant had neither counsel nor funds, the court appointed William B. Bunker to look after his interests.

For much of Wednesday the outlaw was discussing his case with Bunker, a deputy remaining in close attendance throughout. Every now and again Ketchum wandered from the point, relating stories of divers incidents in his past life. Bunker and his assistant, John R. Guyer, tried desperately to find some plausible defense for a man whose conviction was inevitable and who appeared supremely indifferent to his own case. Ketchum was somewhat surprised and hurt because no one had attempted to rescue him. "When a man is in, he ain't got no friends," he remarked to someone: but he had lost his friends while he was still out.

Both parties were ready to go to trial on Thursday, September 6th. The case was called at 2.30 p.m., and adjourned four hours later when twelve presumed peers of the accused had been selected. Bunker and Guyer then presented the court with a motion that the first indictment be quashed because the punishment was "unusual and excessive" for the crime of which Ketchum was accused and, as such, contrary to the provisions contained in Article 8 of the Constitution of the United States. "Cap" Fort disputed this, and Mills briskly set the motion aside. The court then rose.

Ketchum appeared "very much bored" and "mean at times." "If I hang, my information hangs with me," he said grimly. His attitude showed that he "would like to make most any kind of a deal whereby he might escape the death penalty."

Court resumed at nine o'clock the next morning for the taking of evidence. On almost every point, the testimony was straightforward and unequivocal. According to Albert Thompson's recollections of the case, one of the few incidents which stirred Ketchum out of his lethargy arose while Charlie Drew, the express messenger, was on the stand.

"You say the prisoner pounded on the door of your car and commanded you to open it?" asked Leahy.

"Yes, sir."

"Well, what did he say to you?" prompted the attorney.

"He said, pointing his gun at me, 'fall out of there damn quick'."

"And what did you do?" Leahy pursued.

"I fell out of there damn quick. What would you have done, Mr. Leahy?" the witness flung back.

The District Attorney did not duck the question.

"I would, too," he responded; then turning to the defendant, he inquired: "Is that true, Tom?"

"You bet your god-damned life it's true," Ketchum declared, amid laughter, "and he didn't lose no time, either."

Unfortunately, most of the lines in this vivid sketch are absent from the official transcript. This was the exchange, as the court stenographer recorded it:

> A. (Drew) ... He covered me with the gun and called out, —Come out of that door, or Fall out of there, or words to that effect.
> Q. (Leahy) And how close was he to you at this time when he pointed the gun in your direction.
> A. Twelve to fifteen feet, I take it to be.
> Q. What did you do.
> A. I got out. There was nothing else to do.
> Q. Did you get out or "Fall out."
> A. I did not fall out. I got out. ...

There are times, alas, when fiction is stranger than the truth.

Although Ketchum had not got his hands on a single dollar in his last hold-up, Leahy questioned the witness closely as to how much money there had been in the express car at the time. Drew said that, as far as he could remember, there had been fifty dollars in the way safe; "the through safe contained valuables, paper and money, but I don't know what it contained, sir. I had no access to it." When asked to add to this statement, he admitted knowing that he had "more than five thousand dollars worth of stuff in the through safe," but emphasized that this was no more than a "rough estimate."

Attorney Bunker found an awkward witness in Fred L. Bartlett. The mail clerk was as hostile as ever towards the man who had shot him. He had been disabled for life and was quite sure that his presence in the witness box owed nothing to Ketchum's good intentions. It was going to take more than a clever lawyer to change his mind about this. Bunker tried:

> Q. Could you get the motion on your head before the bullet struck you, after it was fired.
> A. It is quite evident I did.
> Q. Do you know at what rate one of those bullets travels.
> A. No sir. I never figured it out.
> Q. Don't you know they travel 2400 feet a second.
> A. It is possible.
> Q. That would not give you much time to get your head out of the way.
> A. The motion of putting the pistol (sic) forward might have given me warning.

> Q. Did you see the pistol put forward to shoot.
> A. I did. . . .
> Q. If that bullet hadn't hit the iron plate on the door would it have hit you.
> A. It would undoubtedly have hit me further back on the head.
> Q. Do I understand you to say that if this bullet had have kept its course it would have gone in rear of you.
> A. No sir. If this bullet when it first struck the car had kept on its course it would have hit me farther back in the head or in the body.
> Q. If you had your head in the car could you see the flash of the gun.
> A. I said my head was out of the car leaning forward.

Further cross examination brought out an admission from Bartlett that the bullet, having been fired from below, must have ranged upward. Bunker then proceeded.

> Q. Well, how do you explain to the jury that if the bullet had not struck the side of the car that it would have struck your body farther back or lower down.
> A. It would have struck me about the back part of the head, I think.
> Q. Then it would not have struck your body at all.
> A. My head is part of my body.
> Q. Didn't you swear that you had your head out of the car.
> A. Yes sir, part of it.
> Q. How much of your head was out of the car.
> A. I never figured it out, but I had enough of it out to see out.
> Q. How far was the man who fired the shot from you.
> A. Probably thirty of thirty-five feet.
> Q. And you were in plain view, weren't you.
> A. My head was.

On the whole, the evidence left little room for argument. Frank Harrington and Joe Kirchgrabber, as well as Drew and Bartlett, gave details of the hold-up. Chris Waller, John Mercer, Joseph Robbins and F.F. Clarke related how Ketchum had surrendered and what he had said. Harry Lewis and George Titsworth testified on what he had told them afterwards.

There were three witnesses for the defense: F.W. Hall, Saturnino Pinard, and F.J. Dodge. The purpose of the defense was to show that the defendant had been placed in the custody of the United States shortly after his arrest by Pinard, that he had been brought to Clayton as a prisoner of the United States, and that he was still a prisoner of the United States. Fred Dodge, the veteran Wells, Fargo detective — no "undercover man" was more famous in his own lifetime — was on the stand for a very few minutes. He told Bunker, that he had come to Clayton the previous day with "Mr. Rainey, Division Superintendent of the railway company, Special Agent Reno, United States Deputy Marshal Hall, a man named Saxton, and a man named Kenochan." He added:

"There were two others. I don't know their names. I don't know the names of the train crew running the train. Neither do I know the name of the negro porter. I think that was all."

    Q. Are you sure there was a negro porter on that train.
    A. Yes sir. He got me a cup of coffee.
    Q. An intimate friend of yours, was he.
    A. He was a friend in need.
    Q. I will ask you if the defendant was on that train.
    A. Oh, yes, I forgot "Tom". He was there.
    Q. You overlooked a very important personage.
    A. That is right.

This piece of frivolity concluded the testimony in the case.

As Bunker was taken ill, the task of making the closing speech for the defense fell to John Guyer. He did as well as he could, but the proposition was a hopeless one. The jury needed little time to bring in a verdict of guilty. Albert Thompson wrote later that "Ketchum "evinced no emotion." A newspaperman reported, not without ambiguity, that the outlaw "was much affected by the verdict, but his great nerve kept him from making any demonstration."

Guyer at once moved for a new trial. This request was considered on the following Monday and turned down. Next day, September 11th, the court assembled for sentence to be passed.

"Have you anything to say why sentence should not be pronounced upon you?" asked the court.

"Nothing at all," replied Ketchum.

The jury had fixed the penalty as death; the law gave it no alternative, anyway. It was then the duty of Chief Justice Mills to set a date for the execution, and his privilege to advise the condemned man on how best to occupy himself in the meantime. (There was a convention, generally observed, that this privilege take the form of an expression of solicitude for the spiritual prospects of the condemned; it was almost as if a judge was both the servant of God and the instrument of Justice.) This is how Mills addressed himself to Ketchum:

    It is hereby ordered, considered and adjudged by the court that you, Thomas Ketchum, on the fifth day of October, A. D. 1900, between the hours of ten o'clock in the forenoon and four o'clock in the afternoon of said day, in an enclosure to be erected by the sheriff on the court house grounds in the town of Clayton, county seat of Union county, Territory of New Mexico, you be there hanged by the neck until you are dead by the sheriff of said county of Union, or such person as may be deputized by him. . . .

The court recommends to you that between now and the day of your said execution you prepare yourself by repentance for your past evil deeds to meet your God, and may God have mercy on your soul.

Ketchum smiled and gave his attention to his attorneys.

The judge granted Ketchum leave to appeal. This was tantamount to a stay of execution, as the Supreme Court was not due to meet until January, 1901.

On Thursday evening, September 13th, Sheriff Pinard restored Ketchum to the care and protection of the Territorial Penitentiary until such time as he was required at Clayton to shake hands with the hangman. Tom was now better able to compare notes with "Bronco Bill," who had robbed a couple of trains in 1898 but had escaped the death penalty because he and Will Johnson had killed three members of a posse, and Bill had been convicted of second-degree murder only; or with Elza Lay, whose case had been broadly similar to that of "Bronco Bill"; or with Alverson, Hoffman, and Warderman, who had been convicted in a Federal court for a crime of which they were innocent and he was guilty. His last journey to Santa Fe was an uneventful one, but at Trinidad he had been heard to deride any notion that he would swing.

Hang a man for waylaying a railroad train? It was too ridiculous for words!

Chapter Fifteen

AN AMBUSH FOR GEORGE SCARBOROUGH

After the capture of Elza Lay at Chimney Wells, Tom Capehart rode hard across country until he reached the WS ranch in western Socorro County. At the horse camp, twenty miles from the ranch headquarters, he met Butch Cassidy, who had recently returned from Wyoming, pockets well-lined with his share of the loot from the Wilcox train robbery. Red Weaver was also in the locality, having reappeared in Alma shortly after parting from Marshal Foraker.

Will Carver, traveling by a more southerly route, vanished into Cochise County. With him were two or three willing recruits, one of whom was Ben Kilpatrick. These men were in close touch with the others. There were various rendezvous. One was in the Peloncillo Mountains, forty miles southwest of Frisco, New Mexico. The WS horse camp was another.

Still buried in the mountains of Colfax County was the booty from the second Folsom robbery, discarded by Carver and Lay through their need for as rapid a flight as Lay's partial incapacity would allow. The men planned to have the loot disinterred and distributed, but there were obvious difficulties. Carver could never again risk showing his face in the Cimarron area. Weaver, officially, had a clean bill of health in Colfax County, and probably wanted to get his hands on the lot; but he, too, could hardly expect to be seen there without attracting the wrong sort of interest. So, for the time being, the cache remained undisturbed.

In the meantime, there were other sources of revenue. Las Cruces, where Alverson, Hoffman, and Warderman had been convicted, had a bank owned by George D. Bowman & Son.

Shortly after two o'clock on Monday afternoon, February 12, 1900, two horsemen turned into Main street and rode slowly up to the bank. They were seen by "several parties at the Rio Grande Hotel," who attached no importance to them, "as there was nothing unusual in their appearance." The cream-colored horse ridden by one of the strangers attracted more notice than the two men.

— 132 —

The men dismounted and entered. Cashier James G. Freeman and the woman book-keeper were quickly covered by two six-shooters. Freeman dallied over opening the safe until one of the bandits snapped a pistol in his face a couple of times. The visitors cleared the safe of three or four thousand dollars, which included the payroll for the Torpedo mine, emptied the till, and left after counselling Freeman and his assistant not to make an outcry. Unconcerned bystanders watched them gallop out of town in the direction of the Organ Mountains.

Both men were unknown to the townspeople who saw them. There was never any positive identification but it is highly probable that one of them was Tom Capehart. William B. Childers, who had decided against having Capehart taken to Las Cruces for trial as an accessory to the robbery of the Stein's post office, might not have appreciated the humor of the new situation.

Pat Garrett's posse started out twenty minutes after the robbery. They never made up the time. Instead, they arrested eight or nine men, none of whom had anything whatsoever to do with the robbery. All were released almost at once, and three of them then threatened to sue the county. The posse also "arrested" three horses. One, a broken-down gray, Garrett tried to pass off as the cream horse; if the animal had looked to be cream-colored, he explained, it must have been because he had been ridden through a sand storm. The difference in movement, he said, could be accounted for by the horse being "fagged out" and "only grass fed." No one was quite sure about the color of the horse ridden by the second man; so Sheriff Garrett produced two: a white-faced sorrel and a dun with black mane and tail. The horses, like the men, were released for want of evidence. Newspaper comment, as was the style of the times, began by making it "a pretty safe wager that these bank robbers will soon be rounded up unless they made (sic) a successful dash across the line into Mexico," and closed a few days later with the opinion that "the men and money are gone, likely not to return." The bank, meanwhile, soothingly "adjusted" its loss to a mere $1100, less than one third of the sum first reported.

The two robbers did not make for the International Line. Garrett's posse lost track of them somewhere north and west of the Organ Mountains. Probably, as Garrett believed, they changed mounts in the Organs country, the animals used for the ride-in and getaway being returned to their owners and the bandits fleeing on the horses they had left earlier. They rode north and then west, crossed the Black Range, and finally disappeared in the Mogollons, near the Arizona line, having retraced the route they had taken on their way down to Las Cruces. Their escape was aided by the simple but effective system of horse relays which, from their point of view, had the further merit of ensuring the continued goodwill or, at worst, sufferance of the smaller range men who furnished many of their mounts. The bandits had set up a chain of informal remount stations during the ride to Las Cruces. Subsequently, in the course of their flight, they stopped at each of these to return the horses lent them for the corresponding stage of the first half of the round trip. This naturally meant that no one would lose his livestock for more than a week or two at the most. The bigger outfits, under absentee ownership, were treated less considerately.

As the two fleeing bank robbers bore on toward the Arizona line they were relentlessly shadowed by George Scarborough. Ben Kemp, a rancher in Socorro County with more than a nodding acquaintance with Tom Ketchum and his gang, later told his son of an unsought meeting with Scarborough which must have occurred shortly after the Las Cruces hold-up.

One day Scarborough and a companion rode onto Kemp's range. Kemp does not say whether or not there were a couple of worn-looking horses in his remuda which the officers would have noticed. At any rate, the men were looking for clues or information.

They found Kemp, and Scarborough began to upbraid him for helping the robbers. Kemp tartly replied that it was not his policy to fire questions at strangers who wanted food or shelter. There was really nothing more for Scarborough to say, but he was never one to give up.

Eight months after the Texas Canyon affair Scarborough, with Jeff Milton and Eugene Thacker, had run down "Bronco Bill," Will Johnson, and Daniel "Red" Pipkin, three train robbers who were in sojourn in Arizona after a series of crimes in New Mexico. Scarborough killed Johnson and gave 'Bronco Bill" the wound which effectually terminated an eleven-year career of lawlessness. Scarborough's most recent "exploit," at the time of the Las Cruces robbery, was the recapture of Pearl Hart, the noted "female stage robber." Pearl, in company with a habitual drunkard named Mike McGinnis, had escaped from Tucson. It was their ambition to reach Casas Grandes, and their misjudgment to break the journey at Deming. In the morning Officer Scarborough, learning that the two celebrities had hit town, barged into their hotel room. Pearl informed him, amid much profanity, that she had nothing to wear to jail, as all her clothes had been taken to the Chinese laundry. Scarborough insensitively ordered her to don Mike's garments and stood his ground until she complied. As usual, he had got his man.

During the weeks that followed the bank robbery he stayed on the prowl in western New Mexico, to the growing discomfort of Butch Cassidy, who felt that the officer was trying to corner him. Capehart, too, was sick of being dogged everywhere by Scarborough. In order to eliminate him the gang devised a lethal variant of hare and hounds, in which the roles of hunter and quarry were to be reversed at the kill. Brutal and calculating as their strategy was, its style was not altogether dissimilar to his own, and he ought not to have been deceived by it.

In the Burro Mountains, between Silver City and Lordsburg, Scarborough picked up the trail of three men whose identities he apparently did not know but whom he presumed to be rustlers. He followed the trail down toward Cochise County then, after an exchange of telegrams with Deputy Sheriff Walter Birchfield, secured transportation for his horse and himself from the Southern Pacific. Birchfield met him at San Simon and they struck across the valley for the Chiricahuas. They had not gone very far before they came upon the carcase of a freshly-slaughtered bullock. If Scarborough had any thoughts of giving up the chase, this ensured that he would put them out of his mind. But as the trail wound higher and higher into the mountains he became uneasy. He decided, too late, to turn back.

Near a place called Triangle Springs, some thirty miles from San Simon, the three men who had laid the trail and set the bait had a tryst with two or three others. Two of the gang rode a little way into a canyon, tethered their horses, and scaled the rocky face of the canyon to join their companions.

George Scarborough's progress as an exterminator of outlaws ended shortly before sundown, Tuesday, April 3rd, 1900, when he and Birchfield reined up sharply at the sight of the two saddled but riderless horses. Before he or Birchfield had grasped the situation the five or six outlaws, standing among the boulders high above, poured down a concentrated rifle fire. The two officers drew their revolvers and spurred their horses toward a cluster of rocks, but Scarborough was knocked out of the saddle by a 30-40 bullet before they could get there. As the officer tumbled to the ground, Capehart gave a great whoop. For Scarborough, it was like the huntsman's halloo. Birchfield dismounted, receiving a slight wound as he did so, and ran to help him. Although exposed to a sustained fusillade, Birchfield threw up a barrier of rocks and stones to shield Scarbrough and himself.

Besides Cassidy and Capehart, the ambush party contained Will Carver and at least one of the Kilpatrick brothers. Several, if not all of them, knew Birchfield and liked him. Capehart had worked for him on the Diamond A. They wanted very much to finish off Scarborough; but when it became evident that they would have to kill Birchfield, too, they sheered off. It is probable that they had been shooting around him rather than at him while he was building the wall of rocks. For his part, he did not inform his fellow-officers that he had recognized any of the attackers. But he did his best to save Scarborough.

When it was dark, Birchfield rode through snow and sleet to get help from the San Simon ranch headquarters. Scarborough, with an ugly wound in the leg, was unable to move. He was driven into San Simon and placed on the next train for Deming. Loss of blood and long hours of exposure to the cold had seriously weakened him. He died on Thursday, two days after the ambush.

Henry Brock, who heard the story of the shooting from Birchfield, maintained that his friend had deliberately led Scarborough into the trap: "He didn't tell me he got Scarborough up there in order to get him killed, because he didn't have to."

But it is obvious from Birchfield's actions that he was as surprised as was Scarborough. Brock himself related that Birchfield had improvised a shelter of rocks for Scarborough. The deputy would not have done this if he had been in league with the gang. Nor would he have undertaken a hard ride through foul weather to bring help to the stricken man. No doubt he disliked Scarborough, as Brock stated, and he might not have gone with him had he known whose trail they were following; but this does not mean that he would have involved himself in such underhand (and dangerous) work. Yet it is fair comment on Scarborough's standing that Brock, a well regarded cowman, not only believed what he did of Birchfield, but approved of it.

Shortly after this, Assistant Superintendent Frank Murray, of the Denver office of the Pinkerton agency, came to Alma to investigate reports that currency obtained in the Wilcox robbery were being passed in the locality. Some of it had turned up at the bank in Silver City. Others of the stolen bills had been handled by the store-keeper at Alma. Murray became quite friendly with Cassidy and Lowe while he pursued his enquiries, never suspecting that they were outlaws. The men he was trying to trace were cowboy friends of the gang, who had helped to change Cassidy's loot for him or were prepared to admit having spent the money. But Cassidy sold his saloon soon after Murray's departure and headed north with Red Weaver. Before they started out they stole all the horses from the — 02 ranch, owned by one Ashley, whose rustling activities had incurred their contempt and anger.

Cassidy rather despised and distrusted Red Weaver. By the time they rode into St. Johns, Arizona, he was seeking some way of ridding himself of Weaver's unwanted company. It so chanced that a local officer gave him his opportunity by arresting them both because they looked as though they might be thieves. Cassidy was able to persuade the man that he, Jim Lowe, was a bona-fide traveler. This fellow Weaver, Cassidy went on, had tagged on to him just down the road, and had struck him as a man whose recent history might bear some scrutiny. The grateful officer released Cassidy and held Weaver for further questioning.

Some time later William French learned that a couple of mysterious strangers, equipped with unusually large kyacks (panniers), had visited the camp of a survey party on the old Maxwell Grant. These kyacks were the match of a pair which French had given to Cassidy just before Butch and Red left. The rancher concluded that Cassidy and another man, probably Capehart, had reclaimed the buried Folsom loot. He may have been right; but it is evident that the task of removing the treasure was delegated to Red Weaver — who, of course, had suffered nothing worse than brief detention in St. John's — for, in the late summer or early autumn of 1900, Weaver again showed himself in Alma, well supplied with money and not caring who knew it.

The rest of the gang regrouped further north, probably at Hole-in-the-Wall, where they were joined by Harry Longbaugh, Harvey Logan, and William Cruzan.

Chapter Sixteen

"WILL YOU DIE GAME, BOYS?"

Harry Longbaugh, alias Harry Alonzo, alias Frank Jones, nicknamed "the Sundance Kid", had been a fugitive for ten years. His story, like that of most of his companions, could be told in just three words: cowboy, rustler, outlaw. In the summer of 1892, he was helping to rob stage coaches in Montana. On November 29th of that year he took part in the train robbery at Malta, Montana, on the Great Northern line. Nothing further was heard of his activities until June 27th, 1897, when he was one of the gang who raided the bank at Belle Fourche, South Dakota. He was jailed soon after this, but escaped. Since December, 1897, his movements had not been a matter for public notice.

Up to December, 1894, Harvey Logan, or "Kid Curry", gave no promise of the infamy that was to be his. But two days after that Christmas he rounded off the celebrations in Landusky, Montana, by killing Powell "Pike" Landusky, founder of the town. For the next two years or so he and his brother, Lonny, made their living as rustlers. Later he rode with Longbaugh and three others in the Belle Fourche robbery. Subsequently the Logans, Longbaugh, and George Curry joined Cassidy's gang. Harvey Logan is supposed to have been the outlaw who killed Josiah Hazen, a Wyoming sheriff, three days after the Wilcox robbery. In the spring of 1900 two officers were slain in Utah by a band of horse-thieves said to have been headed by Logan. Even disregarding the apocrypha, it is clear that he was one of the most ferocious and violent criminals of his day. His new partner, Bill Cruzan, had served three years in the Colorado State Penitentiary for Grand Larceny but had yet to graduate from rustling to highway robbery.

Wherever the meeting took place, the outcome was that the enlarged gang split into two groups, each with its own objective.

At 8.30 p.m. on Wednesday, August 29th, 1900, the second section of Union Pacific train No. 3, westbound, was held up just beyond Tipton station, Wyoming, by Harvey Logan, Ben Kilpatrick, Bill Cruzan, and an unidentified fourth man. Newspapers gave it out that the loot was

$55,000. Wells, Fargo said the robbers obtained only $50.14.

On September 2nd Logan, Kilpatrick, and Cruzan reached Jim Ferguson's ranch at the foot of Black Mountain, where they had planned the robbery. They hid out on the mountain for three weeks, waiting for the posses to disperse. At the end of the time Logan and Kilpatrick rode south. Cruzan accompanied them as far as eastern Utah, but then turned back.

In the meantime, on September 19th, Cassidy, Carver, and the Sundance Kid had stirred up some excitement of their own by robbing the bank at Winnemucca, Nevada, of more than $32,000. "Cowboy Bill" Carver, most uncharacteristically, was dressed like a hobo; right down to his hobnailed boots. On his way into town he killed a skunk, but did not come out of the encounter unmarked. For some time thereafter the outlaw could have been readily identified by the smell of his clothing.

Aside from Carver's encounter with the skunk, the entire operation was cleanly executed. About two weeks later the trio rejoined Logan and Kilpatrick, who had ridden down into southern Utah. Early in October the five crawled out of a side-door Pullman at Fort Worth, Texas. After exchanging their trampish apparel for the most fashionable gear on display, they set out for the red-light district and plunged into an orgy of dissipation and debauchery. Carver, using the name "Will Casey," went through a form of marriage with a whore called Lillie Davis. There followed a riotous "honeymoon" in Denver and Shoshone, Idaho, with Harvey Logan and one Maud Walker making up a foursome. But after several weeks of high living and free spending Carver and Logan simply gave the girls some money and jewelry and left them.

On November 21st the five outlaws, somewhat inebriated, visited a photographer's studio in Main street, Fort Worth. They placed an order for fifty prints but, realizing too late the folly of what they had done, did not go back for them.

Fred Dodge, the detective, got hold of the picture almost at once. It was not long before copies were being mailed to law-enforcement officials all over the West.

The gang broke up and scattered. Etta Place, an unusually attractive demi-mondaine, was traveling as Longbaugh's wife when Cassidy and the Kid left town for a trip East, with Argentina their ultimate destination.

Carver, Logan, and Ben Kilpatrick stayed in Texas. They celebrated Christmas in San Antonio, then moved on to San Angelo. Carver heard that Rufus Thomas, who had helped to capture Elza Lay, was now living in the neighborhood and decided to stalk him out. He found Thomas engaged at the poker table, and waited for him to get up from the table. After two whole days of hanging around he lost patience and left.

The three outlaws spent most of February in San Angelo and Knickerbocker, and most of March in the nearby village of Christoval. They drove from place to place in an elegant rubber-tired buggy, representing themselves as horse-dealers. In mid-March they appeared in Sonora, where they purchased a sorrel horse, saying that they thought it might make a good polo pony.

Carver was known personally to a good many people in that country, and Ben Kilpatrick was hardly a newcomer. It is doubtful whether even those who had never met them before gave any credence to their yarn that they were traders buying polo ponies for an outfit in Iowa. The bandits must have figured that the publicity aroused by their recent crimes and the distribution of the photograph taken in Fort Worth would do them no harm in this section of Texas. Carver's status would be precisely what it had been when he was riding with the Ketchums: so long as he and his partners got up to no mischief near home, hardly anyone would interfere with them.

This placid picture was ruined, allegedly, by the outsider, Harvey Logan, who was passing as "Walker" in some places and as "McDonald" in others.

In the last week of March the gang showed up at the Kilpatrick farm in Concho County. Ed Kilpatrick was there, along with the rest of the family. The outlaws meant to lie low for a while before riding out to strike at some train or bank.

There were no impartial witnesses to the incident which disrupted the plans of the gang. The details depend wholly on the word of several of the Kilpatricks who, truthfully or otherwise, testified that the stranger called "Walker" was the guilty party.

On Wednesday, the 27th, Harvey Logan was in the yard of the Kilpatrick place with Ben, Ed, and George. The four were engrossed in a game of croquet when a man named Oliver Thornton came up and ordered the Kilpatricks to keep their hogs from straying onto the pasture of his employer, Ed Dozier. Harvey Logan was armed, even at croquet. Instead of staying out of the quarrel, he drew his gun. Thornton started to run and Logan killed him.

Carver, Logan, and Ben Kilpatrick quickly harnessed their team to the buggy, threw their saddles and range clothing inside, and drove away.

George Kilpatrick arranged to pack some provisions and meet them later on the T Half-Circle range, south of Eldorado. Ed Kilpatrick apparently wanted nothing to do with it, perhaps because there were no charges against him.

The three drove at speed, stopping twice to cut telephone wires. They bought a horse or two in Eldorado, then stole a quarter of beef from the T Half-Circle. Five or six days after the murder they drove into a thicket of live oak, abandoning the vehicle in a small clearing. Here they hastily donned range costume, saddled the horses, and rode on to meet George Kilpatrick. They did not clip the wires between Eldorado and Sonora. This was either a foolish oversight or a serious error of judgment for, late in the afternoon of Tuesday, April 2nd, a call from the T Half-Circle warned Sheriff Elijah S. Briant of Sutton County that the suspects were headed south, toward Sonora. At about eight o'clock that night Carver and George Kilpatrick rode into town, leaving Logan and Ben to wait for them a short distance outside.

Common belief was that the four men were planning to rob the new bank there. While the gang probably had examined the prospects offered by the bank it seems more logical that they were now on their way to Val Verde County to hold up the Southern Pacific. Carver and Kilpatrick wanted nothing more than a few supplies; even after nightfall, they were reluctant to show themselves in the center of town. They first entered a Mexican store on the outskirts, where they purchased some baking powder but failed to obtain the oats they needed for the horses. The two men then tried to buy the grain from a livery stable opposite the bank. Here, too, the owner was unable to oblige; so they rode down the street to Jack Owen's bakery. It never occurred to Carver, a hunted man for four years and seldom so hunted as he was in these last few days, that one of them ought to have stayed outside to keep watch. They had not been in town for more than a few minutes, but it had been long enough for Carver to be recognized as one of the "rubber-tired outfit." The officers were converging upon the bakery while Carver unconcernedly helped the storekeeper to pour grain into the sack.

Sheriff Briant was accompanied by Constable W.D. Thompson and Deputy Sheriffs Henry Sharp and J. L. Davis. Since they were not absolutely sure that these men were two of those wanted for questioning about the Thornton murder, Thompson walked over to inspect the horses. One of them, a sorrel fifteen hands high, he knew for the animal which the men had bought in Sonora a fortnight earlier. This eased away the last shred of doubt.

Sharp was stationed by the side door of the bakery. The other three stepped up to the front door, drawing their pistols before they reached the threshold.

Carver was still at the counter. Kilpatrick was standing nearer the front door. Neither was on the alert as the officers closed in.

When Briant ordered them to throw up their hands Carver instantly let go of the sack and grabbed his Colt .45. As the outlaw was raising the gun, and before he had cocked it, Briant shot him in the right arm and through the lung. Carver dropped the gun and fell. Although there was a double-action Smith & Wesson .38 in his belt, within easy reach of his left hand, he did not try to draw it. He was groping for the Colt when Sharp rushed in and kicked it away. Kilpatrick had responded to the command with the inarticulate, indeterminate movement of a man who did not know whether to fight or surrender. He was immediately shot down by Thompson.

All four officers kept firing until both Carver and Kilpatrick lay still. They were disarmed, carried to the courthouse, and stretched out on the floor. Both were alive. Carver, under sedation, and apparently oblivious of his surroundings, poured out bitter, forlorn words fashioned from hopeless courage and wilful defiance.

"Keep shooting them, boys . . . will you stay with me? . . . will you sweat it out? . . . die game, boys."

Many believed that Carver was "Walker," the murderer of Oliver Thornton. This was denied by both Kilpatrick and Carver himself. Carver insisted that his name was "Franks," until he could see from the number of his acquaintances among the visitors that it would be useless to disown his true identity any further.

He had seven wounds. His right arm was broken in two places, and so was his left leg. Only the first bullet from Briant, which had penetrated the lung, had inflicted a mortal wound. Carver breathed his last at about eleven o'clock that night. His personal estate was insignificant: a few items of expensive jewelry; a horse, with saddle and accoutrements; twenty-five dollars in cash; two gold certificates; his two revolvers and a derringer.

George Kilpatrick had been shot five times. He recovered and was released, since he was innocent of complicity in the Thornton murder. But this narrow escape from an ignominious death did not blunt George's aspirations to outlawry. Two or three years later he began to make some progress in the career which had been retarded by the intervention of Elijah Briant and his men.

Will Carver had been dead for less than a week when luck turned sour on Red Weaver.

For six months or so, Red had disported himself as would befit a gentleman of wealth and leisure, revelling in his position as resident badman of Alma, New Mexico. He was arrested once and charged with horse-theft but of course had no difficulty in raising bond. Then one night he attended a dance in Alma and turned his charm on Lydia Sipes, a relative of the three Holomon brothers, who did a little ranching and some rustling in the neighborhood. Pad, the youngest of the three brothers, objected strongly to Red's behavior and the outlaw was put out into the road. On the following day, Sunday, Weaver caught Holomon in the store, struck him in the face, drew his gun, and demanded satisfaction. Pad claimed to be unarmed but offered to settle up with Weaver in the morning.

Although Weaver was regarded as a four-flusher by Cassidy and William French, no one doubted that he was much too tough for the likes of Pad Holomon. As the hours dragged by, Holomon's friends urged the youth to get out of town while he still had a whole skin. He stobbornly refused to go. By daybreak, however, he had thought it over; and the more he thought about it, the more scared he became. At last he went outside and began to walk toward his horse, carrying his cocked 30-30 in one hand. Weaver was standing in the street, bent on cancelling out his obligation to young Holomon. Pad, turning a corner, saw him at once and instinctively fired from the hip. He did not take aim; he was so frightened that he did not realize he had pulled the trigger. Yet there lay Red Weaver, stone dead, with an undischarged six-shooter beside him and a red splash upon his forehead. In law, it was a simple case of self-defense; in fact, it was a sheer fluke. Thus passed Bruce Weaver, on Monday, April 8th, 1901, to the loss or personal regret of no one.

Tom Ketchum might have sneered at the profligate rashness of Will Carver's last months; probably he had never thought very highly at all of Red Weaver. But from the standpoint forced upon him by his predicament, he must have envied them the style of their taking off. Yet, since a man cannot change the cards he has been dealt, he could do no more than try to play a bad hand well.

"I believe I'll keep my nerve", he had remarked to Saturnino Pinard and his deputy, Tom Gray, when they were returning him to Santa Fe after his trial and conviction. During the long months of his imprisonment, he rarely showed any sign of giving way to fear. When the time came, he too would die game.

Chapter Seventeen

OFF WITH HIS HEAD

Twenty months and a few days spanned Tom Ketchum's arrest and his dispatch into the hereafter. This allowed him ample time for reflection, but he never yielded to repentance. He regretted nothing except that he had been caught and that he had not killed Harrington or Kirchgrabber. He felt sour towards Bronco Bill and Elza Lay because they were merely serving out terms of imprisonment—yet he would declare that he would rather be hanged than die of old age in a prison cell.

At intervals news would come through of his former associates. Bud Upshaw had been arrested at Globe, Arizona, on December 6, 1899. W. H. Kelly was taken into custody at Penasco, New Mexico, on the same day. Dave Atkins was traced to Butte, Montana, and captured on March 12, 1900. All three were claimed by the authorities of Tom Green County to face trial for the murder of "Jap" Powers. There was no move to extradite Tom from New Mexico to Texas, probably because it was realized in San Angelo that such a request would stand no chance of being honored.

Ketchum outlived both Will Carver and Red Weaver, but only by a few weeks. He affirmed his belief that "the gang" would rescue him, and many of the officers feared that he might have genuine cause for optimism. Their worries, although perhaps understandable, were wholly irrational; as far as is known, the dwindling and scattered remnants of the outlaw freemasonry never even gave a thought to helping Ketchum escape.

In appealing to the Supreme Court of the Territory, Ketchum's attorneys again invoked the eighth amendment to the Constitution of the United States, contending that the death penalty was a "cruel and unusual" punishment for the offense charged. Bunker and Guyer submitted this argument on January 25th, 1901, before Justices Crumpacker, McFie, McMillan, and Parker. It had not swayed Chief Justice Mills, the trial judge, and it did not impress the Supreme Court. The plea was rejected, and official policy coldly restated, in the opinion delivered by Justice Frank W. Parker. Three years earlier Parker had shown, by his reaction to the acquittal of the men falsely accused of having held up the mail train at Stein's Pass, that he was hardly a fountain of objectivity. His response to the plea of Ketchum's attorneys was reasoned but inexorable. He cited the judgment in the case of William Kemmler, the first man to die in the electric chair, discussed three rulings of the Appeal Court of the Commonwealth of Massachusetts, and went on to quote the comments of the judge who had handed down the opinion in the cause of the State of Missouri v. Williams:

> The interdict if the Constitution [is] against the infliction of cruel and unusual punishments as amount to torture, or such as would shock the mind of every man possessed of common feeling, such for instance as drawing or quartering the culprit, burning him at the stake, cutting off his nose, ears, or limbs, starving him to death, or such as was inflicted by an act of Parliament as late as the 22 Henry VIII, authorizing one Rouse to be thrown into boiling water and boiled to death for the offense of poisoning the family of the Bishop of Rochester. . . .

Parker cited a number of other cases before stating his views on the act of 1887:

> It is hardly necessary to recall the incidents attending the ordinary train robbery, which are a matter of common history, to assure everyone that the punishment presribed by this statute is maost salutary provision and eminently suited to the offense which it is designed to meet. Trains are robbed by armed bands of desperate men, determined upon the accomplishment of their purpose, and nothing will prevent the consummation of their design, not even the necessity to take human life . . . If the express messenger or train crew resist their attack upon the cars, they promptly kill them. In this and many other ways they display their utter disregard for human life and property. . . .

His colleagues concurred with his opinion that the statute was "not in violation of the eighth amendment to the Constitution of the United States" and it was ordered that the sentence be executed on March 22nd. But late in February the execution was postponed until March 27th, and on March 19th Governor Otero granted a stay of thirty days to give Ketchum's attorneys an opportunity to produce new evidence. It is not apparent what sort of evidence they were looking for, as the case against Ketchum was absolutely clear-cut. About all they could hope for was that Tom might part with enough information to induce the Governor to exercise clemency. In default of this, Ketchum would hang on April 26th.

During his eighteen months as a prisoner in the Territorial Penitentiary, Ketchum received numerous visitors. Some of these were officers who tried to sound him on the activities and associates of various outlaws still at large. One whose motives were rather different was Ben Clark, Sheriff of Graham County, Arizona. In April 1897 Clark, then a deputy under William Birchfield, was a member of the posse which killed Black Jack Christian. Nearly thirty years later Clark wrote that he visited Ketchum "in order to remove all doubt" as to the identity of Black Jack. This makes very little sense. Clark had seen the body of the man slain by the posse, and if there were doubts about the identity of the dead outlaw they were not going to be resolved by an inspection of Tom Ketchum. No matter; Clark visited Ketchum, in company with Sheriff E.L. Hubbell, of Bernalillo County, New Mexico, and listened attentively while Tom gave them an untruthful account of his movements in Arizona.

Miguel A. Otero, Jr., the six year old son of the Governor, was a regular visitor to the outlaw's cell and Tom, apparently, always liked to see him and would reminisce to him at some length. J. S. "Rox" Grumbles, a prominent cattleman from Lincoln County, called on Ketchum a number of times. Grumbles was "much of a warbler," according to Jack Culley, and Tom would get him to sing a ballad" "with a sad refrain at the end of each verse about 'a prisoner for life'."

Berry Ketchum went along to the penitentiary on one occasion, but Tom refused to see him. More than this; he charged that Berry had introduced Sam and himself to train robbery. The three of them, Tom alleged, had obtained about a hundred thousand dollars, but Berry had held onto nearly all of it in order to set himself up as "a real Christian gentleman."

This was fabrication, but it may have been engendered by a genuine sense of injury. Envy of the respected and prosperous elder brother could not have wholly accounted for his malevolence.

Whatever reasons underlay Tom's animosity toward him, Berry went to Governor Otero to express his disappointment. Before he left Santa Fe he gave the warden some money, to be spent on keeping Tom well provided with candy and cake and such trifles.

There was never any possibility that the sentence would be commuted by the Governor. Yet there were grounds, constitutionally unassailable, on which a reprieve could have been secured without recourse to Otero.

In law, any bill passed by the Territorial Legislature was invalid until it had been ratified by Congress. The statute which stipulated the death penalty for those convicted of train robbery had not been presented for ratification. Technically, therefore, it was null and void. In the event, Bunker and Guyer did not cite the point until Ketchum was beyond their help. Perhaps it did not occur to them in time; perhaps, on the other hand, they felt constrained from using the argument by the enormity of its implications.

As the day appointed for the execution drew close, the authorities, preserving as much secrecy as was possible, laid out plans for the delivery of Tom Ketchum from the Territorial Penitentiary to the Union County Jail. At midday on Tuesday, April 23rd, Ketchum was told he would be leaving for Clayton that afternoon—two days earlier than had been advertised. Shortly after three o'clock, he was placed, heavily manacled, in a steel-lined mail car. Among the guards were Sheriff Harry C. Kinsell, of Santa Fe; Salome Garcia, who, as Sheriff of Union County, was to act as executioner; Tom A. Gray, Garcia's deputy; H.J. Chambers, a detective from Chicago, who had been invited to assist Garcia in the hanging; W. H. Reno, as official representative of the Colorado and Southern Railway; Joe Napier; Harry Lewis; and Sheriff Putnam, of Elbert County, Colorado. The prisoner, it was reported, "chaffed good-naturedly" with his escort and "nonchalantly said good-bye" to the officials of the penitentiary.

He was taken to Clayton via Lamy Junction, Las Vegas, Raton, and Trinidad. The strained nerves of the guards were badly jarred when the train came to a sudden and unscheduled halt on the stiffest grade on the Raton Pass. For a few moments they imagined that friends of Ketchum, bent on a rescue act, had held up the train.

"I don't want ever to be so scared again," said Joe Napier, in relating the incident to Jack Culley. "A rescue by Tom Ketchum's gang wasn't goin' to be a garden party exactly. I don't reckon it was more than a few minutes till we knowed what had happened, but it seemed to me a week."

The cause of the delay was soon found to be a minor and rather commonplace accident: the couplings had broken apart on the grade, cutting off the car occupied by Ketchum and his guards. It was a simple matter to reconnect the train, and the journey was completed without further alarum.

At half-past five on Wednesday morning Ketchum rode into Clayton for the last time. He noted the stockade which had been erected outside the courthouse yard to prevent all but the privileged holders of tickets from witnessing his final moments, and suggested that it should be torn down so that everyone could watch. He was given permission to examine the scaffold and eyed it critically.

"It looks good," he opined. "But I think they ought to hang Harrington on it first, and if it works all right, they might try me."

Eight o'clock on the Friday morning was the time set for the execution. Ketchum retained throughout both his composure and his waggish if somewhat malicious sense of humor. He slept soundly and ate heartily of the food carried to the jail from the Eklund Hotel. Altogether he was more assured and at ease than those who were charged with the task of accomplishing his quietus.

There were officers everywhere in town. Two men were posted on either side of the gate to the prison yard. It was their duty to turn away anyone who could not show a pass, and to admit no one without having first made a search for weapons. Otero, still afraid that the plans might fall awry in spite of all the elaborate precautions, sent Lewis "Cap" Fort to Clayton with instruction to supervise Sheriff Garcia's preparations for the execution. Fort, Garcia, and Chambers, it turned out, held very diverse opinions on the rudiments of an art in which none of them was expert.

A fifteen foot rope, "of first class Manila hemp," had been supplied at a cost of $20.80 by the Chief of Police at Kansas City, along with a suggestion that there should be a drop of seven feet. Chambers disagreed emphatically; as he saw it, "four feet six inches would be plenty for a man of Ketchum's weight — 193 pounds." Fort then lengthened it to five feet six inches, only for Garcia to extend it by a further six inches. Fort and Chambers, perhaps anxious to have the final say, then got together and altered it to five feet nine inches. There the grisly comedy was concluded.

Sheriff Garcia, already nervous, was thrown into consternation by a message, bearing what appeared to be the signature of Governor Otero and the Great Seal of New Mexico, which ordered him to postpone the execution for another thirty days, at the request of President McKinley. The telegram was handed to Garcia at about eight o'clock on Thursday night. He wired Otero for confirmation, and received a disclaimer. The author of the "bogus respite" was never unmasked. Whoever he was, he caused a good deal of excitement and succeeded in allowing Ketchum to remain breathing for five hours longer than the authorities had decreed.

No Baptist minister squandered his time by visiting the outlaw; if the tenets of that faith had ever drawn any credence from Tom Ketchum.

he had long since disencumbered himself of these and all other religious pretensions. As was usual in such circumstances, a Catholic priest undertook to interest himself in Tom's future welfare. Father Dean's efforts met with an immediate and decisive rebuff.

On Thursday night Tom was asked whether he wanted to see a priest. He replied that he would rather have some music; but they sent the priest in to him anyway. Dean began by inviting the condemned man to make his confession. Tom signified his willingness to do this, provided only that the priest would confess to him too. If the priest would get a fiddler, added Ketchum, they could dance together.

Tom Ketchum slept well that night, and ate well on the morrow. Attired in a black suit and white shirt, with a black tie and black Oxford shoes, he would make a neatly turned out corpse. At about 9.30 a.m. John Guyer called to see him, accompanied by Albert Thompson and several newspapermen from out of town. Earlier Tom had intimated to Guyer that he wanted to make a statement about the Stein's Pass hold-up. This was the first item of the day. The message was addressed to President McKinley, drafted by Guyer, and signed by Ketchum. A copy was handed to the press at ten o'clock.

> ... There are now three men in the Santa Fe penitentiary, serving sentences for the robbery of the United States mail at Stein's Pass, Ariz., (sic), in 1897, viz: Leonard Alverson, Walter Hoffman and Bill Warderman. They are as innocent of the crime as unborn babes.
> The names of the men who committed the crime are Dave Atkins, Ed Bullin, Will Carver, Sam Ketchum, Bronco Bill and myself. I have given to my attorney in Clayton means by which articles taken in said robbery may be found where we hid them, and also the names of witnesses who live in that vicinity, who will testify that myself and gang were in that neighborhood both immediately before and after the robbery.
> ... I wish to do this much in the interest of these innocent men, who, as far as I know, never committed a crime in their lives. ...

Probably it was nothing more than spite which led Tom to implicate "Bronco Bill" in the Stein's Pass affair. While Bill's whereabouts at the time of the hold-up are unknown, it seems plain enough that there were only five of the robbers and that he was not among them. It is likely, too, that the first meeting between Ketchum and he occurred in the penitentiary at Santa Fe.

Afterwards he talked to the reporters in the jail corridor. He spoke scathingly of Berry:

"The assistance he has rendered me in my present trouble was to send me $150. I don't call that much".

His sentence, he thought, was "a little unjust" for the crime:

"The lawmakers of this Territory did not make the laws to protect the people, but to protect the moneyed corporations".

"The crimes that I have committed", he continued, "I do not deny at all — none of them:" but before he finished speaking he had denied some of them.

After giving a detailed account of the Stein's Pass episode he reiterated that he had not meant to wound the mail clerk, Fred Bartlett in his last hold-up. Next he discussed Black Jack, refused to divulge his real name but maintained that he was not the man killed near Clifton in 1897 and that he was still alive.

"There are a dozen men in southern Arizona who will swear that I and Black Jack are two different persons," he said. This was an understatement—but none of them had thought enough of Ketchum to come forward with this information after his arrest. Black Jack, he said, "was the cause of my becoming an outlaw. Les Dow, the officer, saw Black Jack at the Deer Creek tank affair, and in 1898 he told me that if I was ever tried for Black Jack's crimes I would never get free, for I looked too much like him. I thought if I was going to be hanged for another man's crimes I might as well have some of my own". But Ketchum had been a fugitive killer for eight months when Black Jack's gang began operations. Moreover, it seems unlikely that he and Dow could have had any such conversation, as the officer had returned to Eddy almost directly after the fight and was murdered there less than three months later. Tom erred in citing 1898 as the year, for Dow had been killed in February of 1897.

There followed assorted lies:

"I never killed anyone in my life, and never shot but three men in my life.

"I know exactly who killed Herzstein at Liberty in 1895 (1896); but I don't wish to tell you. They are men I don't wish to get into trouble. I was crippled in Texas at the time. Then the men who committed that murder are alive and free. Yes, Sir; alive and got their liberty, while I have merely tried to hold up a railroad train and have got to die for it." He declared that he was in Alamosa, in southern Colorado, at the time of the first of the three hold-ups near Folsom, but generously gave himself credit for having planned the robbery. Next, he proceeded to accusations of the sort which have always been difficult to substantiate:

"I feel that my attorneys did all they possibly could, but the prosecuting attorney and all were bought by the railroad company, and it was cut and dried from start to finish to hang me. I believe they used money during the execution and conviction both. I have been told that, but I do not wish to tell exactly who told me. I have been told that they put up money to Mills and to others to prosecute me: also that they put up money to see that the execution went off."

Before he moved on from the general to the particular he referred to the personal oversight over which he had brooded ever since his arrest:

"If I had known that it was a capital offense for robbing a train in your Territory I would certainly have killed someone." Very glib; as he said, he could easily have shot down Kirchgrabber, or Drew, or Scanlon, after Harrington had wounded him: but the chances are that, at the time, he was too badly hurt to think of anything but flight.

"I feel sore against Harrington," he vouchsafed. "And hope that I will meet him in hell inside of six months. I also hold ill will against old Fort and against Reno, and hope that I will be able to meet them there inside of a year... I think I will have a supper ordered for them." Fort and Reno, no doubt, were gratified by the degree of magnanimity afforded them.

"I can't tell exactly, but I believe if there is a hell there will be a lot of people out of this Territory that will go there.... My belief is to treat everybody right. I can take the Bible and prove or disprove anything. From reading the Bible, if I profess any religion, it will be the Holiness religion.

Having delivered himself of these thoughts on hell, life, and divinity, he spoke briefly of the Powers murder. At no point did he mention the killings at Camp Verde or the train robberies in Texas.

Both Pinard and Garcia, he admitted, had treated him well. In fact, he left everything he owned to Saturnino Pinard. He recalled a jest made by Will Carver one day when the gang were hiding out in Hole-in-the-Wall, probably in the winter of 1898-99: "Tom, if the law ever captures and hangs you, come back and tell me how it feels. I might want to try it myself some day!" One good thing about going to hell, he then remarked, was that he would have two good arms after he got there.

A photographer took two pictures of him. He asked for copies to be sent to a kinswoman, Eva Prodman, who was living in Lodi, California, and to Lee Smith, an old friend in San Saba County.

"Bronco Bill told me before leaving Santa Fe prison that if it did not hurt to let him know as he wanted to be hung, too," he confided, with another flash of spite toward the man whose great offense, in Ketchum's eyes, was not that he had killed, but that he had dodged the scaffold.

Guyer, a good amateur musician, had sent for his violin and a guitar player named Epimenio. Together, at Tom's request, they played "Just as the Sun Went Down." The outlaw listened in silence as they played the Amelia Waltzes and the "Mocking Bird" with variations. He was served fried chicken for dinner and attacked it with relish, avowing that he didn't "want to go to hell hungry because it's a long time till supper." Guyer waited for him to finished before saying goodbye:

"Well, Tom, I've done all I could for you and unless you especially request it, I do not want to see the end. I feel that I cannot witness your execution."

They shook hands and Tom answered, "Yes, Guyer, you have done for me all any man could have done. I will not ask you to see me die."

Guyer must have been alone in his sensibility that day. As the hour approached, just about everyone else became affected by a craving to partake vicariously in the forthcoming event.

All the stores were closed. The saloons were open and trading briskly. Idle talk flowed with the liquor. It was generally held that the man should not die for the crime of which he had been convicted, but probably few of those present thought too strongly about the issue. The atmosphere, as reconstructed by the newspaper reporters—none of them strangers to hyperbole—was that of a macabre and somewhat muted carnival.

At about twelve o'clock the first of the invited guests sauntered into the stockade. Several photographers were perched upon a platform above the wall of the jail. One man set up his camera by a gap in the fence but the hole was covered and he had to seek a vantage point elsewhere. By one o'clock the yard was over-run with expectant onlookers, including some latecomers without tickets. Almost the last to arrive was Dug Clark, a cowpuncher from one of the ranches over the Colorado line. He was known to a number of people in Clayton; but none of the assembled officers had ever seen him before and they watched him keenly as he walked over "to a spot where he could command a good view of the jail door and of the scaffold."

The scaffold stood close to the north wall of the jail. From the windows on the second floor of the courthouse, almost directly above the gallows, Cap Fort, Albert Thompson, and several others watched for the appearance of the principal actor and his entourage. Sheriff O.T. Clark of Las Animas County, Colorado, was waiting on the scaffold. So was the priest, whose patience evidently exceeded his powers of persuasion. The crowd was tense and quiet. Those who were unable to get into the yard gathered in morbid little groups outside the stockade and on the sidewalks, or simply stayed in the saloons.

The morning had been clear and bright. At one o'clock the sun lay shrouded and the wind skimmed the dusty prairie in sharp gusts from the south, scattering sand and grit amongst the crowd. The wind was buffeting the stockade at thirteen minutes past one when the door of the jail opened and Tom Ketchum emerged, flanked by Sheriff Garcia and Detective Chambers and followed by several deputies and jailors. Although his left arm was chained to his side, he walked firmly to the corner of the jail. There, it seemed to those who were nearby, "a distinct and unmistakable look of recognition" passed between Ketchum and the cowpuncher. Without pausing, Ketchum turned the corner and quickly ascended the thirteen steps.

Besides Ketchum himself, the party on the scaffold comprised Sheriffs Garcia and Clark, Detective Chambers, Trinidad C. de Baca, Doctor J.C. Clark, and Father Dean. Reymundo Arguello, the jailor, was standing against the wall below, with John McCandless and a Doctor Slack. McCandless was to lift the body and Arguello would cut the rope when Slack pronounced Ketchum dead.

Ketchum had declined to address the crowd. He stepped directly onto the trap and looked down.

"It's all right," he said, perhaps relieved because he could safely stand there. He told Garcia that he wanted no pictures taken, but the photographers were already snapping away and nothing could or would be done to stop them. He had another request to make:

"Please dig my grave very deep."

Then, or so it was thought, "his eyes straightway sought the stalwart cowpuncher and rested upon him with a peculiar expression for fully ten seconds," the other man returning the look.

"Hurry up, boys," he said impatiently, as they were binding his legs, "Get this over with."

The noose was pulled down and adjusted, Tom helpfully moving his head from side to side. Finally the black hood shut out his view of the prairie beyond the stockade.

Garcia, grasping the hatchet, was standing by the control rope. Because the thought of the part he must play had made him nervous, he had fortified himself from the bottle and was now "a little tipsy."

"Are you ready?" he inquired.

"Ready. Let 'er go," Ketchum muttered through the hood.

Tom needed all his nerve. Garcia took a huge swing at the control rope and missed it, burying the blade deep into the boards.

Beneath the scaffold the crowd was laughing and smiling while Garcia was struggling frantically to wrench the hatchet loose. A witness reported that it took the sheriff several minutes to tear it clear, and it must have seemed so; but actually the time was just seventeen minutes past one when Garcia was ready to try again. His second blow smote cleanly through the twine, the trap flew back, and Ketchum plunged downward—all the way to the ground.

The spectators in the yard saw the body jerk, then tumble toward the earth, to alight on its feet for an instant before it pitched forward, blood spurting forth from the black cap.

Unbeknown to the sheriff, his father, young Fructuoso Garica was watching through a large knothole in the fence. Fructuoso admitted to feeling faint. Someone behind the courthouse windows, seeing the rope leap up, went hysterical with rage. Thinking that Ketchum had survived the drop, the man yelled: "Hang him again! Hang him again!"

As Fructuoso Garcia remembers it another voice, or perhaps the same one, bawled: "Get another rope for that son of a bitch. Let's hang him right this time."

The words of Reymundo Arguello tell most accurately and most vividly just how Ketchum died, and give the nay to at least one hardy tradition:

> ... Then Sheriff Garcia cut the rope. We were under there waiting. It was awful down there. I was scared. Then the body came hurtling through the trap door. The body didn't stop and hang as I thought it would. I was supposed to cut the rope after McCandless lifted the body up. I reached down and turned the body over. Blood spurted out. It went all over my clothes. I looked away, toward the photographers. In the pictures my eyes stuck out of my head. The head [Ketchum's] didn't fall over one side and the body the other, as people say. The black hood was pinned to Black Jack's shirt with *muy grande* pins, horse blanket pins, I guess. If those pins hadn't held the hood in place the head would have rolled away. It had been jerked off right where the hair comes around.

Officers looked about them for the cowpuncher, whom they were convinced was one of Ketchum's gang, but he was gone. Days later they learned his identity. There is no explanation for the apparent understanding between Ketchum and Clark. They may have known each other; or the entire scene could have been a delusion projected in overstressed minds.

Dr Slack had not needed to feel Ketchum's pulse, but the county required his services in another capacity. He was asked to sew the head onto the trunk, and did so most skilfully.

The crowd had dispersed quickly. Not all of them returned to the saloons. One, a lawyer, arrived home with his shoes all bloody. His wife made him wash them in a trough before she permitted him to enter the house by the back door. His nine year old daughter, now Clara Toombs Harvey, also brought back first-hand knowledge of the hanging. She had been out riding, and happened to be passing the stockade when the trap dropped.

At half-past two the plain white coffin was lifted onto a spring wagon and trundled out of the courthouse yard. Fort and Thompson followed this informal hearse to a hill some way north of town, arriving just as the gravedigger was about to lay the coffin to earth. The casket was opened at Fort's behest and the men started down at the remains, admiring the dexterous handiwork which had restored the head to the body. Then the lid was replaced, the coffin lowered, and the soil shovelled into the hollow. There was no mourner, no minister, and no monument for Tom Ketchum.

Billy Reno, the great man of words, proclaimed loudly and at length that he disbelieved practically everything Ketchum had said. Perhaps, when all the circumstances are taken into account, he had an excuse for scoffing even at those of Tom's statements which were quite truthful.

Many theories were tendered as explanation of why Ketchum was decapitated. It was intended that way to ensure a mercifully instantaneous death; it was intended that way to ensure that Ketchum should not set up a precedent by surviving the drop—these were the premises of two of the numerous conjectures.

A more tenable hypothesis was argued thus: On the Thursday night the officials decided to test the rope, or the mechanism, by attaching a two hundred pound sandbag to the noose and dropping it through the trap. The rehearsal went off beautifully, but the participants neglected to remove the sack. In the morning the rope was as rigid as wire.

Some maintained that Tom had hurled himself forward when the trap dropped, so as to be sure of avoiding death by suffocation. This would have been a rare feat, more especially because his legs were bound.

The explanation most commonly accepted was the obvious one: between them Fort, Garcia, and Chambers had hopelessly botched the job. Several newspapermen reported that the drop was one of seven feet. If this were true, it would seem that, after Fort and Chambers had set the drop at five feet and nine inches, someone must have meddled with the apparatus yet again. So, either the Chief of Police at Kansas City, who had recommended a seven-foot drop, did not know what he was talking about, or something must have been amiss with the rope. An unidentified newspaperman who telegraphed the story to the San Francisco *Chronicle* implied as much: he reported that "the noose was made so it slipped easily. . . . the weight of the body, with the easy-running noose, caused the rope to cut the head clean off." Clearly, he meant that the rope had been treated. In his manuscript, though not in his book, Albert Thompson was more specific. According to him, the substance used was soap, and the man who applied it was Sheriff Garcia. Thompson said that Garcia, "mortally afraid" that some of Ketchum's erstwhile running-mates would attempt a rescue, "decided to soap the rope to make sure that it slipped properly."

In the end, the blame rested with Fort, since he was the Governor's emissary, sent out to make sure that there were no mistakes. Garcia, however, was the main target of the critics. One newspaperman went so far as to say that the sheriff planned to present the rope to his daughter as a keepsake. Garcia's response to the sneers and accusations was ineffable:

> Tom Ketchum's head being severed from his body was caused by him (sic) being a very heavy man. Nothing out of the ordinary happened. No bungling whatever. Everything worked nicely and in perfect order. Salome Garcia, Sheriff.

Although the means may have been questionable—perhaps "cruel and unusual", even—the result was beyond all quibble: the worst desperado and killer in the Southwest was no more.

Yet, though in a grotesque way, those who had prophesied against the event were proved right. Gerome Shields had offered to bet boxes of cigars against it, many other officers had predicted against it, and Tom Ketchum himself had repeatedly made his promises against it.

They never hanged him.

Chapter Eighteen

EMPTY SADDLES AND LONELY GRAVES

It was, perhaps, as much a sign of the changing times as an argument for the deterrent effect of capital punishment that there was no really serious outbreak of outlawry in New Mexico after the execution of Tom Ketchum. Several banks were robbed during the early 1900's, there were numerous minor hold-ups, and in July of 1904 a Rock Island train was held up and robbed at Logan, north east of Tucumcari. This rather spoiled the theory that Ketchum's fate, and the retention of the law which had brought it upon him, had guaranteed the railroads immunity from the attentions of bandits. One man who thought that New Mexico was still the land of opportunity for the would-be outlaw was Ed Kilpatrick, brother of Ben and George. He left Texas, took the name "Ed McCorkle," and teamed up with Henry Hawkins, once leader of the "Mesa Hawks," a bunch of third-rate bad actors whose operations had attracted a lot of publicity for a few weeks in the winter of 1901-02. On Wednesday afternoon, December 10th, 1902, Hawkins and Kilpatrick stuck up the Sierra County Bank at Hillsboro. They rode out of town with several thousand dollars, vanished somewhere beyond the Black Range, and were never caught. But exploits such as this were few, for the outlaw game was getting to be a hard one to play in New Mexico. Elsewhere, too, trains would still be held up, or occasionally a bank would be raided, in the style which had been reproduced so often in the last decade or so of the old century. By about 1908 outlawry of the old horseback kind was practically extinct in the United States.

Staidness and outward respectability were steadily overtaking the last of the wilder communities of the West. There were still desolate and almost trackless stretches of open space and the isolated, mountainous localities where an outlaw could find allies as well as cover; but the rapid development of the telephone network greatly lessened the chances of escape to such places after a robbery. Progress, as it is called, was beginning to manifest itself in other ways, too. The "horseless carriage" of the early nineties was derided by all but a handful of novelty-seekers.

In 1899 the "locomobile" commanded small bands of enthusiasts in the bigger cities but remained something of a freak to the ordinary public, who regarded its advocates as dangerous eccentrics. In 1902 the automobile was in vogue with the wealthy, and in 1904 its manufacturers were peddling the notion that every household was entitled to own one. Several years elapsed before the new mode of transport even started to make any real impression on the West, and by then most of the bad old ways were dying out side by side with most of the good old ways.

A few gangs of outlaws arose at different times in the first years of the Twentieth Century, but almost always their first major crime was also their last. As for the men who had taken to outlawry when the Ketchums were still riding, they carried on until they were caught or killed, unless they read the omens in time to leave the United States for Central or South America.

Without a doubt the plans discussed in Texas between Carver, Logan, and the Kilpatricks had included robbery and dispersal, perhaps to Mexico and South America. It may be supposed that Carver knew exactly where to find the loot from the second Folsom robbery, since Elza Lay had received word of its whereabouts even though he was in jail. Whether or not Carver was interested in resuming his somewhat erratic "courtship" of Laura Bullion, who was then staying with her uncle, James Lambert, near Douglas, he would not have skipped the country without first returning to southwest New Mexico to collect his share of the money stashed away there. In the event, he was killed before the gang was ready to go into action, and his death meant that Harvey Logan and Ben Kilpatrick had to revise their own plans.

Apparently the two men were camped just outside Sonora on the evening of April 2nd and must have been alerted by the sound of gunfire, for the posse which went out in search of them after the shooting found no trace of either. Some days later the pair were seen in New Mexico, going north. Perhaps by chance in Hole-in-the-Wall, more likely by prearrangement in Montana, they met Orlando Camillo Hanks, a thirty-seven year old Texan, just released from the Montana State Penitentiary at Deer Lodge.

"Charley" Hanks had left his home in DeWitt County, Texas, to evade a charge of criminal assault. He worked on the northern cattle ranges for a few years, tried his hand at rustling, then reached for bigger things. On the night of August 25th, 1893, he and three others stopped an eastbound train on the Northern Pacific near Greycliff, Montana, and robbed the express car and all the passengers. One month later the gang were trapped on the Blackfoot Reservation and three of them were killed, along with a posseman named Schubert. Camillo Hanks, last of the Greycliff robbers, was tried for the murder of Schubert and convicted on January 10th, 1894, under the name of Charles Jones. His term of imprisonment at Deer Lodge expired on April 30th, 1901. Almost at once he got in touch or was put in touch with Logan and Kilpatrick. Barely two months later the three men held up westbound train No. 3 on the Great Northern Railway near Wagner, Montana, a mile or two west of the scene of a robbery by the Sundance Kid more than eight years earlier.

The robbery, one of the most celebrated of the era, began at twenty minutes past two on Wednesday afternoon, July 3rd. When it was over the three bandits were in possession of a sum of money amounting to something between $41,000 and $70,000. More than forty thousand dollars of the booty comprised banknotes enroute from the Treasury to the Montana National Bank at Helena which, except for nine bills that had been sent to Washington as specimens, lacked the signatures of the president and cashier of the bank.

The posses were out for nearly a week without sighting the robbers. Only one of the three, Harvey Logan, was correctly identified. Another, probably Kilpatrick, was mistaken for Harry Longbaugh, the Sundance Kid. Later the Pinkertons were to name George Parker, alias Cassidy, as one of the gang. Before the case was solved Hanks was misidentified at different times as Logan and Cassidy, while Logan, as well as Kilpatrick, was confused with Longbaugh.

Three weeks after the robbery James Winters, who in 1896 had killed Johnny Logan, a brother of Harvey, was ambushed on his ranch near Landusky. Although there was no direct evidence, it was commonly believed that Harvey Logan had ridden back on his tracks to dispose of his old grudge against Winters.

Presently Logan, Kilpatrick, and Hanks turned up in Fort Worth, scene of much of the gang's foolishness the previous autumn. Logan kept company with both Annie Rogers and Lillie Davis, Carver's former "wife"; but it was Charley Hanks, not Logan, who subsequently took Annie on a trip through Louisiana, Arkansas, and Tennessee. Annie was arrested in Nashville on October 10th. On the 26th of the same month two policemen attempted to capture Hanks, but he lunged free, fled down the street, and eventually got out of town on a stolen horse.

EMPTY SADDLES AND LONELY GRAVES

It was in Fort Worth, too, that Ben Kilpatrick came to an arrangement with Laura Bullion. She said afterwards that Bill Cheney, who was a friend of both Carver and Kilpatrick, had "sort of felt sorry" for her after the death of Carver and had given her enough money to travel from Cochise County to Fort Worth where, as she primly expressed it, she was "introduced" to Ben. In fact, she had known Kilpatrick for something like ten years before this.

Using various names, and forging signatures to the Montana banknotes whenever funds ran low, Kilpatrick and Laura made their way to St. Louis. But on the night of November 5th Ben was arrested in the red light district of that city. Laura was taken into custody the following morning just as she was on the point of leaving for the railway station. In December both were convicted of currency offenses, Ben receiving a sentence of fifteen years imprisonment in the Federal Penitentiary and Laura a five-year term.

Harvey Logan had returned to Tennessee, his home State. A pool room brawl in Knoxville led to a gunfight in which the outlaw was wounded by a policeman. Less than two days later, on December 15th, the fugitive, bleeding, bedraggled and exhausted, was found shivering in the snow near Jefferson City, thirty miles east of Knoxville.

Charley Hanks reputedly went to Calaveras County, California, after his narrow escape from the officers in Nashville. In the spring of 1902 he reappeared in Texas, traveling in from the east. He got as far as San Antonio. There, on April 17th, he was shot dead in a saloon by an officer who had been summoned to suppress Charley's rowdy behavior.

Remnants of the old gangs, reinforced by some newcomers to the profession, were still operating from the traditional hide-outs in Wyoming and Utah. Four of them chose the unconventional hour of ten o'clock in the morning to waylay a Denver and Rio Grande train crammed with tourists admiring the scenic grandeur of the wild Saguache country. They halted the train at the foot of a steep mountain pass near Sargeants, Colorado, dynamited the two express safes, and rounded off the entertainment by inviting the sightseers to form a line beside the coaches and to hand over their money and valuables.

This robbery occurred on Monday, July 14th, 1902. There was another about a year later, also in Colorado. Bandits led by Bill Cruzan held up the Denver and Rio Grande Western at Unaweep, west of Grand Junction, robbed the express car, crossed the river by boat, and quickly disappeared from the ken of the posses.

DYNAMITE AND SIX-SHOOTER

None of this could compare with the coolness, cleverness, and audacity of Harvey Logan's escape from the jail at Knoxville, Tennessee, on June 27th, 1903. Logan rode out of town on the sheriff's horse, lost his pursuers in the mountains of North Carolina, and then vanished for months on end. There was no shortage of rumors as to his whereabouts, but the officers had to wait until the following spring until there was a really promising lead. Logan, it was then thought, was with the unreformed George Kilpatrick and others in the neighborhood of Ozona, Texas. This report went the way of the others: the men left while the officers were still discussing what action should be taken.

Kilpatrick, the presumed Logan, and the unknown third man made their next recorded appearance in Colorado, late on Tuesday night, June 7th, 1904. Once again the Denver and Rio Grande Western was held up and robbed, this time at Parachute, between Grand Junction and Glenwood Springs. The robbers employed the standard technique. So, in announcing its loss as only $10, did the Globe Express Company. The company's statement was contradicted by witnesses who saw the robbers the next day and claimed that all three horses were heavily burdened with loot.

Hard pressed by the posses, the men were forced to abandon their horses and, allegedly, to cache the plunder. On Thursday evening they were trapped in rocky draw near Glenwood Springs. Two of them managed to scramble to safety; the third, wounded, fought off the possemen for as long as he could, then killed himself.

In the pocket of the dead outlaw was found a letter from Ola Kilpatrick, addressed to Tap Duncan—a brother of Bige, who had married Elizabeth Ketchum. When it was learned that Tap was alive and in Texas, the body was identified as that of Jim York, another Texan. Later still it was given out that the dead man was none other than Harvey Logan; the famous Kid Curry. The Pinkertons swore to it; the West would not accept it. On November 1st two men robbed the bank at Cody, Wyoming, and murdered the cashier, Frank Middaugh. For several days afterwards the papers were full of stories that Logan was one of the robbers. Two local thugs whose ambitions far exceeded their capabilities were the next suspects, but were soon shown to be innocent of this particular crime. Nothing happened that would still the rumors about Kid Curry. He had got out of the mountains disguised as a prospector, it was said, and away to South America.

William E. Lay, alias William McGinnis, was a model prisoner and a "trusty" at Santa Fe. Possibly his fellow inmates thought of him less warmly. Twice he helped the authorities to subdue mutinous convicts; on the second occasion he was actually asked to ride out of the prison gates to summon the Territorial militia. Sometimes, too, he would accompany the warden on buggy-rides around the city. At the time of the second of the prison riots, Miguel A. Otero, who had been sympathetic toward Lay ever since the outlaw's trial, was still Governor. Almost at once he commuted the sentence of life imprisonment to one of ten years. This meant that Lay would have to serve a total of only six years and three months, the balance having been deducted as remission for good conduct.

Prison records indicate that Lay was released on January 10th, 1906. In fact he was permitted to leave the penitentiary in December, 1905, probably as a token of seasonal goodwill. William French's statement that the former bandit went to Alma after being let out of prison, which Charles Kelly attempts to refute, is borne out by H.A. Hoover, a resident of Alma in 1905. Hoover noted in his diary that he had seen "McGinnis" in town on Christmas Day, and later talked with Louis Jones, with whom Lay boarded for about eighteen months.

Louis and Walter Jones, originally from Texas, had lived in western New Mexico since 1885 and had opened a large general store in Alma a year or so before Lay was discharged from the penitentiary. Apparently he had never met either of them until he approached them for accommodation shortly after his arrival in 1905 but, as Louis observed, he seemed to trust them. Louis Jones told Hoover that Lay wrote a number of letters in the hope of tracing his sometime partners. When the last of his letters was returned to him, marked "unclaimed," like all the others, he announced that he was going off to dig up a box of money which was "buried under the root of a juniper tree on the Mexican border" and that, all being well, he would be back within two weeks. Thirteen days after his departure he rode up to the store with fifty-eight thousand dollars "wrapped in a slicker."

French surmised that Lay had headed for Alma after his discharge simply to collect his share of the Folsom loot. Hoover believed that the $58,000 " was not from the Folsom train holp-up" but "more than likely . . . from some other train robbery." His grounds for this assertion are that the messenger saved all the money in his care on the occasion of the second hold-up at Folsom; that as Folsom is four hundred miles from the Mexican border, the gang could not possibly have reached the border before Lay was caught; and that Lay himself was supposed to have remarked that the express company had been tipped off, "for they got nothing" out of the hold-up. French, almost certainly, was right and Hoover wrong.

The fatuous tale that has an express messenger hiding money to which he had no access seems to have obtained far more credence than it deserved. French himself tells of how and why he formed the conclusion that the booty had been cached in Colfax County and that Butch Cassidy had set out to recover it. Obviously the rancher never knew for sure that the money had been brought south, and he did not venture to guess who might have brought it. But then he did not look for the explanation behind the sudden affluence of Bruce Weaver. As for Hoover's third point, it is hardly surprising that Lay would not want it to be thought that he proposed to collect and live off the proceeds of the Folsom or any other robbery. In any case, when express company officials expected an attempt at robbery they did not hold back their scheduled money shipments. They hired guards.

There is, finally, the question of how Lay was able to learn where the money was to be found.

Charlie Siringo, the "cowboy detective," who for years moved unsuspected among the friends and confederates of the outlaws, claims that he was asked to "smuggle" into the Santa Fe penitentiary the key to a code through which Lay would be able to keep in touch with his comrades outside. He visited Lay, whom he describes as "a pleasant fellow but a hard-looking 'mug'," in the fall of 1900. The cipher, if Siringo is to be believed, was childishly simple: a confidential message would be conveyed by every fourth word of an ordinary note. Siringo does not say whether or not he informed the penitentiary officials of this, but probably he did not. Had he done so, Lay would not have retained the exemplary prison record which enabled him to earn maximum remission after the commutation of his sentence, while Siringo himself would have been unmasked as soon as Lay's contacts realized that their code was no secret to the authorities. By using this device, or something similar to it, any of those few who knew where the Folsom loot had been secreted could very easily have passed the word to Lay. The message could have been sent by Cassidy, Carver, Weaver, or possibly Tom Capehart. Weaver, no doubt, had been directed where to bury the money and, whatever disloyalty he may have practised earlier, he would not have attempted a double-cross over this, especially if he was expecting

Carver to show up in the near future.

Thus, Elza Lay's impeccable conduct whilst he was in prison should not be wholly ascribed to his mild temperament and persuasive manner.

Lay stayed on with the Jones brothers for several months after his trip to the border. During all this time the money, covered by gunny sacks, reposed in a corner of the small stockroom next to the main store building. Finally Lay, and the money, went to Wyoming. He remained a wanderer almost to the end of his life, but was esteemed and trusted wherever he went. His reformation owed much to his strength of character; but that fifty-eight thousand dollars must have helped, too. Lay's first marriage had broken up long before he entered prison. He married again shortly after his return to Wyoming, and wrote to tell the Jones brothers that he had invested $40,000 in a cattle ranch. In the years that followed he knew many vicissitudes. For a time he was an oil-field scout. He opened saloons at various places, and was once employed as a payroll guard. At the time of his death, in 1933, he was superintendent of a waterworks in Los Angeles.

Berry Ketchum, unlike his brothers, was a family man. He married in the 1880s, and had three daughters: Alice, Nora, and Barshie. A year or two after Tom Ketchum was executed, Berry bought a ranch nine miles west of Sheffield, Texas, seventy miles southwest of Knickerbocker. H.A. Holmes, now a Justice of the Peace in Pecos County, remembers him well:

> He was a tall heavy set man with a full beard. He was rough spoken. I have seen him many times. That was before the days of the automobile and he drove a pair of mules to a small buck board.

Louis Montgomery, a native of San Saba County now living in nearby Brady, has a story which nicely illustrates Berry's reputation for toughness:

> When I was rodeoing they had a mean bucking horse that came off of the Ketchum ranch and they called him Berry Ketchum because he was so tough.

But if Berry Ketchum was known as a hard man, he was always a straight one. Jim Harkey, a nephew of Dee Harkey, was in his employ for twenty years and told Mr Holmes that "he never worked for a better man than Old Man Berry Ketchum."

Berry died in March, 1914, at San Angelo, a rich man and a respected one.

The Kilpatricks moved southwest at about the same time as Berry Ketchum, making their new home in Crockett County, not far from Ozona. Boone Kilpatrick married Truda Sheffield, daughter of the man after whom the town was named. Truda's brother, Dan Sheffield, was an outlaw and so, by now, was Felix Kilpatrick, whom Mr Holmes characterizes as "fully as mean as Ben, if not meaner. George Kilpatrick left home in the spring of 1904 to take part in the Parachute train robbery and never returned. In 1913 Felix fell out with Dan Sheffield and was killed by him. But Felix had outlived his brother Ben by a year.

Ben served nine and half years in the Federal Penitentiary at Atlanta, Georgia, before being released on June 11, 1911. He traveled back to Texas at the expense of Concho County, where he was under indictment for the murder of Oliver Thornton. After the jury had voted for his acquittal, he went on to his mother's place. On several occasions he called on Marvin Hunter, editor of the weekly paper at Ozona. Hunter was favorably impressed:

> He was a genteel, likeable fellow, who looked you square in the eye, and had nothing about him that would lead one to ever believe that he had trodden the outlaw's trail. One day in my office Kilpatrick told me had had "gone dead wrong", to use his own language, and that he realized the folly of it all. He said he had fully reformed in prison, and it was his intention to lease some land near Sheffield, get a flock of sheep, and convince the world that he could be a good citizen instead of an outlaw. And I sincerely believe that was his intention; but alas, for good intentions!

Two weeks after his last interview with Hunter. Ben Kilpatrick rode up to the Berry Ketchum ranch with Nick Grider, a first cousin of Jim Harkey. Jim shod two of Berry's horses and gave them to Ben and Nick. This was the preface to what was surely the last train hold-up ever attempted in the tradition of that fading figure, the badman of the Old West.

Kilpatrick and Grider rode down through Terrell County to the Southern Pacific tracks, less than forty miles south of the Berry Ketchum ranch. By Wednesday, March 13th, 1912, their preparations were complete. That night Kilpatrick stepped into the locomotive cab as the westbound express, now known as Number 9, pulled out of Dryden, halfway between Sanderson, the county seat, and Lozier, scene of Tom Ketchum's first train robbery.

All went according to the old-established pattern as the train was stopped and the mail and express cars were run up the track a mile from the detached passenger coaches. Grider came up and kept the crew under guard while Kilpatrick went through the two cars. But the express messenger, David A. Trousdale, cleverly distracted Ben's attention then smashed his brains out with three blows from an ice mallet. Trousdale took the dead man's rifle and waited for the second bandit. Growing impatient, the messenger fired a couple of shots. As Grider started to climb into the car Trousdale shot him through the head.

The bodies were taken on to Sanderson and photographed. Kilpatrick was identified almost at once. There was some controversy over the identity of the other man. Some said it was one Ole Beck. Others named him as Howard Benson; and others yet as Ed Welch. Jim Harkey kept quiet about it all for some forty years. Finally, on his eightieth birthday, he told H.A. Holmes what he knew of the hold-up and revealed the identity of Ben's companion, saying that "it had been so long since it happened that he knew there would never be anything done about it."

Most of the "wanted men" of the American West were following the example of Butch Cassidy and the Sundance Kid by going to one or other of the South American republics. Here there could be peaceful oblivion for those who sought it. For those who did not care to settle down, there was immense scope for banditry. Cassidy and Longbaugh lived quietly for five years before going back to the old ways of robbing and dodging. The second phase of their outlawry lasted a further five years and ended when they were shot dead in 1911. William French says Tom Capehart accompanied Cassidy to South America, and that he died alongside Cassidy; but here, surely, French confuses Capehart with Longbaugh. Henry Brock heard that Capehart was in Peru, with Cassidy and others. Alverson knew that Capehart had become an outlaw but never learned what afterwards happened to him. Perhaps he really did ride with Cassidy in South America. It is very easy to show that Capehart and Longbaugh were two different men: at the time of Capehart's arrest for the Stein's Pass affair, Longbaugh and Harvey Logan, having escaped from the Deadwood jail, were being hunted in Montana and Wyoming for the robbery of several post offices.

Alverson himself, along with Bill Warderman and Walter Hoffman, received a full pardon from President Theodore Roosevelt on March 29th, 1904—nearly three years after Tom Ketchum had publicly stated that none of the three was implicated in the Stein's Pass hold-up, and one year after Antonio Borrego, Assistant Cell-house keeper at the New

Mexico Territorial Penitentiary, had sworn before a Notary Public that Sam Ketchum, three or four days before his death, had likewise dissociated them from complicity in the attempted robbery.

Roosevelt told them that he knew they were victims of a "great injustice" and, characteristically, suggested that each should return to Arizona and "face the world like a man". Only Alverson took the advice. Jess Benton, who had so wanted the ranch in Texas Canyon, took possession shortly after the men were convicted. Alverson maintained that Benton and his partner, Jim Wolf, simply filed homestead rights and moved in. Benton's version is that John Cush had to mortgage the property in order to pay the lawyer who defended him; the lawyer then sold the ranch and cattle to Benton.

Most of Alverson's own cattle had been sold to meet lawyers' bills. After his release he went back to claim those that were left. All he found was "one big red steer." He stayed in Cochise County and in 1938 dictated his reminiscences to Mrs George F. Kitt.

Luckier than most was Bill Cruzan, who had taken part in the robberies at Tipton and Unaweep. When Charlie Siringo called at his hideout somewhere in the Colorado mountains, Bill was not at home. He was never captured. Ed Kilpatrick was not brought to book for his part in the Hillsboro bank robbery, but died in an accident some few years later.

Sam Ketchum now lies under the main road between Santa Fe and Albuquerque. His burial place was near the corner of the Odd Fellows cemetery. Much later, when plans were made to widen the road by thirteen feet, the authorities had the choice of arranging for the body to be moved to a new grave and leaving it undisturbed. They decided upon the latter course.

The grave of Tom Ketchum was not left undisturbed. In 1933 it was announced that the body would be disinterred and taken to the new cemetery, a half mile east of the old graveyard. Ketchum was to be raised at 2 o'clock, on the afternoon of Sunday, September 10th. The committee in charge of the proceedings included Carl Eklund, Tom Gray, and Albert Thompson, all of whom had witnessed the execution, thirty-two years earlier. Another of the members was Jack Potter, who had known Ketchum as a trail hand, back in 1894.

The people came to see, and the ceremony went off as planned. There was an audience of more than a thousand for Henry H. Errett, Superintendent of Schools for Union County, when he climbed onto a truck beside the open grave to begin his discourse on Ketchum's life and death. He began by explaining that they had not met to honor or pay homage to Ketchum, "but rather to drive home to everyone that crime eventually exacts the toll of suffering, misery, death and disgrace." He finished by stating that the inner casket would be opened so that the crowd could inspect what was left of the outlaw.

Those who crowded up to the coffin were struck by Ketchum's durability, for the body was "in a fine state of preservation."

> His jet black hair and long thick mustache had turned a maroon red. His skull was in fine condition. The black suit he wore had turned to a reddish gray color and was decomposing. The lower jaw had dropped, his eyeballs were gone but their deep sockets were intact. Very little flesh covered his face. The coat sleeve was neatly folded over the stump of his right arm.

At four o'clock the body was put into a new coffin and driven away to the cemetery. There was some talk of a commemorative monument being erected, and highway signs being put up outside Clayton "advising tourists of the tomb of one of New Mexico's reputed most infamous and bloody killers;" but today there is still no marker over the grave.

It is always tempting to seek to fit a character into perspective by comparing him with his equivalent in modern times. Such comparisons, at best, are meretricious and superficial. Tom Ketchum was one of the most daring and dangerous criminals of his own generation and type; yet he hardly stands in close affinity with such as Floyd, Dillinger, or the Barkers, and was infinitely superior to the slimy and loathsome creatures of a city underworld. Further than that one can barely go, but Jack Culley has this to say of Ketchum and his like:

> And if you are an admirer of the simple qualities of courage and endurance and self-reliance in men—well, these men had them....
> If we ever thought about the moral aspect of the matter, we were likely to argue that our Western bandits were better people than the robber barons, ... who preyed upon the public in the industrial field. They did not rob widows and orphans. Be that as it might, we recognized the bandits as cowpunchers like ourselves....
> Such exploits as theirs, indeed, have the stuff of the great sagas and ballads in them, the hero-tales that have thrilled mankind in all ages.

Idealized and over-simplified this may be. Yet a mountain of factual assertion cannot stand in the way of a rivulet of romantic imagery. Perhaps, then, the undeniable appeal of legend and folklore is the touchstone to a higher and more elemental truth than the sort of truth which is a matter of record.

But perhaps, again, the whole question is resolved more decisively, more in the spirit of the range, and more impartially by another of Tom Ketchum's contemporaries.

The flowers which Jack Potter placed in the open casket, that September afternoon in 1933, were accompanied by a card bearing these six words:

"To a cowboy who went wrong."

TALES THAT WERE TOLD

ONE DEAD MEXICAN	172
HELD UP AT GRANTS	174
"THEY GOT JOHN LEGG"	178
THE IDENTITY OF G.W. FRANKS	180
MURDERED ON THE ROAD	184

ONE DEAD MEXICAN

Among the droll items beloved of hack-writers who like to string motley fiction around real personalities is the story which relates how Tom Ketchum, keen to try out his new rifle, and determined to settle a wager as to which way a man would fall from his horse after being shot, deliberately picked off a Mexican who was riding some distance away from the gang.

It is rather odd that this colorful yarn was first committed to cold print in Albert Thompson's book *They Were Open Range Days*. Thompson, one of the pioneers of Clayton, interviewed Ketchum on a number of occasions and was, probably, better versed on the experiences of the gang in north-east New Mexico than anyone else.' The original draft of the manuscript for his chapter on Ketchum is far longer and more informative than the published version; yet it contains not a word of the episode described so minutely, and with the accompanying conversation between the members of the gang "recreated" in such detail, in Chapter 21 of the book. Thompson says that the shooting took place in "the Big Hatchet Mountains, southwestern New Mexico," and that Ketchum admitted it to Jerry Leahy.

Whatever Leahy told Thompson, it might be instructive to cite two newspaper stories — quite dissimilar in detail but with one important feature in common — which appeared shortly after Ketchum had been captured. The first is taken from the Trinidad *Chronicle-News,* as quoted by Titsworth:

> . . . One day a Mexican rode into San Angelo, Texas, wearing a magnificent sombrero, all a-glitter with silver braid. Black Jack coveted it, and he knew but one way to get it. The Mexican was not quick to give up the hat, but soon had no use for it, for dead men's heads are just as well uncovered. Ketchum looked very well in that hat.

About a month later, the El Paso *Herald* carried a piece which was reprinted in the Santa Fe *New Mexican* on October 7th, 1899.

ONE DEAD MEXICAN

> ... The nature of the man is shown by a well authenticated story to the effect that, during his boyhood days on the ranch, one of his chief sources of pleasure was gained from a somewhat peculiar habit he had of hiding behind the chaparral on some lonely hill and from this vantage point shooting at — and seldom missing — the Mexican herders on the plains below. ...

These tales, themselves untrue, may have been the earliest forms of this enduring fabrication. Thompson shifted the locale and concocted a fresh set of details; others, not to be outdone, have more recently added further embroidery.

There are two incidents in the life of Tom Ketchum which may have been twisted by word of mouth into something which suggested a basis for such creations as these. One was the murder of John "Jap" Powers, who quite certainly was not of Mexican ancestry, but who was ambushed near San Angelo. The other was the murder of Merejildo Gallegos—who, if not a Mexican, was at least of Spanish descent. Ketchum, in his talk with Leahy, might have made some vague allusion to one or other of these crimes. If he told Leahy that he had killed a man merely to put a rifle to the test, then surely the District Attorney was being ribbed.

HELD UP AT GRANTS

The town of Grants is about midway between Albuquerque and the Arizona line. In 1897 it was little more than a station and shipping point on the Atlantic & Pacific Railroad (reorganized as the Santa Fe-Pacific in July of that year, but generally referred to by the old name for some time afterwards).

It was on November 6th, 1897, that the eastbound express, No. 2, was robbed of a large sum of money just outside Grants. Sheriff E.L. Hubbell of Bernalillo County later learned that the booty came to $90,000. Two more trains were held up at Grants during the next nine months, but the first robbery was the only one to give rise to sustained excitement and controversy. Tom Ketchum, as has been stated, was able to convince some of his acquaintances the hold-up was his work.

Joseph "Mack" Axford, whose *Around Western Campfires* is one of the best written and most reliable books of reminiscence to come out of the Southwest, was one of those who heard the story from Tom. Mr Axford believes that Tom and Sam Ketchum and Dave Atkins were the Grants robbers.

Lorenzo Walters does not specifically mention the Grants robbery in his book *Tombstone's Yesterday,* but he does report that the Ketchums robbed a Santa Fe train in the Fall of 1897 and escaped into Mexico—circumstances which fit the Grants robbery and no other. There is no indication whether Walters' informants were people who heard this from Ketchum, or from friends of Ketchum; or whether the whole thing is just part of his general confusion over which crimes were to be laid against Ketchum's gang and which against Christian's bunch.

The salient facts are these.

During the summer of 1897 U.S. Marshal Foraker was kept closely informed on the movements of the remaining members of the Black Jack gang. Jim Shaw, who had once belonged to the gang but whose treachery had led to the killing of Black Jack in April, 1897, sometimes acted as a Field Deputy under Foraker. The Marshal was pleased with Shaw's efforts and spoke highly of him in two letters to the Attorney General. In August the outlaws made two unsuccessful attempts to ambush Shaw; on October 16th Foraker was informed that the turncoat had been killed a couple of days earlier and replied that the news came as no surprise. Incongruously, though, Foraker did not mention the incident to his superiors in the Department of Justice.

Three weeks later came the Grants robbery. Foraker at once declared that the bandits were members of the Black Jack gang, who had headed north even as he was trying to arrange for extradition papers to be drawn up. A few days after this the officer temporarily changed his mind about the whole thing. He told the *New Mexican* that the guilty parties were "two or probably three Arizona men," but refrained from releasing their names. He was less reticent in his letter to the Department, dated November 12th. Amazingly enough, he named one of them as the till-lately esteemed James M. Shaw. The other, he said, was a certain Mace Slaughter. Nowhere did he make any allusion to his earlier understanding that Shaw had been killed. He did comment sardonically that Shaw would hardly push his claim to money owed him for posse service as "evidently he [Shaw] is now helping himself and will not need it." It would be interesting to know the identity of the gentleman who peddled his information to Foraker; but the matter is of small consequence, for within a few days the Marshal had sure evidence that his original surmise was correct.

The three robbers had crossed into Arizona, joined up with the rest of their gang, and ridden back into Mexico. There followed the riotous Thanksgiving performance in Fronteras which led to the detention of "Tom Anderson," "Jesse Williams," and Theodore James and the discovery on their persons of more than $9,000 in greenbacks.

Two officers in Bisbee, Arizona, some thirty-five miles north of Fronteras, then made the premature announcement that the three men were already in their custody. This prompted the New Mexico authorities to apply for a writ of requestion on the Governor of Arizona. Within a day or so it was learned that the Arizona officers had been anticipating developments which did not materialize, but a move to have the outlaws extradited from Mexico had scarcely been initiated when, on November 29th, a courier from Fronteras arrived in Bisbee with the news that the trio had "bribed the Mexican officials to release them." Marshal Foraker was loud in his condemnation of "official red tape" and two posses carried their disgust a stage further by actually making a foray into Mexico in the vain hope of securing a more peremptory execution of justice. Almost simultaneously Marshals Foraker and Griffith heard that outlaws were planning to hold up the Southern Pacific near the Arizona-New Mexico Territorial line, and assumed that this latest mischief was the design of the Grants robbers. Then came the Stein's Pass hold-up and the arrest of men who were friendly with both sets of robbers but who had taken part in none of the crimes of either. Amid all the confusion the Ketchum gang got away. So did Bob Christian, George Musgrave and Theodore James. It seems beyond dispute that these were the three Grants robbers. They dispersed in January of 1898 and nothing more was officially heard of any of them until December, 1909, when Musgrave was arrested for murder.

But if there were genuine doubt about the identity of the bandits the Ketchums would be the least likely suspects. To begin with, they were most probably in southern Arizona or northern Sonora at the time of the robbery. They had gone to Cochise County in September with the intention of striking at a Southern Pacific train; they persisted with the plan, put it into effect, and remained in the border country until about March of the following year. The reasoning, and the facts which support it, are by themselves nearly enough to exclude the Ketchum gang from blame for either the robbery at Grants or the murder in Colorado, three nights earlier. The style in which the robbery was accomplished, too, was all very typical of the operations of the Christians and George Musgrave: the train was seized in a mad rush and scurry, with a lot of wild yelling and shooting; and the bandits assiduously refreshed themselves from the whiskey bottle while they were pillaging the express car. They also joked boisterously with the fireman whom they had made prisoner. There was never any of such nonsense when Tom Ketchum was at work. Moreover, it might be appropriate to reiterate the obvious: if the Ketchum gang really had robbed the A & P at Grants, they would not have gone into action again at Stein's Pass, barely a month later.

The second of the Grants robberies took place between midnight and one o'clock on Tuesday morning, March 29th, 1898. C.C. Lord was the express messenger on this occasion, just as he had been on the night of the earlier encounter. This time, however, he had the company of a guard, Charlie Fowler. There were five of the bandits: Billy Swingle, alias Kid Swingle, alias William Raper, alias William Walters, but usually known as "Bronco Bill"; Daniel "Red" Pipkin; Will Johnson; Jim Hightower; and Jim Burnett. Their target was No. 1, the westbound express, but the scheme fell badly apart. Charlie Fowler repelled the attack on the express car. Jim Hightower was wounded. The outlaws robbed the train crew and at least some of the passengers but on the whole they had very little to sing about. Lathrop, the railroad fireman, was shot in the leg by someone at some stage of the proceedings.

Nearly two months later Bronco Bill, with Johnson and possibly Pipkin, stopped a Santa Fe train at Belen and got away with a worthwhile haul. Bronco and Johnson were soon overtaken, but they killed three of the posse and fled into Arizona. A further two months passed before they ran up against Jeff Milton and George Scarborough. Bronco Bill was wounded and captured; Johnson was killed; Pipkin showed a sharp turn of speed and escaped unhurt.

The arrest of Bronco Bill set off a rush of highly-colored and ill-prepared newspaper stories on his recent misdeeds. Some reporters— perhaps badly informed, perhaps in deliberate courtship of the sensational — gave him credit for the first of the Grants robberies instead of the second. Red Pipkin, meanwhile, was raising a gang for another attack on the westbound train at Grants station. The attempt was made on August 14th, and was defeated by Charlie Fowler and two messengers named Goodman and Comfort. Pipkin and his friends held the train for a couple of hours but got no booty of any description. Pipkin was arrested in Utah in March, 1899, and spent several days in the Winnemucca, Nevada, jail with some men who were supposed to have robbed a train at Humboldt the preceding July. He was taken to New Mexico and tried for the second of the Grants hold-ups, only to evade sentence because of an error in the indictment. In the end he was convicted in Arizona on a charge of horse theft.

That is about all there is to the story of the various Grants hold-ups, except that many people remain convinced that the bulk of the loot from the first robbery is still buried in the Malpais country, somewhere south of Grants.

"THEY GOT JOHN LEGG"

Of all the officers who were involved in the hunt for the Ketchum gang, William H. Reno was the most garrulous and publicity-conscious. He gave numerous accounts of the Turkey Canyon fight, no two of them alike. Reporters—since he was so amenable—credited him with a degree of courage and sagacity which finds little or no basis in hard fact. Others who came into contact with him, such as Marshal Foraker, William French, and Mason Chase made him the object of a good deal of sarcastic, contemptuous, and sometimes abusive comment. Although it is evident from a study of the Turkey Canyon engagement that the cowardice imputed to him could be charged with greater fairness to one or two of his companions, it does not require very much perception to understand why the man was disliked.

After the execution of Tom Ketchum, Reno declared that the outlaw was "lying all the time" in his last statement. The detective's interpretation was somewhat inaccurate; besides, he could tell a pretty tall story himself. One reporter, an avid listener as Reno was holding forth during the train journey back north, recorded the following specimen:

> Sitting at the window of a Pullman car yesterday morning, Billy Reno looked out over the brown, uncompromising plains and smiled, inscrutably. 'They got the man who started me on this chase," he said, with charming insouciance. 'Who was he?' someone asked. 'John Legg. He wrote me in 1897 that Black Jack [Ketchum] and his gang were coming north. A little later they did the job at Folsom, N.M. Next year they killed Legg at Fort Sumner, N.M.' Again that smile, and the train put behind a few more of those sad New Mexico miles.

Legg worked for several years as a Deputy Sheriff in Lincoln County and sometimes served as a Deputy United States Marshal. In August, 1894, he killed one William McLehaney, known as "Portales Bill". His part in the pursuit of Tom and Sam Ketchum after the murder of Herzstein and Gallegos has been told. In October of the same year, 1896, he rode with one of the posses which made a feeble pretense of giving

— 178 —

chase to Black Jack Christian's gang, who held up four stage coaches during that month. He was shot and killed at Fort Sumner, but not by the Ketchums or any other outlaw band. The fracas which resulted in his death arose from a quarrel over a Poker hand. Legg was killed by James Blanton—like Legg a gambler and a hardcase, according to the Roswell *Record* — on March 22nd, 1899. A shot fired by Legg, apparently intended for Blanton, wounded a man named Gillespie.

It is quite possible that Reno truly believed that Legg met his death at the hands of the Ketchum outlaws. If he did, this is yet another case of an officer laboring under the double burden of an untrustworthy informant and his own naivety. The failings of many individual lawmen, and the need for greater co-operation between the different agencies of law and order, were sorely exposed during the campaign against such groups as the Ketchum band. In theory, this ought to have had the healthy and constructive effect of awakening the public into electing or securing the appointment of better men. More than one writer on western outlawry has contrived a tidy conclusion by propounding this as though it were an actuality. One might assert with an equal regard for consistency that the current prevalence of violent crime is proof of the very reverse. In truth, today's officers, like those of yesteryear and times more distant, are no more and no less than a fairly typical sample of humanity in general.

THE IDENTITY OF G.W. FRANKS

Perhaps the most gratuitous, yet certainly among the more recurrent of the fictitious malformations of the history of the Ketchum gang and the Hole-in-the-Wall outlaws, is no more than thirty years old. It is the one in which Harvey Logan, alias Kid Curry, is substituted for Will Carver as "G.W. Franks," the man whose shooting so unnerved the posse in Turkey Creek Canyon. Its origins are easily traced.

The story was introduced by Charles Kelly in *Outlaw Trail*. The source, purportedly, was William French's book, *Some Recollections of a Western Ranchman*. Kelly also cites French's book as his authority for the absurd statement that Tom Capehart was actually just another alias for Harvey Logan. Thus it is Kelly's assumption that G.W. Franks, Tom Capehart and Harvey Logan were all of them the man who held back the posse in the Turkey Canyon fight. James D. Horan, in *Desperate Men* and elsewhere, follows Kelly and provides a few touches of purple prose. Brown Waller, whose book on Harvey Logan, *Last of the Great Western Train Robbers*, is largely an ill-organized but interesting pastiche of contemporary newspaper accounts, strikes a curious compromise between the evidence of his own extensive research and his regard for the work of Kelly and Horan by concluding that there must have been two Tom Capeharts and that both Logan and Carver used the alias "G. W. Franks." All highly perplexing.

It is time to take a look at what French actually wrote. French does not state or even imply that Capehart was or might have been Harvey Logan. Nor does he say that Logan was or might have been Franks. In fact, he does not make one single solitary mention of or allusion to Harvey Logan in the course of the entire book. What he does say is that he believed Capehart to be Franks.

French relates how Cassidy told him that Tom Capehart had just returned to the WS range with news of Lay's capture, then describes his own subsequent conversation with Capehart:

> I then asked Tom, whom (sic) it was evident must be the man

THE IDENTITY OF G.W. FRANKS

> Franks, how Mac [Lay, alias McGinnis] had been taken.
> ... That he did not intend to commit himself was evident from the start, for he made no direct allusion to the cause of Mac's trouble, saying merely that he had been wounded, shot twice through the body. ...

Capehart's account of the arrest of Lay, as he heard it from Lusk and retold it to French, has been cited in Chapter Twelve. Tom also told French that he had been afraid of being taken for the fugitive "Franks," since from the description that was issued he might have been Franks, or again he might not. French deduced from this that Capehart really was Franks. This poses a separate question, but before it is entered into something should be said about the whereabouts of Harvey Logan at the time Charles Kelly says he was at Alma, Folsom, Turkey Canyon, and Chimney Wells.

It is certain that Logan was one of the six who robbed the Union Pacific at Wilcox, Wyoming, on June 2nd, 1899. This occurred during the time Sam Ketchum, Lay, and Franks were staying in the vicinity of Cimarron, New Mexico — three hundred miles to the south of Wilcox. The investigation disclosed that Logan, with two companions, was roaming through Wyoming for several weeks prior to the robbery. Cassidy and Lay were still working for William French during the earlier part of this period. Lay, as has been related, quit the WS either very late in April or early in May; Cassidy left shortly afterwards, in time to join Logan and the others for the Wyoming robbery. The six Wilcox robbers split into two groups of three directly after the hold-up. Logan and two others, probably George Curry and Bob Lee, drew the keener pursuit and killed Sheriff Hazen a few days later. Since they are known to have retreated north, it is perfectly clear that Logan could not possibly have been in New Mexico at the time of the Folsom robbery. Nor could he have joined Lay after the Turkey Canyon fight.

Another who put Harvey Logan among the Folsom bandits was Miguel A. Otero, and for the oddest reason. He thought that G.W. Franks and Will Carver were both aliases for Harvey Logan.

Sam Ketchum, in his first account of the fight, referred to one of his companions as "the Kid." Charles Kelly seizes upon this as a reference to "Kid Curry" (Harvey Logan). But at the time he made this statement Sam refused to name his companions, and he could have been talking about either of the two, since both were much younger than he.

Kelly, incidentally, says that Lay was one of the Wilcox robbers.

This is no less untenable than the assertion that Logan was at Folsom, since there is cast-iron evidence that Lay was in northeast New Mexico throughout the month of June, 1899.

Jack Culley accepted French's conclusion that Tom Capehart was Franks, in preference to evidence adduced by George Crocker that Franks was Carver. Undoubtedly French reported truthfully what he had seen or heard. But Capehart, as French admitted, "did not intend to commit himself"; he told French no more than what he thought French was entitled to know. Capehart only learned of the arrest of Lay several hours after it had taken place, and so could not have been the man who had accompanied Lay to Lusk's camp the previous evening and who was watching from the hill during Lay's struggle to escape from the posse. If Capehart did not mention the presence of Will Carver or any other third party, it would have been because he thought it best that French should not be told.

French's story may be taken to show that Capehart was in Lay's company after the Turkey Canyon affair; but there is unquestionable evidence that "G.W. Franks" was Will Carver. There are the findings of Carl Livingston, whose information usually came from people who were in a position to know; there is the evidence heard by the United States Grand Jury which indicted Carver as one of the three bandits; there are the statements of Albert Thompson and George Crocker, both of whom could draw upon first hand knowledge and were close to others who had the same advantage. Mack Axford's account of the events is derived chiefly from what he was told by Carver. When the *San Angelo Standard*, in reporting Carver's death, said that Carver was Franks, it was merely repeating something that was regarded as an established fact.

Just before his execution, Tom Ketchum did his best to throw the question wide open.

"The name of the man in the Turkey Creek canyon fight, supposed to have been Franks", he said, "I won't tell, because he is alive and at liberty. I know the man well enough—have known him for fifteen years, but I won't tell who he is".

Since Ketchum knew of Carver's death in Sonora, three weeks earlier, it is impossible to hazard a guess as to whom he might have had in mind. Franks definitely was Carver, and the chances are that Ketchum must have been well aware of this. One explanation could be that here, as elsewhere, he was lying—perhaps deluding himself into the hope that by withholding information, or by appearing to withhold it, he might miraculously gain a last-minute reprieve.

THE IDENTITY OF G.W. FRANKS

Stories are still afloat that G.W. Franks was a "mystery man" with no other known identity who returned to Colfax County many years later to dig up the loot. Whoever first told this one may have heard that someone — sometime — came looking for the buried money and that a man whom many swore could only have been Franks was seen in the locality long after the robbery. Both rumors sprang from actual incident, but there was no connection between them. The money, as has been stated, was taken out of the ground about a year after the robbery: the man alleged to have been Franks was an obscure drifter and recluse who called himself Bob McManus. Deputy Sheriffs George Titsworth and William Thatcher heard about him and arrested him on April 5th, 1905. He was taken to Trinidad, and thence to Raton, New Mexico. Then, says a dispatch to the *New Mexican*, someone with a good memory for faces declared that the man was Frank Potter, one of the three or four members of the old Hawkins gang who were still at large. McManus spent several weeks in jail before the authorities were satisfied that he was neither "Franks" nor Potter.

MURDERED ON THE ROAD

The mystery of the disappearance of Colonel Albert Jennings Fountain and his eight year old son Henry on the road between Tularosa and Las Cruces is a synthetic one in almost every respect. It is certain that Fountain's political arch-rival, Albert Bacon Fall, was the prime instigator of the scheme whereby the Colonel was waylaid and murdered, and that the killing was done by several of Fall's cohorts: Oliver Milton Lee, James Robert Gililland, William McNew, and perhaps one other. The murders are unsolved only in this narrow technical sense: the bodies were never found, and Lee and Gililland were formally acquitted. Over the years that followed, the silence of those with an intimate knowledge of the facts, and the vigorous assertions made on behalf of Fall and Lee by people who would not believe or at any rate would not admit that these two men could have been capable of complicity in the murders, helped to build up a formidable illusion of mystery.

There were other obfuscating factors. Chief among these was a statement by Bob Lewis, a former peace officer living at Magdalena, New Mexico, that Tom and Sam Ketchum, with an unidentified third party, were the men who had murdered the Fountains. Lewis knew this (so he said) because Sam had told him that Tom killed Fountain, Senior, and then proceeded, over Sam's protests, to take the life of the little boy because he, Tom, "wanted to destroy all evidence." The alleged motive was that Fountain had been "too successful in prosecuting their friends" for rustling.

Much—maybe too much—has since been written about the Fountain case. Several writers have referred to a "theory" that Tom Ketchum was the killer; but the "theory" consists only of the story told by Bob Lewis and the overlying reluctance of historians and others to deploy evidence and argument either to buttress or to dispose of Lewis' contentions. It could well be that the more perspicacious writers have excluded the "theory" from proper and detailed consideration because of the sure evidence that the guilt lay elsewhere; if it is established that A killed B, and that C was not connected with he crime in any way, then there is no urgent need to know just what C was doing at the time of the murder. Nevertheless, the enquirer who is primarily concerned with Tom Ketchum is more interested in sealing off the allegation from Ketchum's end.

It is not known when the conspiracy to murder Fountain was evolved, although in essence it was a revival of a scheme devised in 1894; but the first overt move in the 1896 version was made on January 12th, — just a few hours after he had begun his journey from Las Cruces to Lincoln — when his buggy team was run off. The horses were recovered and he reached Lincoln without further mishap. There, in his capacity of special prosecutor for the Southeastern New Mexico Stock Growers' Association, he helped to secure numerous indictments for the larceny of cattle, including two against Lee and McNew. He was shadowed by different relays of horsemen almost from the moment he drove out of Lincoln, on January 30th, up until the time he approached Chalk Hill, the place appointed for the ambush, on the afternoon of February 1st. If one pretends, for the sake of argument, that the Fountain affair is a genuine mystery, it is at once evident that if gunmen had been called in especially to execute the final stages of the plan, they would have had to be in Dona Ana County, New Mexico, by the middle of January at the very latest.

There are strong indications, but no documentary evidence, that Tom and Sam Ketchum were in Tom Green County, Texas, at the time of the Fountain murders. Be that as it may; the brothers can be eliminated from the Fountain case by a straightforward process of ratiocination.

It will be recalled that Tom was one of the men who killed "Jap" Powers, near San Angelo, on December 12th, 1895. This was his first essay into murder; the first distinct sign that he possessed the traits of an assassin. To accept is as a possibility that he and Sam were the Chalk Hill killers would be to presuppose that the men who plotted Fountain's death could learn of the Powers murder, ascertain that Tom was involved in it, locate him—and Sam, get them into the vicinity of Tularosa, persuade them to undertake the assassination of Fountain—all in a matter of four weeks, at the very outside. It would be to presuppose, moreover, that the conspirators knew the Ketchums well enough to be able to trust them to carry out their instructions with discretion and efficiency. Among the facts which would have to be disregarded are these: officials in Tom Green County did not connect Tom Ketchum with the Powers murder until the summer of 1896; Sam Ketchum was never accused of complicity in this particular crime; and at no time were the names of Tom and Sam Ketchum brought into the Fountain case, by anyone, until 1949. The Ketchums had a fair knowledge of the Tularosa country, and must have met most of the ranchers in the area at one time or another; but they were transients, and had never stayed in the neighborhood long enough to be drawn into the darker intrigues of Dona Ana County.

One is left wondering over what it could have been that led Bob Lewis to speak as he did. There is no reason to doubt that he knew both Tom and Sam Ketchum; his remarks on their character are generally consistent in tone with the recollections of other men who had been acquainted with the brothers. It is possible that Sam merely told Lewis what he himself had heard about the killings, expressing disgust at the murder of the child, but without naming anyone as culprit; Lewis might have concluded from this that Sam was implicating himself and his brother by indirection. Whatever the true explanation behind Lewis' "revelation," Tom and Sam Ketchum had nothing in the world to do with the Chalk Hill murders.

Political influence and personal wealth were at issue in Dona Ana County. The chief elements in the unpleasantness were the vendetta between Fountain and Fall and the struggle between the large cattle outfits, who employed Fountain, and the smaller ranchers, led by Ed Brown and Oliver Lee under the aegis of Fall. Parallel with this was Lee's murderous campaign against those of the small ranchers who opposed him or stood in the way of his wishes. Fall, Lee, and their cronies emerge as the most ruthless and sinister bunch of assassins, thieves, and thugs ever to rise up and flourish in New Mexico; but it is only fair to remember that, in the beginning, they had to fight bitterly hard for their own survival: it is certainly true that their opponents were as determined and as tough as they, and in some cases very nearly as unscrupulous. The murder of the child, Henry Fountain, imparted a horrific quality to the grim drama and it may be this, rather than the memory of old animosities, which still tends to inhibit discussion of the case.

That Albert Fall—unquestionably the prime mover in the affair—should head the defense for Lee and Gililland when they stood trial for the murder of the boy, is hardly less than grotesque. The prosecution was in the hands of Richmond P. Barnes, District Attorney of Grant County, Thomas B. Catron, the old master string-puller of the Santa Fe Ring, and William B. Childers, the man who had hounded the alleged

Stein's Pass robbers into jail. Childers, a former political ally of Fall, had been retained by the Masonic Order; Catron, the dominant figure in the Republican party, had been assigned to the case by Governor Otero. Frank W. Parker was trial Judge.

It has been justly charged that Fall turned the trial into a political free-for-all, but there is some reason to suspect that the prosecution was not wholly committed to serving the ends of justice. William McNew was due to precede Lee and Gililland to trial for the murder of the elder Fountain, but the Territory dropped the case against all three simply through fear that the testimony of its witnesses, if used against McNew, would help Fall to determine his strategy for the defense of the other two. It appears that the main object of the prosecution was to topple Fall from political pre-eminence by knocking his chief prop, Oliver Lee, out from under him. In the final event it was decided that Lee and Gililland (but not McNew) would face trial at Hillsboro, the seat of Sierra County, for the murder of Henry Fountain. The jury, to its disgrace, rendered a verdict of "Not Guilty" and the crowd, to its shame, erupted with joy.

NOTES

THE BOLDEST OUTLAWS.

Although much of the material which forms the basis of this book has been collected from a variety of archival and other unpublished sources or from contemporary newspapers, numerous books were also consulted. Hence, some brief assessment should be offered here of the principal published works in which the Ketchums and their gang figure at all prominently.

There have been two books on Tom Ketchum: Ed Bartholomew's *Black Jack Ketchum — Last of the Hold-up Kings*, and Father Stanley's *No Tears for Black Jack Ketchum*. In common with practically everything else that has been written about Ketchum, their subject matter is mostly restricted to the three hold-ups at Folsom, New Mexico, the fight in Turkey Canyon, the trial of Tom Ketchum, and his execution. Both attribute to the Ketchum gang many of the crimes actually committed by Black Jack Christian's gang in the summer and fall of 1896; in contrast, their banditry in Texas is almost totally ignored. Stanley makes extensive (though uncritical) use of the files of the Santa Fe *Daily New Mexican* and of Miguel A. Otero's book *My Nine Years as Governor of the New Mexico, 1897-1906*, and his account of the trial of Lay, or McGinnis, owes much to this latter source. An original exhibit in Stanley's book is a long quoted passage from the unpublished reminiscences of Mason Chase, a ranchman who lived near Cimarron and who was a friend of "Billy" (James H.) Morgan, a posseman in the Turkey Canyon affair, Ed Bartholomew traveled through and took close note of much of the country traversed by the Ketchums; on the Philmont Scout Ranch, in the mountains near Cimarron, he photographed a huge carving of a face, uncommonly like the face of Tom Ketchum, chipped out of the side of a boulder. Otherwise the best feature of his book is the chapter on the death of Will Carver; much the same material also appears in Bartholomew's *Kill Or Be Killed*.

One of the earlier accounts may be found in a book first published in 1928— *Tombstone's Yesterday*, by Lorenzo D. Walters. Much of what Walters wrote about the Ketchums (in a chapter consisting mainly of thinly—paraphrased newspaper reports) ought rightly to have been placed in his chapter on Black Jack Christian. Walters has been followed by Bartholomew and others in charging the Ketchums with hold-ups at Nogales, Rio Puerco, San Simon, Huachuca Siding, and other places in Arizona and New Mexico. He does point out, however, that Ketchum was confused with Christian, and includes one or two interesting anecdotes which refer specifically to Tom Ketchum.

Carl B. Livingston, of Roswell, New Mexico, seems to have been the first to state in print that Tom Ketchum was never called Black Jack by those who knew

NOTES

him and by those who knew the real identities of the members of the different bandit gangs in the Southwest at the turn of the century. His articles were published in the Roswell *Record* and in *Wide World*. Most of his material came from eye-witnesses, and much of it is accurate. One or two of his informants, however, seem to have exercised the imagination more than the memory.

B. D. Titsworth's *Hole in the Wall Gang* appeared as a two-part article in *True West* some twelve years ago. It consists chiefly of newspaper clippings collected by Titsworth's father, a Texan who served for many years as a peace officer in southern Colorado. Someone inserted the year into the dateline of each of the newspaper items—an unfortunate interpolation, since in some instances the year indicated is not the right one.

Around Western Campfires, by Joseph "Mack" Axford, is a highly interesting record of what the author did, saw, and heard—and he did, saw, and heard a great deal—in the West of sixty and seventy or more years ago. Reassuringly unpretentious in tone, and always entertaining, it is one of the best books of frontier reminiscences.

Captain the Honorable William French's oft-misquoted fragment of autobiography *Some Recollections of a Western Ranchman* also proved valuable on occasion. The man French, incidentally, has at various times been described as an Englishman and an Irishman. In fact, he was neither—or perhaps both; he was a member of the Anglo-Irish Protestant "ascendancy" — a class which, in general, managed to become more Irish than the Irish whilst yet remaining more English than the English.

Cattle, Horses and Men of the Western Range is another first rate book. Its author, Jack Culley, was one of those typically untypical Englishmen of a breed now almost extinct. He was also a top notch cowman—unpalatable as that might be to writers of the sort who characterize all Englishmen in the New Mexico cattle industry as drunken clowns or boorish, arrogant oafs.

From time to time, use has been made of numerous other writings on the Ketchum gang, including those of Miguel A. Otero, Albert Thompson, Jack Potter, and others who had known or at least met individual members of the band. Brief comment has been made wherever seemed most appropriate—generally in the Notes to a specific chapter. Special reference must be made here, however, to Larry Ball's thesis, *Southwestern Conditions and Outlawry at the Turn of the Century,* which was subsequently published (though without the footnotes) in the *Brand Book* of the Denver Westerners. It was the first serious study on this theme and the first account in which most of the crimes of Tom Ketchum were pinpointed and set out in the proper sequence.

Descriptions of Tom Ketchum's character and appearance are plentiful, and there are several for Sam Ketchum. Just about everyone who recorded his impressions of Tom took especial note of the outlaw's eyes—Otero, to cite a further example, said they were like "black coals of fire"—and this cannot altogether be explained by the conventional implication commonly found in the literature and journalism of the nineteenth century that the eyes were the windows of the soul.

The description of Will Carver is taken, in the main, from the San Angelo *Standard,* as quoted by Ed Bartholomew in *Kill Or Be Killed* and *Black Jack*

Ketchum; that of Dave Atkins from the details compiled by the Pinkerton agency and reproduced in *Pictorial History of the Wild West,* by James D. Horan and Paul Sann — a book with some very good illustrations and some very bad textual matter. Tom Ketchum, in a loquacious mood at Clayton, New Mexico, where he was under trial, made jocular reference to "Tommy Atkins" in the course of conversation with his attorneys.

Marshal Griffith's letter is one of the many invaluable items in Department of Justice file 13065-96. This particular letter was written on December 9th, 1897. The rule that federal officers and possemen could claim expenses only on production of receipts and vouchers irritated and frustrated the marshals more than any other of the numerous obstacles. Griffith's counterpart in New Mexico, Marshal Foraker, hoping to be able to employ Will Loomis—chief deputy under the previous marshal—as an undercover man, found the Department sympathetic but powerless; they were bound to enforce the regulations, which were laid down by Act of Congress. Foraker, who could wield a weighty subjunctive, expressed his case thus:

"I would have him authorized to render on oath an actual expenses account, to be approved by myself, and the U.S. Attorney and the judge, but not supported by vouchers, as he would as well take a brass band with him if he be required to advertise himself by procuring vouchers for expenses as a government officer. . . . That it is important to the government to suppress this gang I presume I need not argue. That my request to put a single man in the field is not unreasonable I will also not discuss. . ."

Foraker's letter, dated October 9th, was carefully studied in Washington. In the end it was decided that Loomis could be so employed, but that he could not be given the power to make arrests. This was not quite what Foraker had wanted.

Tom Ketchum, while he waited to be taken to the gallows, mentioned his acquaintanceship with Bill Lutley. Some years later Lutley talked about Tom Ketchum to Walter Noble Burns, author of *Tombstone.* Lutley also appears in an anecdote in Axford's book.

At the time of Lay's arrest there was little or nothing in the newspapers to imply that V.H. Lusk might have known the members of the Ketchum gang (excepting Lay himself) for several years. Axford, whose information came in part from Carver, said that the band "had formed a friendship" with Lusk and often stopped at the ranch on their journeys to and from Texas. Major Aud Lusk, the rancher's younger son, in a recent interview with Phil Cooke, was explicit. He stated that the outlaws had been using the place "as a transfer point for horses between train robberies" and that Lusk had finally decided to put an end to this.

The quoted passages about the gang spending their life "in the bush" and "leading a solitary outdoor life" are from Texas press dispatches published in the summer of 1897, after their names had been connected with the Lozier train robbery.

CHAPTER I

The family name is found as both Ketchum and Ketcham in the States

NOTES

mentioned, and in others in New England and the Middle West, in the 1850s and earlier. The surname of the Texas members was often mis-spelled "Ketcham"— for example, in the returns for the Federal Census for San Saba County, 1870.

In this chapter, and throughout the book, occasional use has been made of statements offered to the Press by Tom Ketchum an hour or two before he met his death on April 26th, 1901. Many newspapers published a selection of his remarks. Comparison makes it plain that no one version is complete, but most of what he had to say is contained in one or other or both of two separate stories in the Denver, Colorado, *Rocky Mountain News*. There are any number of variations in the wording of phrases attributed to Ketchum, and one or two quite serious discrepancies. The reason for this is that few reporters knew shorthand (and those that did were seldom called upon to use it); as a rule, the newspapers furnished what was at best a close paraphrase, and at worst the general sense, of the subject's remarks. Here, in the case of Tom Ketchum, subeditors may have been responsible for the odd word (such as "depredation") which Tom himself would hardly have thought of using. There is one peculiar point about these statements made by Ketchum: he said quite clearly that he had passed his fortieth birthday in October, 1900. The evidence of the census returns, together with newspaper dispatches from Austin and San Angelo—contributed by people who obviously had talked to acquaintances of the Ketchum family—shows that Tom must have added three years to his age.

J. Marvin Hunter and others have written that the father of Sam and Tom Ketchum was a physician. There was a Doctor Ketchum in San Saba town, but this was N. Ketchum, the drug store proprietor. Tom himself, just before his death, said that his father had been a "cowman." Rogan, one of the nearest neighbors of Green B. Ketchum, was the only doctor in Richland Springs in 1860.

Misleading reports of Tom Ketchum's educational attainments began to appear in 1897; the culminating nonsense, garnishing him with a degree from Harvard, seems to have found its genesis in a rollicking extravaganza wired from El Paso, Texas, on March 20th, 1898. This dispatch was a haphazard brew of fact and fiction about a figure who was a composite of Tom Ketchum, Black Jack Christian, and a minor desperado named Howard McDonald.

Much of the background material for this chapter has been drawn from the *San Saba News*, although few of the issues for the year 1885 and for the early months of 1886 could be located. Because of this gap in the author's copy of the *News* file, and owing to the unavailability of court records, it is impossible to check Dee Harkey's account of the early errors of Tom and Sam in San Saba County; if Harkey's story is the truth, the incident must have occurred in the middle 1880s—when Dee (who was born in 1866) was old enough to act as a deputy under his brother, Joe Harkey — and it would certainly have been mentioned in the newspaper. One is inclined to accept what Harkey has to say hereof, though those familiar with his book *Mean as Hell* will not need to be told that it contains no word of the pecuniary misadventures of Sheriff Joe and is just as silent on Dee's handling, in later years, by various grand juries in Eddy County, New Mexico.

A note on the Dick Duncan case: Dick and a man named Landers murdered the widow Naomi Williamson, her widowed daughter Lavinia Holmes, her son Ben, and her younger daughter Beaulah (affianced to Dick) in February of 1889. Duncan and Landers battered the Williamsons to death and pitched the bodies into the Rio Grande. Dick was arrested several months later, taken to Eagle Pass, and convicted. After a lengthy debate over the question of the competence of the Texas court, Dick was hanged in 1891. Landers was never apprehended.

The history of the San Saba Mobs is best told by C.L. Sonnischen, in *I'll Die Before I'll Run*.

CHAPTER II

Different versions of the tale of the Ketchum inheritance occur in several of the newspaper articles written at about the time of the outlaw's death. There were Ketchums in New Jersey but they do not seem to have been related to the San Saba family except, perhaps, very distantly.

The information (regrettably meagre) on the Snake Valley interlude is taken from Charles Kelly's book, *Outlaw Trail*. Kelly had access to the written recollections of Tom McCarty, who apparently described the ranch as an outlaw hangout. Matt Warner's *Last of the Bandit Riders* also has some word of the Ketchum ranch in Utah, but does not name Sam and Tom as the Ketchum brothers who ran the place.

In the reminiscences of Thomas Edgar Crawford, edited by Jeff C. Dykes and published as *The West of the Texas Kid* (Crawford, like most of those who bore a nickname with "Tex" or "Texas" in it, was not a Texan) there is an account of the narrator's experiences whilst, allegedly, he was in the company of "a character by the name of Black Jack Ketchum," also in the late 1880s.

Now Crawford had the gift of imparting great verisimilitude to anecdotes which invite investigation and which do not survive it intact. With such a paucity of documented material available on this period of Ketchum's life, it is impossible to assess the degree of reliability in Crawford's story of their travels together; all the same it would be just as foolish to reject it in its entirety as to accept it without any reservation. Here is the gist of Crawford's narration:

At the time of their meeting, Ketchum was living in a cabin "on the middle fork of Purgatoire River," a tributary of the Arkansas. (This would place Tom in Las Animas County, Colorado, some twenty miles east of Trinidad, the county seat). The two men teamed up and rode down into the Pecos Valley. Afterwards they visited such places as Taos, Cimarron Canyon, Ute Park, Santa Fe, and Wagon Mound—all in New Mexico; Holbrook, Arizona; the Snake River country of southern Idaho; and Jackson Hole, in western Wyoming.

There is quite a lot to be said for the story; most of those places in New Mexico are intimately connected with Tom Ketchum's history in later years, and he might well have drifted through northern Arizona, Utah, Idaho, Wyoming, and Colorado during this period Tom McCarty (or Charles Kelly) states that he and Sam were ranchers in Utah; there are other stories, connecting him with northern Arizona and Wyoming at different times in the years before he became an outlaw,

NOTES

and he himself talked at least once of having lived in Idaho.

Against it there is Crawford's knack of telling a tall tale and making it look absolutely authentic.

Of course Tom Ketchum was never called "Black Jack" by anyone who met him or knew him before his arrest in 1899, and never spoken of as "Black Jack" until 1897. It was only in the latter months of 1897 that the newspapers started to apply the sobriquet to Ketchum. This does not mean that Crawford made up the story: it is more likely that he referred to Ketchum as "Black Jack" because this was the name by which Tom would be most readily recognizable to the reader.

The rancher Ann Basset (the celebrated "Queen Ann," of Brown's Hole) said that Tom Ketchum went gunning for William G. Tittsworth after Tittsworth had killed Charley Powers, allegedly a friend of Tom's. This is told in that fascinating and superbly illustrated work *Where the Old West Stayed Young*, by John Rolfe Burroughs. But the killing occurred in the early 1880s, when Tom was still a youth in San Saba County, and Ann was a little girl of seven or eight. Tittsworth's book *Outskirt Episodes* is a sort of autobiography in which most of the names are fictitious ones.

Gerome W. Shields was first elected to the post of Sheriff in 1888. Many years later, in a letter to Albert Thompson, he said that he had arrested Tom Ketchum in 1892. But in 1899 he had told a reporter in Santa Fe that Tom Ketchum was the first man he ever arrested, from which it would appear more probable that Tom turned the dog loose on the congregation one Sunday in the early part of 1889. The author was unable to get hold of material from the San Angelo newspapers, unfortunately.

Phil Cook, during a series of interviews in Clayton, New Mexico, heard all about Tom's involvement with the unnamed ranch wife from around Amarillo way. Otherwise the account of Ketchum's trail driving years is put together mostly from the Albert Thompson manuscript and Potter's recollections. The VV outfit (the brand was V pitchfork V), whose headquarters were near Ruidoso, should not be confused with the VVN, of Eddy County. Potter thought that Tom Ketchum might also have worked for the latter company.

Eve Ball, in *Ma'am Jones of the Pecos*, gives a second version of Tom's encounter with the locomotive engineer. Her spokesman, in this instance Charles Nebo "Nib" Jones, says that it happened after the cowboys reached Clayton with the S Cross herd. Shortly before the end of that drive, according to Jones, Tom got drunk, slit the throats of a sheep dog and her pups, and claimed that he and another of the S Cross hands, a fellow who called himself Billy Morgan, had committed the murders for which Dick Duncan had been convicted. Nib adds that he was certain that Tom himself had nothing to do with the murders but that Morgan was furious with Ketchum and came near to killing him. Morgan fled camp, after forcing Nib to steal a horse for him. Jones seems to imply that he believed Morgan to have been Dick Duncan's missing accomplice.

The material on Will Carver, the Kilpatricks, and Laura Bullion is drawn from a number of sources, including the census returns for 1860, 1870, and 1880; newspaper reports of the killing of Carver and of the arrest and interrogation of Ben Kilpatrick and Laura Bullion; Marvin Hunter's article *Black Jack Ketchum and*

His Gang, in *Frontier Times,* April 1939; and letters to the author from H.A. Holmes, of Sheffield, Texas, who knew several of the Kilpatricks and whose stepmother was "a second or third cousin" to Will Carver.

CHAPTER III

The author could locate neither the court records nor the San Angelo newspapers of the period; consequently the account of the Powers murder is based chiefly on a couple of dispatches—one reporting the killing, and the other giving details of the arrest of Mrs Powers—which appeared in the San Antonio *Express,* the St. Louis *Globe-Democrat,* and various other papers, and on Tom Ketchum's own statement, which must have been somewhat prejudicial to himself. Albert Thompson, who got some information on the crime from Gerome Shields, stated in his Manuscript that Tom Ketchum was tipped off by Will Carver. Evidently Shields did not advise Thompson as to the approximate date of the crime, for Thompson—making a wild guess, and a bad one—wrote that the murder occurred in the 1880s. He also placed the scene of the crime in San Saba County, probably through careless haste.

The principal newspaper sources for particulars of the Ketchum's service with the Bell round-up, the subsequent murders, and the pursuit, are the Santa Fe *Daily New Mexican* and the *Roswell Record.* The latter paper also doled out a fair measure of comment about the derelictions of Sheriff Perry. References in James D. Shinkle's interesting book, *Reminiscences of Roswell Pioneers,* to "Charles C. Perry" seem to be the result of mistaken presumption: although nicknamed Charley, Perry was actually named after Christopher Columbus.

A dispatch from Santa Fe, dated February 6th, 1897, and carried by a number of papers, states that the brothers had joined "Wilson Waddingham's ranch" as line riders in July 1896. In point of fact Waddingham had relinquished control of the Bell ranch in 1894 and the Ketchums had left the place early in June of 1896. But this article is another of those which confuse the actions and identities of the Christians, the Ketchums, and the man McDonald.

The Bell cowhands told Jack Culley that the man who showed such prestidigital skill with the pistol was Tom Ketchum. Culley, unaccountably, says that they were wrong and that the man was Sam Ketchum. Yet since, according to Culley himself, the man was wearing a black beard, it seems clear that he must have been Tom, rather than Sam.

Another account of the chase for the Ketchums and the malfeasance of Sheriff Perry is that of Dee Harkey, who says, mistakenly, that Will Carver was one of the murderers. Harkey mentions the arrest of the suspects in Mexico, and his reticence is further evidence that the officers had caught the wrong men: if he and his companions had bagged the Ketchums, Dee would have had a great deal more to say on the matter.

Much could be written on the earlier life of Bob and Will Christian. Will was about fifteen when he had his first brush with the Federal Court at Fort Smith, Arkansas. He was acquitted of the theft of three head of cattle "of

NOTES

the value of ten dollars each and of the total value of thirty dollars" from one Samuel Alvison, a resident of the Choctaw Nation, on March 10th, 1886. In 1890 William Mark Christian, father of the boys, and his brother, Daniel L. Christian, were "regular (sic) peddling" whiskey in the Nations and were "very sharp . . . selling all the time now but very sly," according to a report from Deputy United States Marshal John Childers. The Christian ranch, just within the borders of the Creek Nation and near the boundaries of the Seminole and Choctaw Nations, was a resort for thieves and outlaws. Bob and Will roamed through most of what became the state of Oklahoma, and were friendly with such worthies as "George Thorne," perhaps the slipperiest horse thief and escape artist in the Nations, whose real name was George Weightman and who is usually remembered by his nickname, Red Buck. The Bob Christian gang of bandits was formed in the Choctaw Nation, late in 1894. At least two newspaper accounts named a man called Christian as one of the participants in the celebrated train robbery at Dover, Oklahoma, on April 3rd, 1895 (the others were Red Buck, Tulsa Jack Blake, Bitter Creek Newcomb, Charlie Pierce, Zip Wyatt, and Bill Raidler) but this could hardly have been Bob or Will; the man to whom reference was intended may have been Dan Clifton. On April 20th of that year Bob Christian killed an officer, William Turney or Turner, in Pottawatomie County, Oklahoma. Bob and Will were convicted of manslaughter but broke jail and, in between dodging posses, robbed a number of stores and post offices during the summer and autumn of 1895. They had numerous confederates and followers. Although never identified as such, they were probably at the head of the band who held up a train near Curtis, Oklahoma, on the afternoon of September 12th. Less than a month after this, they were accused of a second train robbery, at Caston tank. Four other men were eventually convicted for this last crime, albeit on the shakiest and most unreliable sort of testimony. Bob and Will Christian arrived in New Mexico early in 1896 and returned to outlawry in July.

The story of the meeting between Tom Ketchum and Black Jack is from an astonishing document entitled *William Christian, alias Black Jack*, by Ben R. Clark, which appeared in *Progressive Arizona and the Great Southwest*, December 1929 and January 1930. Clark, a deputy sheriff of Graham County, Arizona, was in the posse which killed Black Jack; he was elected sheriff in the fall of 1898. In a letter to William K. Meade, U. S. Marshal of Arizona, dated May 2nd 1897, Clark said that "the dead body was positively identified to be Tom Ketchum alias Black Jack—it was recognized as such by men, women and children." A telegram to Hall from Fred Higgins, who fired the fatal bullet, stated that a number of witnesses had identified the dead man as Tom Ketchum; but Hall himself, after having studied a transcript of the evidence before the Coroner's Jury, wrote to Meade on May 31st to say, among other things, that Speck was the only person who identified the body as that of Tom Ketchum.

CHAPTER IV

The Samuels train robbery took place on Wednesday, September 2nd, 1891.

For J. Ernest Smith, the express messenger, the hold-up was not a novel experience. Nearly four years earlier he had killed a couple of would-be train robbers near El Paso, setting an example which, it was hoped, would make train robbery a thing of the past. But Smith himself was held up for a second time, near Stein's Pass, in February 1888, and his express car efficiently plundered. After the Samuels hold-up he offered his resignation.

Accounts of the first Comstock train robbery and the capture of the bandits were taken from the El Paso *Times*, a dispatch from Del Rio to the Abilene, Texas, *Reporter*, and dispatches from San Antonio and Houston to the St. Louis *Globe-Democrat*.

The last named paper also contains a number of dispatches on the pursuit of the gang after the Lozier robbery, although its account of the actual hold-up is rather disjointed. Messenger Joyce's reminiscences were published in *Mainline*, the railroad magazine. "Kit" Carson, of Albuquerque, kindly provided the author with a copy of this item. In dictating the story, in 1922, Joyce erroneously gave the date of the hold-up as May 10th; further, he forgot to mention the incident of the parrot (which he had described with great gusto, twenty-five years earlier) but lingered on the story of the aggressive bulldog (which did not figure at all in his original report). Another version of the Lozier robbery was found in the *San Francisco Chronicle*.

W. H. Hutchinson's fine biography of Eugene Manlove Rhodes, *A Bar Cross Man*, is the source of the statement that Sam was staying with Rhodes in the summer of 1897. Rhodes said that Tom and Sam tried hard to persuade him to join them in the Folsom hold-up but that he declined because he was "flush just then." Apparently Tom had once spent a winter at Rhodes's ranch; the year is impossible to determine, but it must have been some time prior to 1894.

In the main, the story of the first Folsom robbery comes from the newspapers of the day; the most detailed of the accounts used is contained in a dispatch from Fort Worth to the *Globe-Democrat*. Otero's description, in *My Nine Years as Governor*, is the best of those derived from later writings, but is far from accurate; in particular, Otero is grossly at fault in associating Elza Lay and "Bronco Bill" with this hold-up. First reports put the loot at $12,000 to $15,000; Otero and Livingston place the figure at $3,500; Tom Ketchum said that the members of the gang got about $500 each. Titsworth describes the Poker game at Moore's saloon. Other material for this part of the chapter is drawn from Livingston and from newspaper stories on the arrest and trials of "Collins." The conclusion that Collins and Weaver were merely two different names for one man is the author's; the facts which make it an obvious one are as presented in Chapter X.

The Gulf, Colorado and Santa Fe Railroad was reorganized as the Colorado and Southern Railway some time shortly after the events described in this chapter.

CHAPTER V

A dispatch from Tombstone, Arizona, dated August 15th, 1897, gives a brief history of the Hoffman-Richards feud.

NOTES

Foraker attempted to put the blame for the killing of Richards onto the Black Jack gang in a letter to the United States Attorney General, dated October 9th, 1897.

The most specific references to the friendship between the Texas Canyon cowboys and Christian's gang are to be found in Alverson's manuscript and in a letter from Jesse Smith Lea to U. S. Marshal Hall, dated May 24th, 1897.

The hold-ups at Grants are dealt with under *Tales That Were Told*.

Tom Ketchum himself spoke of Atkins' carelessness with the bottle, which led to the band's flight into Mexico.

Information on Charley Perry's death in South Africa was passed to Colin Rickards, in London, by Mrs. Emmett White, of Roswell, New Mexico. Mrs. White is related to Perry's family.

Other sources are as cited in the text.

CHAPTER VI

There was some controversy over the question of Ed Cullen's true identity. Officers in El Paso believed that he was a certain Victor "Sandy" Collins and ridiculed the claim that he was anyone called Hespatch, even though letters found on the body pointed to the man's connection with Colorado City. Tom Ketchum apparently stated that the slain outlaw was Ed Bullion; the surname was spelled Bullin or Bullen in newspaper accounts of Ketchum's "confession." *Kill Or Be Killed*, by Ed Bartholomew, contains the statement—unsourced—that Ed was a brother of Laura who had been a cowpuncher in Texas with the Kilpatricks, Ketchums, and Carver. J. Evetts Haley tells in *Jeff Milton: A Good Man with a Gun* of how Ed came to be called "Shoot-em-up-Dick." (The restaurant owner was a well-known character who passed under the name Sam McCoy.) Axford describes how "Shoot-em-up-Dick" dealt with the high-and-mighty magnate.

Details of the movements of the posses in the Stein's Pass area, of the robbery of the station and post office, and of the train hold-up have been pieced together from many sources: the letters of Marshals Foraker and Griffith, numerous newspaper reports and interviews, Tom Ketchum's account, and Haley's. Both Messenger Adair and Mail Clerk Albright were interviewed in Los Angeles, at the end of the run.

Adair, as it turned out, was not finished with train robbers. He was held up by the Alvord gang near Cochise station, Arizona, on September 9th, 1899. In this instance Adair's hands "went up above his head in a jiffy."

CHAPTER VII

J. Evetts Haley's *Jeff Milton: A Good Man with a Gun* is a very fine book but it is not an impartial biography. There were certain incidents (one such will be cited in due course) wherein Milton's role was smaller than the one assigned to him in the book. Again, Milton—like any other courageous man—had his moments of weakness, though Mr. Haley hints at none of these. John Wesley Hardin and Jeff Kidder, the bravest of the brave, must have experienced failure, too, but it is difficult not to be skeptical of any protrayal of these two as blubbering abjectly before Jeff Milton or anyone else.

Leon Claire Metz, in *John Selman: Texas Gunfighter,* has closely explored the nature of the relationship between Hardin, Milton, Selman, and George Scarborough.

The author's evaluation of Scarborough was formed after a comparison of the appraisals—contrasting in many respects, but by no means mutually irreconcilable —of Haley, Metz, James H. McClintock *(Arizona: The Youngest State),* Marvin Hunter (J. Marvin Hunter and Noah H. Rose, *The Album of Gunfighters),* Henry Brock (reminiscences, in conversation with Lou Blachly), Ed Bartholomew *(Kill or Be Killed),* and Ben C. Kemp (recalled by his son, Ben W. Kemp, and edited by Jeff C. Dykes, as *Cow Dust and Saddle Leather);* and from material in a collection of newspaper accounts of various episodes in which Scarborough figured.

George's father, G. W. Scarborough, was a clergyman at Cameron, Texas.

Jesse James Benton describes how Scarborough arrested Hoffman. Benton misspells the officer's name as "Scarber"; Carl Livingston gives it as "Scharbaugh"; James Emmit McCanley, in *A Strove-Up Cowboy's Story,* writes it as "Scarbrough". Each of these, presumably, represents an attempt at phonetic spelling.

In telling Mrs George (Edith Stratton) Kitt of his experiences after his arrest, Alverson named the man who, he claimed, drank himself to insanity; but Mrs Kitt judiciously suppressed the name from her typescript.

Jim Fielder, the attorney, seems not to have believed that the courts should be the rightful arbiters of all matters of dispute. In October, 1895, he fell out with C. L. Cantelly, Marshal of Silver City, and killed him in a gunfight.

There must be doubts about the veracity of Alverson's charge that Pat Garrett loaded the jury against the defendants at their second trial, for there is not a morsel of evidence to back it up. What is certain is that there was a rotten deal, and that Alverson, Hoffman, and Warderman were on the wrong end of it.

CHAPTER VIII

Allen A. Erwin's notable work of biography *The West of John Horton Slaughter* is the source of the story of how Tom Ketchum had second thoughts about trying conclusions with "Little Black John." Erwin got the story from Fred Moore, who was with the outlaws at the time. While no date is mentioned, it is reasonably certain that the day in question fell sometime between the autumn of 1897 and the spring of 1898, because this was the only period when all four members of the gang were together in the locality, except for a very short spell early in 1899.

A dispatch from El Paso to the San Francisco *Chronicle* gives a fairly good account of the second Comstock robbery, although at one point the correspondent mistakenly described the train that was held up as the eastbound one.

Coleman, Texas, had been the scene of a successful train robbery in the spring of 1893. In the summer of 1899 it was claimed in a number of newspaper articles that the bandits got $30,000 in the 1898 Coleman robbery, but this must have been the result of confusion with either the hold-up at Comstock or the one at Stanton. It is certain that the robbers were driven off before they had a chance to blow the through safe, and it appears that they did not even get their hands on the contents of the local safe. A very few days after this, Bud Newman and Bill and Jeff Taylor were arrested on the Newman ranch near Carta Vista, north of Dél Rio. Newman escaped punishment by turning State's evidence against the Taylors; but Bill Taylor broke jail and killed Newman. The fight is described by Louis Montgomery in a letter printed in *Real West*, September 1968. Mr Montgomery, who lives at Brady, Texas, later provided the writer with some information on the Newmans. He worked on the Newman ranch in the 1890s. Pierce Keaton fled to Mexico. He was detained in Juarez but was not surrendered to the Texas authorities until September, 1899. Officials who were handling the extradition procceedings, and contemporary newspapers, invariably call him John Keeton. In the 1880 Federal Census for Kimble County, Texas, however, he is listed simply as Pierce Keaton, third of the six sons of Charles H. Keaton, a fifty-nine year old Irishman. (Pierce's three sisters are enumerated as Lelia, Lulu, and Dodo).

Andy Jones owned the horse branded 8D Connected which was recovered more than a year later at Chimney Wells, New Mexico, when Elza Lay was arrested.

The newspapers of San Antonio, Dallas, St. Louis, Denver, and San Francisco carried little or nothing on the Stanton robbery apart from the report issued by General Manager Thorn of the Texas and Pacific Railway. Thorn's claim that there were six robbers was probably derived from the assertions of witnesses who mistook one or two of the trainmen for bandits. An item in the Abilene *Reporter*, although brief, contains some further details and states that only three robbers were seen but that it was believed there were four of them involved in the hold-up.

French relates in *Some Recollections of a Western Ranchman* that he went to Jerusalem not very long after the German Emperor visited the city. Kaiser Bill entered Jerusalem on October 29th, 1898; French was absent from the ranch for no more than a few weeks; and the Ketchums returned from Wyoming to the border southwest at about the same time as Cassidy and Lay moved into Cochise County. Hence, it is easy to work out roughly when Tom and Sam called at the WS.

The prison records at Santa Fe, New Mexico, show that Lay gave his place of birth as Coles County, Illinois. This can be accepted as the truth; Lay must have had some family connection with eastern Illinois in order to have heard of Coles County.

Joseph Axford's book and *Riata and Spurs*, by Charles A. Siringo both have worthwhile material on the WS and some of the men who worked there.

CHAPTER IX

The horse-stealing incidents are described by Carl B. Livingston and by two items in the Roswell *Record*, May 12th and August 18th, 1899.

Springer, incidentally, was summed up as a somewhat dreary little place by William French.

Comments on the sources of information on what the outlaws did in northeastern New Mexico during that summer will be found in the notes to the next three chapters.

Ernest Gentry was arrested in Redding, California, in July and taken back to New Mexico by Sheriff Charles F. "Doc" Blackington of Socorro County. Blackington, discussing a friend of Gentry's, who was planning an attempt to rescue the bandit, declared: "Say! I've simply got that fellow lashed to the mast, and if he gets too sociable I'll make him look like a dirty deuce in a new deck." A year or two before the Alamogordo robbery, Gentry had married an Apache woman. He and his cronies, red and white, had been very troublesome to the officers of Navajo and Gila Counties, Arizona.

The papers of Roswell, El Paso, Santa Fe, and many other towns and cities published a great deal on the capture of the thieves in Otero County, on the controversy over their identities, and on the different means whereby the men evaded the charges against them. Dee Harkey named one of the band as Will Morrow, but the man concerned was Sam Morrow: Will was a respectable rancher. Harkey, of course, awarded himself all the credit for the capture of the four but — for once—he seems to have been entitled to whatever honors were going.

Little variation is to be found in the accounts of the Camp Verde shootings. It is of little moment whether the gunman, just before he killed Rogers, said "That won't do, Mack," (as Frank Wingfield recalled it), or whether the words were "Don't do it, Mack," (as Maurice Kildare reports them): the first version sounds the more apt, but the message would have been pretty much the same in either case.

In a dispatch from Prescott, dated July 3rd, it was alleged that the killer had an accomplice who remained outside the store during the shooting. This may have been the belief of the excited messenger who carried the news to Prescott, but it was quickly found to be incorrect.

Who Killed Rogers and Wingfield? by Maurice Kildare (Gladwell Richardson), an article published in *Real West*, July 1968, is a thorough and absorbing reconstruction of the background, the crime, and the pursuit. But Kildare—almost presupposing Ketchum's innocence—concludes that the whole affair is a mystery. The great defect in Kildare's argument is the total absence of any attempt to trace the movements of Tom Ketchum or to go into the evidence against him: a commonly-held belief (quite firmly based, as it happens) cannot be rebutted merely by the recital of a tenuous string of plausible but unsubstantiated alternatives. Kildare shows quite plainly that the murder of Rogers may have been premeditated, and that—contrary to the popular and obvious theory—robbery was not the object of the gunman; but his contention that the murder of Clint Wingfield is proof that the killer had been nursing a hatred for *both* men hardly bears a second's serious reflection. Much the same can be said of his opinion that the Wingfields affected

NOTES

to believe in Ketchum's guilt because it suited them to do so. Frank Wingfield felt so strongly about the murder of Clint and threw so much energy into the pursuit that it is difficult to picture him as standing idly aside if he had reason to think that the killer was still at large. His version of the events, as told to Richard W. Sturgis, appeared in *True West*, August 1963, under the title *I Trailed Black Jack Ketchum*. He never doubted that Ketchum was guilty.

Another resident of the Verde Valley, Elmer Isaac Jones, always thought that the killer was "obviously a robber" and said that the folk of Camp Verde "never did find out who the killer was." His reminiscences of the Valley can be read in *The "Old-Timer" of Verde Valley*, by Harold Farmer *(Pioneer West,* November 1967).

It is impossible to judge whether the evidence then available might have been strong enough to have Ketchum fairly convicted. The eye-witness Boyle subsequently identified Ketchum; but he would have found it difficult to convince a jury (or, at least, an impartial jury) that he could not have been mistaken. Taking all in all, Tom Ketchum's guilt can be asserted with something more than a reasonable degree of confidence but less than utter certainty.

CHAPTER X

The rather complicated sequence of developments from the time Lay and Weaver gave notice to French up to the night of the second train robbery at Folsom was pieced together from the writings of French, Culley, and Erna Fergusson, from what little was said of this interlude in the newspapers in the days following the hold up, and — especially — from the testimony of Morgan, Hunt, and Correy at the trial of Lay. The trial evidence is especially valuable in that each incident is tied down to a date. French, on the other hand, is always vague with dates; and in the few instances where he does give an approximate date, his memory is almost invariably astray. He says that it was probably October when Lay announced that he was about to quit the WS; in fact, it was early in May. Both Culley and Fergusson quote a story of George Crocker, a youth at the time but later a prominent cattleman of that locality, that Lay put up at the St. James Hotel (which still stands, although it has been renamed the Don Diego for no very good apparent reason). He might have done so briefly, but this hotel is not among the places mentioned in the court testimony.

Many of the details of the robbery itself are taken from the testimony of Tubbs, Harrington, and Scott at Lay's trial. Tubbs, it should be added, had moderated his story somewhat during the intervening months: his earliest effusion was taken down by a reporter a couple of days after the hold-up and may be found in Titsworth. The newspaper was, most probably, either the Denver *Post* or the Trinidad *Chronicle-News*. Fred Higgins' account appeared in both the Denver *Rocky Mountain News*, which deilt at length with the robbery, and the Santa Fe *New Mexican*. Other papers, such as the Trinidad *Advertiser-Standard*, carried compartively little copy on the hold-up but kept closely in touch with the pursuit of the outlaws. Practically every published account of the Ketchums, whatever it does not have, has a story on the second Folsom robbery; all are inaccurate in one respect or another, although the broad facts of the case leave little scope for disagreement. The oddest divergence occurs in Livingston's version, wherein it is related that some unnamed member of the gang, posing as a cripple, was helped onto the train by members of the crew; having ascertained that the trainmen were unarmed, this man supposedly scribbled a note to that effect, left it where it would be found by his partners, then dived out of the window. A search for corroboration led—perhaps not unpredictably—to the conclusion that this tale was entirely fictitious.

A few weeks after the hold-up, Foraker told a newspaperman that the outlaws had obtained thirty thousand dollars. The interview was published in the Albuquerque correspondence of the Chicago *Chronicle* and copied in the San Francisco *Chronicle* of September 14th, 1899. Otero, however, must have been in an even better position to learn the full extent of the booty, for he was the more closely involved (and on better terms) with representatives of the railroad and express company interests. Further reasons for accepting his figure of seventy thousand dollars as the correct one will be made apparent in Chapter XVIII. On the witness stand, as elsewhere, Expressman Scott trotted out the story that the bandits got nothing except a saddle tree and some peaches.

CHAPTER XI

The material for this chapter comes from the following sources: the testimony of James Hunt, Agapito Duran, James H. Morgan. Juan Maria Apodaca, Juan C. Martinez, James Correy, C. M. Foraker, George Titsworth, W.H. Reno, Wilson Elliott, Perfecto Cordova, David Farr, Miguel Lopez, and William H. McGinnis (Elza Lay) in *Territory of New Mexico vs. William H. McGinnis, Cause No. 2419, Murder;* numerous contemporary newspaper reports, but principally those in the Denver *Rocky Mountain News,* Santa Fe *Daily New Mexican,* and Trinidad *Advertiser-Standard* during the period between the robbery and the death of Sam Ketchum; Foraker's statement on the fight, as cited in the notes to the previous chapter; the San Angelo *Standard* of July 17th and August 15th, 1899, quoted by Bartholomew in *Black Jack Ketchum,* which carried Elliott's version of the affair; an unnamed paper (Probably the Trinidad *Chronicle-News)* quoted by Titsworth; Mason Chase's manuscript, as quoted by Stanley; the accounts of Axford, French, Livingston, as cited; and that of Brown Waller in *Last of the Great Western Train Robbers.*

Foraker's belief that negotiations between officers and criminals who were contemplating treachery should be closely confidential was stated in a letter to the United States Attorney-General, dated November 6th, 1897. In this letter Foraker was critical of certain officers who had made careless talk about the circumstances of the Cole Creek Canyon ambush. It is noticeable that, as time went on, Marshal Foraker—brother of Senator Joseph B. Foraker, of Ohio, one of the leading figures of the Republican party—wrote fewer and fewer letters to the Attorney-General's office.

NOTES

It is hardly surprising that the fight in Turkey Creek Canyon should have set off a heated controversy. The engagement was a resounding defeat for the posse —and none knew it better than they; a lot of things needed to be explained. Reno was so placed as to have the advantage of being the first combatant to show himself before the public. To begin with, he concentrated on justifying his own actions, never criticizing Elliott's party except once, and then only by innuendo. Elliott, as a cover for his own irresolute performance, resorted to exaggeration. Foraker, however, defended Elliott chiefly by censuring Reno in the fiercest terms. The arrest of the badly-wounded Sam Ketchum, by Reno's posse, did nothing to lower the temperature of the exchanges between Foraker and Reno. The detective's undisguised elation at this success, which proved that the defeat in Turkey Canyon was not absolute, did not help matters. Other participants in the fight and in the capture of Ketchum came out with statements for or against Reno. The whole rumpus was reported — or enacted — in the columns of the *Rocky Mountain News*. Even before the ill-feeling was allowed to sink below the surface, several other papers had published Reno's version of the fight—or versions, for it is difficult to find two that are alike in all material particulars. In one of them, for example, Reno said that Farr was killed instantaneously; elsewhere, though, he stated that the mortally wounded sheriff was granted time enough to ask Reno to say goodbye for him to the Farr family. Apparently, too, Reno talked or wrote at length to Carl Livingston, whose highly colored and highly original account of the fight appeared thirty years after the event; here it is alleged that the three bandits were engrossed in a game of cards as the posse bore down upon them, and that, after Lay and Ketchum had been wounded, Carver kept the officers at bay by rapid fire from his two six-shooters, all the time dodging from tree to tree. There is nothing on those lines to be found in any other description of the affair. One of the many curious facets of Lay's trial—and it is ironical, too, in the light of the detective's generally irrepressible loquacity on the subject of the fight—is that Reno's testimony did not even touch upon the shooting. One can but guess as to whether this was because the prosecuting attorneys so wished it or whether it was in accordance with some request of his own: a logical hypothesis could be constructed from either premise.

The dispatch in which the slain sheriff was identified as an outlaw—as both "Franks" and "McGinnis" at the same time, in fact — was telegraphed from Springer on July 17th, and widely published. This was a spectacular stroke of incompetence by a reporter who was actually on the scene when the body was brought into Cimarron. Still other error in reporting arose from the use of interviews with men whose information came from second hand or hearsay, where misunderstanding, ignorance, or slip of memory could be grafted onto misstatement. On the afternoon of July 17th Marion Littrell, a stock inspector (sheriff of Colfax County a few years later), arrived in Las Vegas with the news that the fight had taken place at five o'clock in the morning and that there were six in the posse; these details were incorrect, but Littrell was only passing on what he had been told, or thought he had been told, in Springer. The item appeared in the *New Mexican* that afternoon. Then, in a story in the Trinidad *Advertiser-Standard* of July 19th, the posseman Love was miscalled Smith and Turkey Canyon referred to as "Chicken Canyon." This story came from Webb, superintendent of the Colorado and Southern, and B. B. Sipes, the local coroner, both of whom had just returned from Springer with Farr's body. But they were in a position to dismiss allegations that the outlaws had been using "explosive bullets" (expanding bullets, or dum-dums); it had not been realized at first, they explained, that the thigh of Smith (they meant Love) had been pierced by the blade of his own knife as well as by a bullet.

There remain three important points of issue which cannot simply be attributed to the discrepancies in contemporary newspaper stories and which cannot therefore be settled by comparing what is left of each account after the obvious flaws have been explained and eliminated. The questions are these: Who was G. W. Franks? Did the posse open fire on the suspects without having first called upon them to throw up their hands? Which of the men killed Farr?

The answer to the first question is that reference to the source material leaves not the faintest flickering suspicion of a shadow of a doubt that Franks was Carver. However, one or two people thought that Franks was Tom Capehart, and others have seen fit to maintain that he was Harvey Logan, or even that Logan was both Capehart and Franks. The matter is discussed at length in "Tales that were Told."

For the sake of conciseness, the second point had better be treated as a plain question of fact, and kept firmly isolated from such obscurantist debate as would weigh fair play against common sense, lawful obligation against practical consideration, the abstract against the real.

Reno always insisted that the outlaws had started the shooting after he and Farr had demanded their surrender. Several others of the posse either agreed with this explicitly or said that, in any event, the officers did not open fire until the bandits had shown that they intended to resist. One of the possemen, Morgan, contradicted this both informally and on the witness stand. Another, Cordoba, was known to have said in conversation that Lay was unarmed when the posse began to shoot; when placed on the stand, however, he responded obediently to the careful prompting of the prosecution. Governor Otero, who sat through the trial and took note not only of the testimony but of the manner in which it was delivered, and who was fully aware of the pressures which governed the conduct of the trial, believed Lay and Morgan. So, in the main, did the jury; their verdict says as much.

It was established almost directly after the fight that Carver had done most of the shooting for the outlaws. Opinion at this time was divided as to whether it was he or Sam who had fired the shot which killed Farr. Elliott thought that it must have been Carver. Reno—after his posse had captured Sam—maintained that Ketchum was the killer. On this point, if on no other, Foraker took the same view as Reno. Some people may have believed Sam's dying declaration of guilt, but it is certain that the outlaw was not telling the truth here any more than he had been a few days earlier, when he stated that he was wounded right at the beginning of the fight and took no part in it. Elza Lay, it can be stated with complete certainly, was the man who killed Sheriff Farr.

The story of Lay's part in the fight is told by Axford in convincing detail.

NOTES

Axford is mistaken, however, in saying that Lay's shooting accounted for other members of the posse beside Farr and that witnesses at Lay's trial did their best to put him in the clear by alleging that he, rather than Carver, occupied the higher ground in Turkey Canyon.

It is generally stated that Sam made his way unaided to the McBride place. But Wilson Elliott, speaking of the matter directly afterwards, said that Sam had been taken there by the other two, and Axford, passing down the story as he heard it from Carver and from people who had talked to Sam, relates the circumstances in some detail. The other version had the effect of sparing the McBrides a certain amount of embarrassment.

Mason Chase, as quoted by Stanley, said that Reno kicked Sam Ketchum.

The surname of Earl Clause was sometimes mis-spelt Clouse or Claws; Jack Culley and Erna Fergusson call him "Pearl Claws."

Reno made the capture whilst armed with Ed Farr's Winchester. The detective acquired Sam's stag-handled Colt forty-five (years later he showed it to Albert Thompson) and his "special railway watch, 17 jewels, with Waltham movement."

References in some of the contemporary press to "Lambert's ranch" as the scene of the arrest were not incorrect: Henry Lambert owned the property, and the McBrides rented it.

A dispatch from Springer, published in the Trinidad *Daily Advertiser-Sentinel* on July 22nd, contains the following fatuities: "Dave Carver, a Texas desperado, who has for some time been operating through New Mexico, and William McGinnis, alias W.B. Franks, are supposed to be the two men still at large." This "Dave Carver" seems to have been created out of confusion between Dave Atkins and Will Carver. When the news came through that another suspect was being questioned, someone must have assumed that this man had to be "Dave Carver." Later, it was learned that the man was Weaver, subsequently referred to as "Wheeler" in newspaper accounts and court testimony.

One further incidental point: although Cimarron had no telegraph office, the village was connected to Springer by telephone. This apparatus was used by both Foraker and Reno; but it was no good at all if direct communication were needed with someone in Denver or Santa Fe.

CHAPTER XII

The story of Sam Ketchum's last days is derived from Jack Culley's account, from material gathered by George Fitzpatrick, and from items in many of the sources cited in the notes to the previous chapter.

Sam admitted his participation in the Stein's Pass hold-up, and stated that Hoffman, Alverson, and Warderman were innocent of the charges, to Robert Law, the cell-house keeper at the Territorial Penitentiary, Santa Fe, and to Law's assistant, Antonio Borrego. Nearly four years later, on April 17th, 1903, Borrego swore an affidavit to this. Sam also talked about the Stein's Pass affair to a doctor who attended him and to John Hart, a convict.

The conclusion that Carver, Lay, and Capehart were the three members of the gang who visited Tom Green County less than two weeks after the Turkey Canyon fight may at first seem far-fetched, but the known facts permit of no other interpretation. The question of Capehart's presence is also discussed in *Tales that were Told*. In the last days of July dispatches were sent out from San Angelo to newspapers all over the United States.

There is, mercifully, very little scope for argument about just how the law caught up with Elza Lay; the different accounts often complement one another, seldom conflict. The main sources for the story as it is told here are Major Aud Lusk (interview with Phil Cooke); Axford, Culley, French, Livingston, Titsworth, and Waller, as cited; the testimony M.C. (Cicero) Stewart at Lay's trial; the Santa Fe *New Mexican* and the *Roswell Record*.

The citizens' vote which banished the town of Eddy from the map of New Mexico and created the town of Carlsbad on the very same spot was held on May 23rd, 1899.

To enumerate the accounts of Tom Ketchum's last hold-up and of his surrender would be to give a recitation of most of the Bibliography; to haul each of them up for comment would require very nearly another book. The following are the chief sources: the testimony of F.E. Harrington, Joseph H. Kirchgrabber, Charles P. Drew, John W. Mercer, C.C. Waller, Joseph E. Robbins, F.F. Clarke, H. D. Lewis, George W. Titsworth, Fred Bartlett, F. W. Hall, Saturnino Pinard, and F.J. Dodge at Ketchum's trial; the manuscript of Albert Thompson, whose information came from Harrington and other eye-witnesses; Jack Potter's book (Potter reproduces the text of a letter from Saturnino Pinard); the Titsworth article; material furnished by Phil Cooke from interviews conducted in Clayton; Jack Culley's book; Livingston's article; and various newspapers. Of the others, one of the best is that of Erna Fergusson, in *Murder and Mystery in New Mexico*, but both she and Culley are well off the mark in saying that Ketchum visited a saloon in Folsom shortly before the hold-up and decided to go ahead with the hold-up only because he had gambled away his money.

Ketchum, as will be seen, kept changing his story, insisting sometimes that he had been alone in the attempted robbery and at other times that he had company. It is clear from examination of the most detailed sources that he was on his own. Perhaps he contradicted himself merely to muddy the issue, for he knew that the authorities were convinced, at first, that others besides Ketchum had been present. At no time, ever, would Ketchum intimate that Sam and Carver had cut him adrift. Officials said at the time, and it has often been restated since, that Ketchum must have been insane to try to rob a train by himself. Maybe he was; but other men took the same risk, and got away with it, both before and after Ketchum's time: Rube Burrow once did so in Alabama, in 1890; Charles Wilson, an apparently inoffensive and dull-witted clerk, bought some dynamite and a pair of cheap pinfire revolvers and robbed a train in Missouri in 1893; someone, technically unknown, single-handedly looted a Union Pacific train in Utah in 1896; and Charles Hammond, one of the worst criminals in Oregon and Montana, performed the lone-robber act on the Northern Pacific in 1902.

It is stated in some accounts that Tom Ketchum was armed only with his pistol when he stopped the train. Those who may be assumed to have been the

NOTES

people most likely to remember—Kirchgrabber, Drew, Harrington, and Ketchum himself — said that the weapon was a rifle. It is true that the mail clerk, Fred Bartlett, once referred to the gun as a pistol; but Ketchum was too far away, and Fred's head was poked into the line of fire for far too short a time, for him to have made out what sort of gun it was—and Bartlett was being questioned, not about the gun itself, but about the wound which he had received when the thing was fired at him.

Chris Waller, who relieved Tom of his six-shooter, described it as a Colt forty-four. Everyone else who saw the piece, or claimed to have seen it, said that it was of forty-five calibre. Waller said that the revolver was loaded in all six chambers and that there were four or five rounds in the Winchester.

CHAPTER XIII

Sources cited for the previous chapter have also served as the basis for this one, but especial reference must be made to the testimony of Lewis and George Titsworth, from the record of Ketchum's trial: the articles by Livingston and B.D. Titsworth; and items from numerous issues of the *New Mexican* during August and September, 1899.

Miguel F. Desmarais was the doctor who amputated Ketchum's arm.

Although Elza Lay was indicted and tried as "William H. McGinnis," he was known to the authorities of the Territorial Penitentiary as "William K. McGinnis." The reason for this discrepancy is unknown but must be immaterial. Lay, one would suppose, never got around to elaborating either variation of his assumed identity by the addition of a middle name.

CHAPTER XIV

Easily the most important sources for this chapter are the trial papers in *Territory of New Mexico versus William H. McGinnis* and *Territory of New Mexico versus Thomas Ketchum;* the *Compiled Laws of New Mexico*, 1897, Sections 1063, 1064, 1065, 1066, 1067, 1068, 1069, and 1151; and the text of the opinion delivered by Justice Crumpacker at the McGinnis appeal.

The *New Mexican*, which also gave a fair summary of the testimony at each of the trials, provided much worthwhile background material. Otero's reminiscences and the Thompson manuscript were useful— albeit that Thompson, in vigorous pursuit of the dramatic image, occasionally left the facts trailing some way behind him.

One account of the Ketchum trial which evidently was based upon a partial reading of the transcript is in Erna Fergusson's book, as cited.

Tom Ketchum's trial, unlike that of Elza Lay William McGinnis, was fairly short and the issues straight forward. In the manuscript he drafted forty years after the trial, Albert Thompson relates that Ketchum, when asked to state his plea, surprised one and all by stepping up to the bench—not to assault Mills, but to ask him to translate the language of the indictment into plain English. The fact that the official court reporter did not make a note of these unorthodox proceedings does not disqualify Thompson's story; it is difficult to believe, however, that the *New Mexican* correspondent would have overlooked them. No such incident was mentioned in the paper, from which it may be assumed that Thompson's memory was at fault.

Even in terms of cold law—ignoring, that is, the politics and perjury—the case against McGinnis, and the reasoning which caused his appeal to be denied, afford a fascinating study in complexity. As to the testimony itself, Wilson Elliott was on the stand for the longest time: more than fifty pages of the transcript are occupied by his evidence. The testimony of Cordova is contained in thirty-three pages, that of Morgan in twenty-six pages, and that of the defendant in twenty-two pages.

Other data for this chapter came from Alverson, Culley, Livingston, *Rocky Mountain News, San Francisco Chronicle*, and from material collated and tape-recorded by George Fitzpatrick.

Steve Roup, the officer who accompanied Stewart to Texts Canyon, was well known in Cochise County as a cowman and as a very handy fellow with a gun. There is a sketch of him in James Emmit McCanley's book *A Stove-Up Cowboy's Story*.

CHAPTER XV

Details of the Las Cruces bank robbery and the farcical investigation were taken from successive issues of the *New Mexican* and from a despatch from El Paso to the *San Francisco Chronicle*. There two papers, and others, published a number of items on Scarborough's activities during 1898 and 1899. J. Evetts Haley's account of the fight in which Bronco Bill was wounded and captured and Will Johnson killed is similar to those which appeared in the newspapers, except that the roles of Milton and Scarborough are reversed. Henry Brock told Lou Blachly that everyone knew that Scarborough intended to kill Bronco Bill and Company if he caught up with them. As Brock put it, "that was Scarborough's scheme [strategy], wa'n't it?"

The meeting between Scarborough and Ben Kemp is described in *Cow Dust and Saddle Leather*, a biography of the ranchman by his son, Ben W. Kemp, with Jeff C. Dykes, and is stated to have occurred "a few months" before the officer was killed. The narrative of this book seems to consist mainly of the younger Kemp's recollections of what he had been told by his father. Hence, wherever Kemp, senior, was speaking of something which he himself knew only by report, the degree of reliability which may be attached to the incident as related in this book is dependent upon the accuracy of two memories besides the content of truth in the original story. In the chapter on Tom Ketchum it is illustrated in several different ways how readily this process lends itself to produce chronological disorder, confusion of personalities and events, and fundamental error. Pro-

NOTES

minence is give to the Hillsboro bank robbery, the story of which is so presented as to imply that Ketchum was one of the two bandits. Neither Ben W. Kemp nor Dykes seems to have realized that the Hillsboro hold-up came off long after Ketchum's death. Elsewhere, it is asserted that Ed Kilpatrick and Ben Kilpatrick were different names for the same man. The Las Cruces robbery is not mentioned anywhere, but from all that is known of the movements of the various parties during the first few weeks of 1900 it looks probable that Scarborough was trailing the Las Cruces bandits when he ran into Kemp and was rebuffed by him.

There are many accounts of how Scarborough was ambushed and killed. Those of Ed Bartholomew, James H. McClintock, and Brown Waller all stick close to contemporary newspaper reports. The story is also recounted by Lorenzo Walters in *Tombstone's Yesterday*. Further important material is included in Livingston's article, in the transcript of one of Blachly's interviews with Henry Brock, and in *The Album of Gunfighters*, by Hunter and Rose.

J. Marvin Hunter, Scarborough's brother-in-law, says that the men who attacked the officers were Max Stein, Tom Capehart, Will Carver alias George Franks, and Frank Laughlin. Probably Scarborough said this just before he died in Deming, but he himself could have recognized only Capehart and, possibly, Carver; Stein and Laughlin were the aliases of two members of the gang who, with Capehart and Carver, had been on the scout in Cochise County for several weeks past. The four were known to have visited Tombstone a short time before the Triangle Springs shooting. It is clear that at least five—and most likely six—men were directly involved in the murder.

Henry Brock, in relating to Lou Blachly the story of the fight as told by Birchfield, named only one of the group: "All at once . . . there was a big yell and Walter said it was old Capehart, he said: 'I'd 'a' knowed him anywhere'."

Lorenzo Walters claimed that Max Stein was subsequently killed after a train robbery in Utah and that Capehart and Laughlin were sent to the penitentiary in Colorado—Capehart for murder and Laughlin for robbery. None of this can be substantiated. It is impossible to tie in the aliases Stein and Laughlin with specific members of the band, but neither of the mysterious pair was Butch Cassidy: the four who left Tombstone did so to establish contact with Cassidy and a companion, who were then riding west from Grant County, New Mexico. Either Stein or Laughlin could have been one of the Kilpatrick boys.

Carl Livingston's version is derived from what he learned from "a reliable man" who had met Cassidy in "a certain republic" in South America and who later went to live in New Mexico. Cassidy admitted that he had decided to kill Scarborough and that he had laid the plans by which this object was accomplished. He said that he had been one of the ambush party, but declined to give the names of his companions.

It is not possible to determine precisely which members of the gang had robbed the bank at Las Cruces, but consideration of all the material at present available leads to the belief that the work was undertaken by Tom Capehart and one other of the four men who were seen together in Cochise County a few weeks after the hold-up.

None of the outlaws who were involved in the assassination of Scarborough could have had anything to do with the murder of two possemen, Frank Lesueur and Gus Gibbons, who were ambushed near Pine Springs, in north eastern Arizona, on March 27th, 1900.

Quite a lot of information on what Cassidy and others of the gang were doing in western New Mexico at sundry times in 1899 and 1900 is provided by Axford, French, and Siringo. The account in Siringo's book *A Cowboy Detective*, first published in 1912, reappeared almost unchanged in one of his later books, *Riata and Spurs*.

It is tempting to surmise that one of the WS hands who was going by the name of Big Johnny Ward (another was known as Little Johnny Ward) was Ben Kilpatrick: French's description of Big Johnny is very close indeed to fitting Kilpatrick—for example, Ward, like Kilpatrick, had a peculiar disfigurement near the iris of one eye.

CHAPTER XVI

In tracing the criminal careers of Harry Longbaugh and Harvey Logan the author has relied mainly on items from the St. Louis *Globe-Democrat*, Denver *Rocky Mountain News*, and San Francisco *Chronicle*. Some of the incidents have been dealt with at length by Waller, Kelly, or Horan; a few were overlooked by them. In general, Waller's treatment of the subject is more detailed but less polished than that of Kelly and Horan.

The prison record of William Cruzan was obtained for the author by Colin Rickards from the Colorado State Penitentiary, Canon City. Cruzan was received at the penitentiary on March 22nd, 1895, and released on May 12th, 1898.

Charlie Siringo spent weeks on the Tipton case, and eventually secured firm evidence against Logan, Cruzan, and Ben Kilpatrick. There was certainly a fourth robber; some of the newspaper reports state that there were five robbers. Butch Cassidy was not and could not have been among the four or five. Assertions that he was present may have arisen in the first place because he and Cruzan were of roughly the same build and complexion.

The Winnemucca bank robbery was one of the most spectacular of all outlaw coups. The newspapers and books cited above furnish, between them, a minutely detailed picture of the hold-up, the long pursuit through Nevada into Utah and northern Arizona, the reunion of the five principal members of the band, and their frolics in Fort Worth and elsewhere.

One of the illustrations in Horan's *Desperate Men* is a facsimile of Logan's Log. a summary of the itinerary of Harvey Logan in his years of outlawry. It gives particulars of his wanderings with Carver and the others between the autumn of 1900 and the following spring. Bartholomew, Livingston, and Waller all reproduce the story as it appeared in the contemporary press. There is hardly the least variation among newspaper accounts of Carver's last fight and of the Thornton murder which preceded it by a few days. It is certain from the descriptions that "Walker", the man said by the Kilpatricks to have been the killer of Oliver Thornton, was Harvey Logan, not Will Carver. Logan was dark of complexion, mustached,

NOTES

slightly bald, and in his middle thirties; Carver was described as light-complexioned, clean shaven, and apparently in his mid-twenties. When Carver's body was examined, a scar was found on the thigh. This was thought to have been caused by a bullet received in the Turkey Canyon shooting. It is much more likely that it was Carver's reminder of the Stein's Pass hold-up.

Bruce Weaver's exit is described in the *New Mexican* and in *Finis for "Red" Weaver*, by Philip J. Rasch. The incident is just barely mentioned by French and Siringo.

Tom Ketchum's remarks to Pinard and Gray were noted by Jack Culley, who was sitting a few feet away from the officers and their prisoner at the time of the conversation.

CHAPTER XVII

It is unfortunate that so little could be learned of the arrest of Upshaw, Kelly, and Atkins and that no record has been traced of the disposition of their cases. The Texas State Archives were unable to help in this respect, and the unavailability of the contemporary San Angelo newspapers was, once again, a serious handicap. Such items as found occur in the columns of the *Rocky Mountain News* and were passed on to the author by Larry Ball, of Boulder, Colorado.

The papers concerning Ketchum's appeal are in *Territory of New Mexico vs. Thomas Ketchum, Appellant—No. 896* the full text of Parker's Opinion may be found in Volume X of the *Reports of Cases Determined in the Supreme Court of the Territory of New Mexico*.

Ben Clark's visit to Tom Ketchum is described in an article by the former sheriff, entitled *William Christian, alias Black Jack*. Culley and Otero, as cited, also wrote of Ketchum's months in the Penitentiary and of the people who visited him while he was there. Miguel A. Otero. Jr, of Santa Fe, recently told Phil Cooke that, when he first went to see the outlaw, his view of the prisoner was blocked by a blanket which covered the bars. On the blanket was a note which read: "See Black Jack, 25 cents." Evidently, then, despite his frequent and vigorous disavowals of the nickname, he was not undisposed to act the part of Black Jack as a means of securing unearned income.

Ketchum's transfer from Santa Fe to Clayton was widely reported in the regional press and in newspapers as far afield as New York and San Francisco.

There are almost innumerable accounts of the outlaw's last forty-eight hours. The events were dealt with in great detail by at least two of the Denver newspapers --the *Post*, quoted by Titsworth, and the *Rocky Mountain News;* the *New Mexican* provided extensive coverage; the San Francisco *Chronicle* also published several dispatches, including a preposterous one from Denver, in which it was claimed that Ketchum had "slain fifty men, women and children" and that President McKinley had granted him a respite (McKinley was not empowered to intervene in any way whatsoever). Of the other sources, these were most valued; George Fitzpatrick, as cited; Phil Cooke, interviews in Clayton, as cited; and Culley's book and the Albert Thompson manuscript, both of which have been cited several times. Additional material and comment can be found in *Clayton, the Friendly Town in Union County, New Mexico,* by Goldianne (Mrs Harry) Thompson and William H. Halley, with Simon Herzstein, which includes information given by John Guyer; *Not So Wild, the Old West,* by Clara Toombs Harvey; and a nicely-produced booklet published by the Fort Jordan Stockade, Clayton, entitled *The Black Jack Story.* Mrs Harvey's father, the lawyer, was O. T. Toombs; her book tells of his visit to the execution, but not of her own presence near the stockade at the time—this last story was among those garnered by Phil Cooke.

The Holiness sect were Protestant fundamentalists whose beliefs were the subject of much newspaper comment during the last years of the nineteenth century.

Almost a year after he bade farewell to Tom Ketchum, John Guyer himself killed a man in Clayton—for which, according to one reporter, he came perilously close to getting lynched. Mrs Harvey, however, states that it was a case of justifiable homicide and that the decision not to prosecute Guyer met with general approval.

A number of witnesses took note of the time as Ketchum walked up to the foot of the gallows, but their reports are not always in accord. Albert Thompson said that Ketchum was brought outside at twelve minutes past one; press correspondents differed as to whether the outlaw appeared in the yard at 1:14 or 1:15, while one man reported that Ketchum ascended the scafford at 1:17 and took the long drop at 1:21. Probably the last-mentioned observer was the owner of a slow watch. It is likely that Ketchum started his last walk on earth a minute or two before a quarter past one and was jerked into eternity four or five minutes later.

CHAPTER XVIII

There is hand-written identification of Hawkins and McCorkle as the two Hillsboro robbers on a copy of the reward poster in the State Archives of New Mexico. Rather more than two years after the hold-up, a couple of tramp bandits were killed at Separ, New Mexico, and one of them was named as McCorkle. It was soon learned, however, that the dead men were George and Edwin Vernon Gates, two of the most-traveled desperadoes in the United States. The Gates boys were wanted for many crimes, including train robbery and murder at Copley, California. In November of 1902, George Gates, at that time calling himself Guy Lacroix, led an unsuccessful attempt to rob a Colorado and Southern train near Trinidad, Colorado.

Ben Kemp, as cited, said that the Hillsboro robbers, one of whom he named as Big Ed Kilpatrick, changed horses at his camp, in the Black Range. Kemp had known Kilpatrick for several years, and he certainly knew something about the Hillsboro robbery, for he himself was at first accused of having had a hand in it.

The principal members of the "Mesa Hawks" were Henry Hawkins, Frank Potter, Frank Isbell, George Cook, Witt Neil, alias Shorty Daniels, John Smith, and George Massagee. They spent several months stealing cattle in eastern New Mexico, then held up the post office at Revuelto, the general store at Tucumcari, and the post office and store at Fort Sumner, where Potter killed a boy named

Henry Beaubien. After this they scattered, but four of the minor members of the band were quickly captured. Hawkins made his next appearance in Hillsboro, then vanished for good. As far as is known, neither Potter nor Isbell was ever caught. It was said for a time that Hawkins and his remaining side-kicks were responsible for the Logan train robbery, but this seems to have been a wrong guess. Three men who most likely had nothing to do with the crime were arrested upon the alleged confession of one Tom Boswell, a horse thief from Oklahoma. Phil Cooke tells the writer that it was, and perhaps still is, believed locally that among the robbers were two men well-known in eastern New Mexico who used their share of the loot to found a bank.

The main newspaper sources for the foregoing are the *New Mexican, Rocky Mountain News,* and San Francisco *Chronicle*.

One of the posse who captured Hanks in Montana in October, 1893, described the action in a letter to the New York *Sun*. This letter was reprinted in the St. Louis *Globe-Democrat,* November 6th, 1893.

Most of the robberies in the 1901-1904 period were covered by one or more of the papers already cited. No contemporary account could be found of the 1903 Unaweep hold-up, but the crime was mentioned in many of the newspaper stories on the later robbery at Parachute, and Siringo refers to it in *A Cowboy Detective* and *Riata and Spurs*. Another train robbery which may have been carried out by range-country outlaws took place near Sandpoint, high in the Idaho panhandle, in the summer of 1902. But by this time criminals of the "yegg" class were a greater menace to banks and railroads than horseback bandits ever were; as a rule, the former were more successful than the latter both at stealing money and at not getting caught.

Those with a thirst for statistics might like to know that in the period between January 1st, 1890, and December 31st, 1903, there were 341 cases of actual or attempted train robbery in the United States and possessions. In the year 1890, the total was a modest dozen; there were more than thirty in each of the years 1893, 1894, and 1895; in 1902 there were twenty-two, and in 1903 only thirteen. The number of causualties associated with this record was 208, including 99 fatalities.

H. A. Hoover wrote of Elza Lay in *Tales of the Bloated Goat* and in *The Gentle Train Robber (New Mexico, January 1956).*

The indefatigable Phil Cooke found out exactly where Sam Ketchum's grave is, and in the *New Mexico Territorian,* June 1962, described the circumstances which made it expedient that Sam should remain at rest beneath the highway. There is no marker to point to the present whereabouts of Samuel W. Ketchum, late of Richland Springs, Knickerbocker, and Turkey Creek Canyon; but then, the Ketchum boys, unlike Billy, the Kid, never caught the fancy of Walter Noble Burns.

All other sources for this chapter are as indicated in the next.

TALES THAT WERE TOLD

Held Up at Grants is derived from a considerable volumn of archival, manuscript, newspaper, and other material on the various crimes and the outlaws mentioned in connection with them. Foraker's letters are in Department of Justice File No. 13065-96. There are accounts of the three Grants (originally Grant's) hold-ups in the newspapers of Santa Fe, Denver, and San Francisco.

Otherwise, the sources for the facts which form the basis of the arguments presented in the five items that comprise this section are cited in the text. It should be restated, however, that the prime purpose of the piece entitled *Murdered on the Road* is to demonstrate that Tom and Sam Ketchum could not have been implicated in the Fountain case: the author is neither competent nor willing to attempt a full examination of the part played by each of those who connived at or participated in the murders, but it seems to him that, in the main, the proven facts of the case and of the events preceding the ambush make the conclusions self-evident. C. L. Sonnichsen discusses the affair impartially, though perhaps not as exhaustively as he might, in *Tularosa*, published in 1960. There is also an excellent review of the Fountain and Garrett murders in *Death in Dona Ana County*, by William R. Smith (English Westerners' *Brand Book*, January and April, 1967). But A. M. Gibson, in *The Life and Death of Albert Jennings Fountain*, ruins what should be an unassailable argument by gross and persistent over-statement, distortion, and over-simplification. With all the subtlety of a Victorian purveyor of penny-dreadfuls, Gibson portrays Fall, Lee, and party as men of unmitigated wickedness and evil, and Fountain as the hero unblemished. Indeed, Gibson's book is just about everything that a work by a professor of history ought not to be. On the other side, it seems that anyone who has the temerity even to suggest that Oliver Milton Lee might not have owned a character that was wholly stainless must perforce be hotly attacked on that score alone. The verdict on Fountain must be that he was an obstinate old man who deliberately exposed himself to menace, refused to accept help from his friends, and duly got himself and his little boy killed.

BIBLIOGRAPHY

PUBLIC DOCUMENTS AND RECORDS, OFFICIAL PUBLICATIONS, etc.

Affidavit: Antonio Borrego to Notary Public, 17 April, 1903.

Acts of the Legislative Assembly of the Territory of New Mexico, Thirty-seventh Session (1907).
(New Mexican Printing Company, Santa Fe, 1907)

Annual Report of the Attorney-General of the United States. 1897; 1898; 1899

Eighth Census of the United States, 1860: State of Texas

Ninth Census of the United States, 1870: State of Texas

Tenth Census of the United States, 1880: State of Texas

Compiled Laws of New Mexico (1897)
(New Mexican Printing Company, Santa Fe, 1897)

Department of Justice File 13065-1896
This file was opened in 1896 and closed in 1901, after the death of Tom Ketchum. It contains all the correspondence received by the Attorney-General of the United States concerning the operations of the Black Jack gang, the Ketchums, Bronco Bill, and others in Arizona, New Mexico, and Mexico, ranging from the reports of the United States Marshals to the complaints of private citizens.

Index to the Probate Cases of Texas — San Saba County, from January 30, 1866 to June 28, 1939.

New Mexico Statutes — Annotated.
Compiled and Annotated by Stephen B. Davis, Jr., and Merritt C. Mechem.
(W.H. Courtright Publishing Company, Denver, Colorado, 1915)

Reports of Cases Determined in the Supreme Court of the Territory of New Mexico.
Volume X — Charles H. Gildersleeve, Reporter.
(E.W. Stephens, Publisher, Columbia, Missouri, 1902.)

Territory of New Mexico versus Thomas Ketchum — No. 136, Assault on Train with Intent to Commit a Felony
(Indictments, Sentence, Testimony and other trial papers)

Territory of New Mexico versus Thomas Ketchum, Appellant — No. 896.

Territory of New Mexico versus William H. McGinnis — No. 2419, Murder.
(Indictment, Sentence, Affidavits, Testimony and other trial papers)

Territory of New Mexico versus William H. McGinnis, Appellant — No. 873

United States of America versus Bob Christian; United States of America versus William Christian, etc.

Various documents of the courts of the Western District of Arkansas and the Eastern District of Texas appertaining to the Christians, members of their family, and certain of their associates in the Indian Nations, 1886-1896.

MANUSCRIPTS

Reminiscences of Leonard Alverson, as told to Mrs Geo. F. Kitt
(Arizona Pioneers' Historical Society, Tucson)

The Ambush of Black Jack — Henry Brock, as told to Lou Blachly.
(Transcription of tape recording; Zimmerman Library, Albuquerque, New Mexico)

Untitled; marked "W.A. Thompson".
(State Archives of New Mexico, Santa Fe)
Evidently a draft for Albert W. Thompson's book "They Were Open Range Days", but containing much material not used in the book.

INTERVIEWS

In June of 1968, Phil Cooke, of Santa Fe, interviewed Mr Fructuoso Garcia and other senior residents of Clayton, New Mexico, obtaining a good deal of unpublished personal reminiscence. Later, in September, 1969, Mr Cooke interviewed Major Aud Lusk — younger son of Virgil H. Lusk — of Carlsbad, New Mexico.

This material was later dictated to the author for use in the present work.

George Fitzpatrick, also of Santa Fe, generously made available the results of his own research on Tom Ketchum. Most of Mr Fitzpatrick's information came from first hand. It was recorded in 1964 and re-recorded for the author by Phil Cooke and Colin Rickards. Among those interviewed by Mr Fitzpatrick were Reymundo Arguello and Miguel A. Otero, Jr.

BIBLIOGRAPHY

THESIS

Southwestern Conditions and Outlawry at the Turn of the Century.
by Larry D. Ball.

NEWSPAPERS

Abilene, Texas, *Reporter* 1894-1900

Denver, Colorado, *Rocky Mountain News* 1896-1901

El Paso, Texas, *Times* December 31, 1896

Oklahoma City, Oklahoma, *Daily Oklahoman* and *Weekly Oklahoman,* 1895.
Times-Journal, July 1, 1895

Phoenix, Arizona, *Arizona Republican* 1896-1897

Roswell, New Mexico, *Record* 1894-1900

St. Louis, Missouri, *Globe-Democrat,* 1888-1898

San Antonio, Texas, *Express* December 29, 1896; July 2, 3, 1898
Light May 26, 1896, April 13, 1897

San Francisco, California, *Chronicle* 1889-1904

San Saba, Texas, *News* 1882-1888

Santa Fe, New Mexico, *Daily New Mexican,* 1896-1905.

Solomonville, Arizona, *Graham County Bulletin,* 1896-1897

Tecumseh, Oklahoma, *Herald* 1894-1896
Leader 1894-1896

Tombstone, Arizona, *Prospector* 1896-1897

Trinidad, Colorado, *Daily Advertiser* November 4, 5, 1897
Daily Advertiser-Sentinel July 12, 19, 20, 21, 22, 1899

BOOKS

Axford, Joseph "Mack." *Around Western Campfires*
(Pageant Press, New York, 1964)

Ball, Eve.	*Ma'am Jones of the Pecos* (University of Arizona Press, Tucson, 1969)
Bartholomew, Ed.	*Kill Or Be Killed* (Frontier Press of Texas, Houston, 1953) *Black Jack Ketchum: Last of the Hold-Up Kings* (Frontier Press of Texas, Houston, 1956)
Burroughs, John Rolfe.	*Where the Old West Stayed Young* (William Morrow, 1952, and Bonanza Books, New York)
Crawford, Thomas Edgar.	*The West of the Texas Kid, 1881-1910* (University of Oklahoma Press, Norman, 1962)
Erwin, Allen A.	*The Southwest of John Horton Slaughter* (Arthur H. Clark Company, Glendale, California, 1965)
Culley, John H. (Jack)	*Cattle, Horses and Men of the Western Range* (Ward Ritchie Press, Los Angeles)
Fergusson, Erna.	*Murder and Mystery in New Mexico* (Merle Armitage Editions, Albuquerque, 1948)
French, William.	*Some Recollections of a Western Ranchman* (Methuen and Co. Ltd., London, 1927)
Haley, J. Evetts.	*Jeff Milton: A Good Man with a Gun* (University of Oklahoma Press, Norman, 1948)
Harkey, Dee.	*Mean as Hell* (University of New Mexico Press, Albuquerque 1948)
Harvey, Clara Toombs.	*Not So Wild, the Old West* (Golden Bell Press, Denver, Colorado, 1961)
Hoover, H. A.	*Tales of the Bloated Goat* (Mogollon, New Mexico)
Horan, James D.	*Desperate Men* (Hammond, Hammond, London, 1952) *The Wild Bunch* (New American Library, 1958)
Horan, James D. and Sann, Paul.	*Pictorial History of the Wild West* (Crown Publishers, New York, 1954)

BIBLIOGRAPHY

Hunter, J. Marvin and
Rose, Noah H.
The Album of Gunfighters
(Warren Hunter, 1959)

Hutchinson, W. H.
A Bar Cross Man
(University of Oklahoma Press, Norman, 1956)

Kelly, Charles
The Outlaw Trail
(The Devin Adair Company, New York, 1959)

Kemp, Ben W., with
J. C. Dykes
Cow Dust and Saddle Leather
(University of Oklahoma Press, Norman, 1968)

McCauley, James Emmit
A Stove-Up Cowboy's Story
(Southern Methodist University Press, Dallas, 1965)

McClintock, James H.
Arizona
(S. J. Clarke Publishing Company, Chicago, 1916)

Otero, Miguel Antonio
My Nine Years as Governor of the Territory of New Mexico, 1897-1906
(University of New Mexico Press, Albuquerque, 1940)

Poldervaart, Arie W.
Black-Robed Justice
(Historical Society of New Mexico, 1948)

Potter, John H. (Jack)
Lead Steer and Other Tales
(Leader Press, Clayton, New Mexico, 1939)

Ringgold, Jennie Parks
Frontier Days in the Southwest
(The Naylor Company, San Antonio, Texas, 1952)

Siringo, Charles A.
A Cowboy Detective
(W. B. Conklin Company, Chicago, 1912)
Riata and Spurs
(Houghton Mifflin Company, Boston, 1927)

Stanley, F.
No Tears for Black Ketchum
(World Press, Denver, 1956)

Thompson, Albert W.
They Were Open Range Days
(World Press, Denver, 1946)

Thompson, Mrs Henry.,
and others
Clayton, the Friendly Town in Union County, New Mexico
(Monitor Publishing Company, Denver, 1962)

Waller, Brown	*Last of the Great Western Train Robbers* (A. S. Barnes & Co. Inc., Cranbury, N. J., 1968)
Walters, Lorenzo D.	*Tombstone's Yesterday* (Acme Publishing Co., Tucson, Arizona, 1928., Rio Grande Press, Glorieta, N. M., 1969)
Warner, Matt.	*The Last of the Bandit Riders* (The Caxton Printers, Ltd., Caldwell, Idaho, 1940., Bonanza Books, New York)

ARTICLES

Benton, Jesse James.	*Cow by the Tail* (Frontier Times, November 1964; January, March 1965)
Clark, Ben R.	*William Christian alias Black Jack* (Progressive Arizona and the Great Southwest, December 1929, January 1930)
Cooke, Phil (editor)	*The New Mexico Territorian* (most issues)
Farmer, Harold	*The "Old Timer" of Verde Valley* (Pioneer West, November 1967)
Hoover, H. A.	*The Gentle Train Robber* (New Mexico, January 1956)
Hunter, J. Marvin.	*Black Jack Ketchum and his Gang* (Frontier Times, April 1939)
Joyce, W. H.	*Hold Up of Southern Pacific Express No. 20... Lozier, Texas* (Main Lines, May-June 1967)
Kildare, Maurice (Gladwell Richardson)	*Who Killed Rogers and Wingfield?* (Real West, July 1968)
Livingston, Carl B.	*Hunting Down the Black Jack Gang* (Wide World, August, September, October 1930; March, April, May 1955)
Rasch, Philip J.	*Finis for "Red" Weaver* (English Westerners' Brand Book, January 1956)

BIBLIOGRAPHY

Romero, Trancito (as told to R. C. Valdez)	*I Saw Black Jack Hanged* (True West, September 1958)
Sturgis, Richard W.	*I Trailed Black Jack Ketchum* (True West, August 1963)
Titsworth, B. D.	*Hole in the Wall Gang* (True West, December 1956, February 1957)

The articles listed above are either written by, or based wholly or in part upon interviews with, people who were involved in or at least in a position to view the events described. Not all of them are accurate throughout, but each has something worthwhile. Ben Clark's effort—which, in any case, has only a paragraph or two on Ketchum—is the most disappointing; much of it is vituperative directed against Christian — not for his crimes, but for his alleged moral licentiousness.

There have been many other articles and features on the Ketchums. None of those that have been seen carries even a drachm of original and genuine material. The best of them seem to have been refashioned from such published accounts as those of Albert Thompson and Lorenzo Walters; the worst are mostly fiction, enlivened in places by memorably asinine dialogue. It would be wasteful to list them.

MISCELLANEOUS

Henry Brock and Lou Blachly. *Tape Recordings*

During the 1940's and 1950's the late Lou Blachly recorded interviews with a number of veterans of the New Mexico cattle industry. This material, comprising several hundred spools of tape, is in the safekeeping of the Zimmerman Library, in Albuquerque. The reminiscences of Henry Brock, who for amny years was superintendent of the Diamond A Holdings in southwestern New Mexico, cover about twenty sides of tape. The recordings numbered 2 and 13 have Brock talking about his outlaw acquaintances.

New Mexico Mounted Police—*Wanted Posters, Book One*

Although the force was not formed until 1905, its records include "flyers" for criminals who had been connected in one way or another with members of the Ketchum gang.

Fort Jordan Stockade, Clayton, New Mexico—*The Black Jack Story.*

This attractive little souvenir booklet contains some information given by Fructuoso Garcia, son of the sheriff who was in charge of the execution of Tom Ketchum.